SHARING THE WEALTH

SHARING THE WEALTH

WORKERS AND THE WORLD ECONOMY

ETHAN B. KAPSTEIN

W. W. NORTON & COMPANY

NEW YORK · LONDON

For information about permission to reproduce selections from this book, write to Permissions, W. W. Norton & Company, Inc., 500 Fifth Avenue, New York, NY 10110

The text of this book is composed in Garamond #3 with the display set in Engravers' Bold.
Composition by Binghamton Valley Composition.
Manufacturing by The Maple-Vail Book Manufacturing Group.
Book design by Judith Stagnitto Abbate/Abbate Design.

Library of Congress Cataloging-in-Publication Data

Kapstein, Ethan B.
     Sharing the wealth : workers and the world economy / Ethan B. Kapstein.
          p.   cm.
     Includes bibliographical references and index.
     ISBN 0-393-04754-7
     ISBN 0-393-97742-0 (pbk.)
     1. Wealth.   2. Income distribution.   3. Working class—Economic conditions.   4. Foreign trade and employment.   5. Economic history—20th century.
     6. Economic forecasting.   I. Title.
     HC79.W4K36   1999
     339.2—dc21   99-14686
                                                        CIP

W. W. Norton & Company, Inc., 500 Fifth Avenue, New York, N.Y. 10110
www.wwnorton.com
W. W. Norton & Company Ltd., 10 Coptic Street, London WC1A 1PU
     2 3 4 5 6 7 8 9 10

CONTENTS

PREFACE

"I WORKED ALL THE TIME to get what I've got, and now it's gone. I thought I had found security." The words were those of recently displaced electronics worker Nancy Blackburn of Shelby, North Carolina. Blackburn had discovered that booming employment figures don't necessarily mean an end to layoffs; her job had just been exported to Mexico. And while she eventually will get a new job, it is likely to come with lower pay and benefits.[1]

Nancy Blackburn is not alone in her anxiety about the future. Today, workers everywhere are being overwhelmed by the raw power of unleashed market forces. From North Carolina to South Korea, from France to Indonesia, working people are all too often finding themselves on the losing end of economic change.

That outcome should give us pause. After all, if globalization and technological change are making countries so much richer, we might well ask how societies are sharing the wealth. And the evidence to date suggests that the gains are highly concentrated in the hands of a few.

This is not how the global economy was supposed to function. Instead, it was expected to unleash a rising tide of wealth that would lift all boats. At the end of World War II, the leaders of the victorious allied powers recognized that the globalization experiment they had launched had to be viewed by domestic societies as contributing to prosperity and peace if it were to succeed. To facilitate these outcomes, they created multilateral institutions such as the United Nations and the International Monetary Fund. But widespread doubts about that postwar order are now being raised, with potentially grim consequences for globalization's future.

This book addresses the issue of how working people, and especially the unskilled, are faring in the world economy. My argument is that they are not doing very well. Unemployment continues to take its grinding toll on both Western and Eastern Europe—and, since the financial crisis of 1997–99, on East Asia and Latin America also. Income inequality is rising in the United States and continues to grow in other industrial countries, while the number of poor continues to grow in regions throughout the world, from South America to Africa, and from the post-communist transition economies to Asia. These facts prompt a simple question: If our economic policies do not help working people enjoy a decent way of life, and instill hope for a better future, what is the point? Fighting inflation, busting budget deficits, smoothing the business cycle, and promoting free trade are empty goals if they do not benefit working people and their children.

All economic change has its social impacts, and one of the great challenges for public policy is to manage those changes in order to maximize overall wealth, while minimizing any harm done to individuals and particular groups. In essence, this book is about how the shift toward a global economy is being managed in terms of its social effects. I will argue that if the world economy is seen by growing numbers of people as being "rigged" in favor of a small number of investors with mobile capital over the masses of relatively immobile workers, then its present structure will not long endure. For globalization is not some inevitable force of history, but rather the consequence of public policy choices. Those choices have undoubtedly promoted our consumption of goods and services, but the interests and concerns of working people have taken a back seat.

To readers who are prepared to dismiss the possibility of a backlash against globalization and the neo-liberal economic agenda, I would point to the period surrounding World War I and its aftermath. The Great War destroyed a global economy that in many respects was as highly evolved as our own, with trade and investment crossing borders at rates that would not recover until the 1970s. That economy was the result of a century of tremendous economic and technological progress, and an accompanying explosion in commerce and finance.

But accompanying these changes was massive social dislocation, including the widespread movement of agricultural workers to cities, and the breakup of traditional community-based support systems. With the failure of national governments to fill this vacuum, workers naturally turned toward radical political solutions in addressing their grim economic fate—communism and revolution, and later fascism and war. The major lesson that the post–World War II leaders drew from this history was that the great catastrophes of the early twentieth century were all products of social disruptions caused by economic change. In their new design, these social disruptions would be eliminated by coupling globalization to a welfare state that would provide workers with safety nets to buffer the hard times.

This was the grand bargain that informed industrial society—albeit not most developing countries, where the welfare state never evolved—and it worked for decades in delivering wealth and opportunity for millions of working people. Today the issue before us concerns how well that system is coping with unimagined levels of capital mobility, trade, and technological change. Can the democratic welfare state still meet its obligations to the least advantaged at a time when government budgets are sharply constrained? Is the global economy delivering prosperity to all participants, or only to some of them? What can we do to ensure that the world's policymakers take into account considerations of fairness no less than efficiency as they plot our economic future? These are some of the questions addressed in this book.

The search for satisfactory answers from the labor standpoint goes well beyond political calculations about the risks of domestic and international conflict. No less important, there is now powerful evidence in the economics literature that points to the material benefits, in terms of sustained growth, of policies that promote greater equality of opportunity and incomes. These measures lead to more stable societies, higher rates of investment, and a more productive workforce. In short, it's possible to state with some confidence that *social justice is good for economic performance.*

But there is an important catch to this argument: Economic globalization may make it more difficult for national governments to distribute scarce resources to meet their broad social goals. Mobile capital will flee the taxation that distributive policies inevitably bring. This means that any effort to reconcile fairness and efficiency cannot be left to the domestic plane alone; international institutions must be empowered in new ways as well. This book takes up the challenge of addressing the policy steps that are necessary to help labor, and especially unskilled workers, cope with the economic forces that have been unleashed.

THE ORIGINS OF THIS BOOK can be traced to Russia, where in the early years of the post-communist transition I had my first sustained experience with working people who were on the losing end of economic change. That's not quite true, for of course I had experienced briefer encounters of this sort throughout my working life. As a merchant seaman during the early 1970s, I often spoke with shipmates about job prospects in that declining industry (they encouraged me to go to college!). Later, as a naval reserve officer, I discovered that a frequent topic of discussion with my active-duty friends concerned how they might "convert" to civilian occupations after leaving the service. Even in American universities, the changing economic environment has meant dramatic shifts in the job market for professors, and my own undergraduate adviser had warned me of the risks of seeking an academic career.

But now, in Russia, I was acting in an official capacity as a principal administrator with the Paris-based Organization for Economic Cooperation and Development. My task was to work with defense-dependent communities from Moscow to Siberia that were struggling in the wake of deep cuts in military spending. I worked with government officials, businesspeople, and members of the foreign donor community in an effort to craft local development strategies and help find new sources of investment and job growth.

To be sure, these defense workers and managers saw no immediate upside to the post-communist transition; their livelihoods were disappearing before their eyes. This raised all sorts of questions in my mind: Did governments have any responsibility to help workers adapt to changing economic circumstances? If so, how should the losers from economic change be compensated? What role should international institutions and bilateral assistance programs play in helping the losers cope with the future? My work was directed toward finding answers on behalf of these people, and quickly.

Since returning to the United States in 1995, I have continued to work on the relationship between economic change and social welfare. One outcome of that ongoing project was an article entitled "Workers and the World Economy," published in the May/June 1996 issue of *Foreign Affairs*. That article seemed to touch a nerve, and it led to the present book.

Following the publication of "Workers," I began a period of near-constant travel in which I had the opportunity to meet with academics, businesspeople, government officials, union leaders, and working people in countries around the world—

from the elite slopes of Davos, Switzerland, to university classrooms in West Africa. I am grateful for all the comments received on the talks I gave in these far-flung places, and I keep powerful and warm memories of the great generosity that people showed me everywhere I went.

In writing this book, I have accumulated more debts than most emerging economies. I must begin by thanking James Hoge and Fareed Zakaria of *Foreign Affairs* for publishing my article and for cheerfully enduring the controversy that followed. I must also thank my editor at Norton, Drake McFeely, for his early interest in the book, and equally important, for his kindness, patience, and good advice.

I cannot possibly list all the colleagues around the world who have helped me with this project. I only hope they recognize all their efforts on my behalf in these pages. Still, I must single out a few of the people who have gone beyond the call of duty in recent years. They include Charles Beitz, John Brandl, Bud Duvall, Joseph Fahey, Albert Fishlow, Jean-Paul Fitousi, Vladimir Gimpelson, Samuel Huntington, Ketil Hviding, Morris Kleiner, Richard Kohl, Bob Kudrle, John Langmore, Patrick Messerlin, Branko Milanovic, Joel Rosenthal, Pierre Sauve, Ed Schuh, Kathryn Sikkink, Sarah Stewart, and Phillip Wheeler. In addition, I have had tremendous research assistance from the following graduate students at the University of Minnesota: Dan Hope, Guang Li, and Ethan Cherin, and all kinds of support from Keith Vargo. I am also pleased to thank the following institutions for their assistance: the Council on Foreign Relations, the University of Minnesota, and the Institut d'Etudes Politiques in Paris.

My wife, Claire, has always stood by me and our family despite my career changes and our disruptive moves. I am ever grateful to her. But this book is dedicated to our daughters, Anne and Laura, who represent the next generation of workers in the world economy. I am confident that they will achieve the "good life" and, equally important, help others to do so as well.

SHARING THE WEALTH

1

WORKERS AND THE
WORLD ECONOMY

*The outstanding faults of the economic society in which we live
are its failure to provide for full employment and its arbitrary
and inequitable distribution of wealth and incomes.*
— JOHN MAYNARD KEYNES, 1936[1]

THE INTERNATIONAL ECONOMY IS IN TURMOIL.
Around the world, working people are questioning whether increasing flows of trade and finance are improving their lot or leaving them helpless in the face of external pressures that national governments seem unable or unwilling to control. Just when workers are most in need of state support to help them cope with rapid economic change, governments are abandoning them.

That is not how things were supposed to work. After all, President John F. Kennedy had reassured us, in words that could have come from a bedtime story, that "a rising tide lifts all boats." The failure of global capitalism to spread its riches poses a rude shock to those who were raised to believe in the promise of the multilateral free-trade regime.

Today, when we hear or read about the global economy, it is usually in terms of the trillions of dollars of goods, services, and investment that circle the planet, with the great increases in national wealth that accrue to states that adopt open policies. But there are other data that usually go unnoticed in these discussions. We hear less about the 100 million citizens in the industrial countries who are classified as living below the poverty line. We hear less about the 35 million in these same countries who are unemployed. We hear less about growing income inequality. And we hear still less about the 1.3 billion people in the developing world whose income level is under $1 per day.[2] For all these people, the global economy has not yet brought either material gifts or the hope of a better life.

The challenges that *these* facts pose are not only to the policymaking and business elites, but also to modern economic "science." At a time when we have mastered inflation and licked the business cycle, poverty, unemployment, and income inequality remain endemic to the international system. This reminds us that if economic theory has a fatal weakness, it's in the area known as "social welfare." Economists can now tell us with great confidence whether a given set of policies will make nations richer or industries more efficient, but they cannot predict whether these same policy changes will leave societies—constituted by individuals with equal rights to the good life—any better off.

In the global finger-pointing exercise about "who's to blame" for the world economy's failure to produce sustained and equitable growth, international organizations have been quick to accuse national governments of all sorts of heresies. It is the governments' responsibility to promote domestic welfare, and no fault for the nation's economic problems can be placed on the open door of free trade, or the hot money that portfolio investors bring to the table and then withdraw just as quickly. To a large degree, this is true, and national governments cannot use globalization as a scapegoat for their political and economic misdeeds, their corruption and mismanagement.

Still, the international economy is not neutral in its effects across countries or classes; multilateral agreements are structured in such a way as to give everyone equal shares of the newly baked pie. Simply stated, there are winners and losers. Further, states have widely differing capacities for managing the domestic, social effects of globalization. If nothing else, that is one lesson that emerges from the East Asian crisis, a region that only yesterday was being hailed as the living example of an "economic miracle."

In most of the popular and journalistic accounts of "globalization," the emphasis is usually placed on the allegedly deterministic forces of technical change that are now creating a world without borders. These analyses miss a central point: that globalization is fundamentally a *political* phenomenon. It did not arise "naturally," but rather was the product of policy decisions taken after World War II among the western allies. The fact that the Soviet Union imposed a different set of choices on its satellites, effectively erasing their contact with the international economy, suggests just how political those decisions really were.

The elites and interest groups that wish to sustain globalization seem to have forgotten that this political deal rested on a basic bargain that governments struck with their working people—their veterans—after World War II. The deal was that international economic integration would increase both national income *and* social welfare; that it would promote both wealth *and* greater equity; that it would advance both prosperity *and* peace. It would do so because good things in economies were supposed to "trickle down" to the have-nots. But after a half-century of experimentation with liberalization, the facts are giving the lie to those claims, with potentially disastrous consequences. If the process of globalization is to be sustained, easing pressure on the "losers" of the new open economy must now be the focus of international economic policy.

It is hardly sensationalist to claim that in the absence of

broad-based policies and programs designed to help working people, political debates in the industrial and developing worlds will soon turn sour. Already we find populists and demagogues on the campaign trails in every country promoting the values of xenophobia and protectionism. These politicians are playing to those who see inequality and unemployment as the flip side of globalization. That perception must be changed if the postwar ideals of world "peace and prosperity" are to be preserved. After all, the fate of the global economy ultimately rests on domestic politics in its constituent states.

Reconciling globalization with social welfare is thus our great task as we enter a new millennium, and this book is written as a contribution to that process. The argument presented in these pages is that there are good reasons emanating from political history, economic theory, and moral philosophy to fashion an economy that is widely viewed by its participants, its workers, as fair. Most people want more—will *demand* more— from their economic and social institutions than efficient output; they also want justice.

Now justice could imply one of two things. It could mean either that the rules of the game are reasonable and fair to all participants (as in *Monopoly*), or that the outcomes are considered equitable. A charged philosophical debate exists among professors over which of these should be the focal point of our concerns. While drawing on those discussions, it is not the intention here to make a contribution to modern philosophy. Instead, the goal is to make a policy-relevant statement about how we can advance the cause of economic justice—defined as equal opportunity for all working people coupled with a social safety net against hard times. And in so doing, we will need to pay attention to both the rules *and* the outcomes.

That social conflict must accompany the spread of free markets should not surprise us, for that is one of the dominant themes of modern history. Markets, which turn goods and services into tradable commodities, are anathema in many respects to fundamental human values. Most of us, after all, do not like to think of love, honor, devotion, and religious belief as tradable goods. More to the point, we do not like to think of *ourselves* as goods at all. People are not commodities, as international society has made clear by rejecting slavery and indentured servitude. In all the industrial countries, and many developing ones, governments have acted—in response to domestic political pressure—to drive a wedge between people and market forces, ultimately providing the array of policies and programs that constitute the "welfare state."

Today, this old theme is being played again around the world, albeit with one significant difference: There is no obvious alternative to democratic capitalism. Neither communism nor fascism currently attracts many adherents, leaving capitalism without the strategic necessity to respond to social pressure.

That, in turn, contains a danger of its own—the danger of complacency. Should working people increasingly come to associate their suffering with the expansion of international markets, they will have little reason to support political actors who make the liberal case. Closure will not seem such a costly route to take, especially if openness has failed to deliver on its promise of greater wealth. Political-economic alternatives to democratic capitalism may be sparse today, but who knows what the future will bring?

There is more than political stability at stake here. A growing body of economic literature links an emphasis on equality to sustained growth. That has surprised many economists and policy analysts, but on some levels it makes perfectly good common sense. The more that countries make productive use of their human resources, the more likely they are to witness improved economic performance.

Beyond these economic and political arguments lies the moral case, and ultimately this is most important; after all, if our social and economic institutions are unjust, what is their value to us?[3] To the extent that we have personal and shared beliefs that transcend our immediate material interests, we will also seek to build a better world for the disadvantaged among us. When viewed as a moral arena, we must find today's global economy wanting, yet we should not doubt that human effort can make a difference to those who have found themselves on the losing end of change. As John Stuart Mill put it more than a century ago, "The distribution of wealth . . . depends on the laws and customs of society. The rules by which it is determined are very different in different ages and countries; and might be still more different, if mankind so chose."[4]

A HISTORICAL PERSPECTIVE

Western leaders at the end of World War II were well aware of the need to rebuild the global economy on a different basis from that which had informed Great Britain's nineteenth-century experiment with international integration. They had no interest in unleashing on European society the market forces that had produced such violent change, nor did they wish to re-create an international financial system—the gold standard—which had earlier made it almost impossible for governments to respond to domestic social requirements. Instead, they sought to create an international economy that, while liberating trade and finance from its territorial shackles, also protected labor, the working man and woman, against the harsh downturns that market forces could produce. In short, they wanted to build an economy that contributed to political stability, economic growth, and social justice.

The postwar elites believed quite deeply that a strong causal connection existed between economic and political instability, between depression and war. Many of them, like John Maynard Keynes, had witnessed firsthand the failures of the 1919 Treaty of Versailles, which had condemned Germany to an impoverished future. They saw the spread of the Great Depression, and the fascism that grew out of desperate populations. They knew that if unbridled capitalism had a tragic failing, it was in its treatment of workers, and that evil ideologies were prepared to profit by this flaw. Indeed, it was the great failures of the nineteenth-century political-economic system—its balance-of-power politics coupled with the international gold standard—that opened the way to new ideas about how the twentieth century's postwar system should be organized.

While political stability and economic growth were the central objectives the new system had to meet, underpinning it had to be some notion of social justice. That is, western leaders recognized that if peace and prosperity were to be achieved, the structures they were building had to be viewed as legitimate, as fair, by working people. The postwar era thus represented an intellectual rejection of laissez-faire capitalism, and in its place stood a social-democratic vision that, while varying greatly from country to country, ensured all workers—at least in the industrial countries—greater opportunities for education and advancement, coupled with a social safety net as insurance against hard times.

The provision of equal opportunity and the knitting of that safety net are among the most significant developments of modern political history, and their present-day erosion places our economic policies at great risk. They were the product of great struggle, accompanying the industrial and commercial revolutions. The fundamental insight of those who agitated for social policies during the nineteenth century was that labor should not be treated as a commodity, that the inherent dignity of man required something better.

The vast gap between what capitalism promised working people and what it delivered had been conspicuous throughout the Industrial Revolution. Writing in *Progress and Poverty* in 1879, the reformer Henry George observed, "At the beginning of this marvelous era it was natural to expect, and it was expected, that laborsaving inventions would lighten the toil and improve the condition of the laborer; that the enormous increase in the power of producing wealth would make real poverty a thing of the past." George chronicled the many technologies, such as the steam engine and the telegraph, that had been introduced in his lifetime, and the great explosion in commerce and trade that they heralded.

But far from ushering in an era of prosperity, "Disappointment has followed disappointment. From all parts of the civilized world come complaints of industrial depression . . . of want and suffering and anxiety among the working classes." George observed that the massive investments in technology had only resulted in increasing returns to capital and falling wages for working people. Thus, "The mere laborer has no more interest in the general advance of productive power than the Cuban slave has . . . in the price of sugar."

Accompanying these technological developments were public policies that facilitated globalization's progress in favor of specific interests. Perhaps the most important example of this was Britain's decision in 1846 to lift the Corn Laws, which had long protected domestic agriculture. With industrialization, the Manchester factory owners needed more labor. The simple solution was to get farmhands off the land. The most efficient way to achieve this goal was to introduce foreign competition in agricultural products, forcing down prices and ensuring that farmers and tenants could no longer earn their livelihood. It should be noted that at the same time, Britain was experiencing "enclosure" of common land, which also drove smallholders off the land. The net effect was that labor flooded the cities, and because the price of food was also falling, it was possible to pay these workers a pittance.

Throughout the Industrial Revolution, various regulations that had long governed economic life—many dating back to the Middle Ages—were dismantled, and rural workers found their traditional way of life torn asunder. Workers became commodities like grain and coal, with demand for and supply of their services a function of market requirements. As people streamed to cities, they lost the social safety net of the rural village, with nothing to replace it. When harvests were bad and food prices increased, people starved. These were the simple market economics of the nineteenth century. Is it any surprise that they turned increasingly over the decades toward radical political movements that promised them a better deal?

In the late-nineteenth-century United States, too, working people sought to control market forces. Under the sway of the "social gospel" movement, a "new political economy" emerged, placing the dignity of the individual at the center of economic policy. These young economists, led by Richard Ely of the University of Wisconsin, would go on to establish the American Economics Association in 1885 as an organization dedicated to bringing "Christian values" to the economy. (Economists today are horrified to learn of the AEA's religious roots!) As historian Sidney Fine has written, "The new school of political economy placed man rather than wealth in the center of the economic stage and subordinated everything to his welfare . . . new-school economists condemned the principle of self-interest as unchristian and advocated brotherhood and a regard for one's fellows in its stead. They called on such ethical agencies as the church, the school, and the state to help guide economic developments."[5]

During the panic of the 1890s, in which unemployment levels reached almost 20 percent of the working population, these economists lobbied government (unsuccessfully) to provide unemployment insurance, promote job creation, break up monopolies, and create better health and safety standards. Despite the inability of the social-gospel movement to advance labor's policy agenda by much at this time, its influence would strengthen over time, with its message carried forward by the Progressives of the early twentieth century and later by President Franklin Roosevelt's New Deal.

Still, if American government has been hesitant to act in

any area, it is with respect to the individual economic welfare of its neediest and least advantaged citizens. For much of its history, the American state cast a relatively blind eye toward individual suffering, and with rare exceptions social policy was not really viewed as a responsibility of the federal government until the New Deal. And even then, in the midst of the Great Depression, political debates over the appropriate scope of public policy stymied a host of possible measures, including those aimed at the promotion of full employment. To the extent that Washington has inclined toward laissez-faire policies in any area, it is with respect to labor. This liberal tradition, well recognized by Alexis de Tocqueville in the early nineteenth century, continues to have a powerful grip on policymaking, and it is that aspect of American ideology that may ultimately endanger its leadership in the global economy.

For such a laissez-faire approach to the fate of workers is inherently unstable, as the philosopher Karl Polanyi taught in his 1944 masterwork, *The Great Transformation*. Drawing on the long sweep of European history, he described the process by which landless working people throughout the continent entered a world of urban poverty, creating a political cauldron. During periods of prolonged depression—made all the more severe by strict adherence to the international gold standard—these laborers fell prey to radical and extreme political forces. Polanyi argued that it was the complete unraveling of economic and labor market regulations and traditions in the nineteenth century that paved the way for the social and political cataclysms of the twentieth—World Wars I and II, the Great Depression, and the Russian Revolution.

Whether or not we now accept this version of history is immaterial; what is important to note is that our postwar leaders brought this view with them to their conferences on economic reconstruction. As U.S. Treasury Secretary Henry Morgenthau said at the opening of the Bretton Woods conference of 1944, "All of us have seen the great economic tragedy of our time. We saw the worldwide depression of the 1930s. We saw currency disorders develop and spread from land to land, destroying the basis for international trade and international investment and even international faith. In their wake, we saw unemployment and wretchedness. . . . We saw their victims fall prey . . . to demagogues and dictators. We saw bewilderment and bitterness become the breeders of fascism, and finally, of war."[6]

The postwar leaders were committed to rebuilding the world economy, but this time with a significant difference. In globalization's nineteenth-century incarnation, under the tutelage of a liberal Great Britain, governments did little to protect working people against the malign effects of economic change. Unemployment insurance and funds for retraining did not exist, and where welfare benefits existed, they reduced workers to pauperism. Having learned from that experience, statesmen now sought to design a liberal world economy that maintained an active role for the state in order to ensure that equity and growth traveled hand in glove. The distinguished political scientist John Ruggie labeled this postwar "deal" between workers and the state the "bargain of embedded liberalism."[7]

Thus the new, American-led global economy would include both domestic and international components. The fundamental idea was that the global economy would be designed in such a way as to generate the greatest possible output and consumption through the adoption of free-trade policies, while the national, welfare state would distribute the product to its citizens according to domestic political preferences. In putting this scheme into practice, the state would thus come to supervise most aspects of economic life. Throughout the industrial countries, employment acts would be passed at the war's end, in order to reassure returning servicemen—whose heads might have been filled with radical ideas on the battlefield—about their future job prospects. Across Europe, ambitious social-welfare schemes were put into place. These policies and programs made clear that labor was not to be treated as a commodity but rather as an economic partner, and the organization of workers into unions was actively encouraged.

Western leaders constructed international regimes for money and trade that were by charter sensitive to the exigencies of domestic politics. When they created an international monetary system in 1944 to avoid beggar-thy-neighbor currency devaluations (that is, the deliberate manipulation of exchange rates in order to gain a competitive advantage for a nation's exports), they created an International Monetary Fund (IMF) as a lender of last resort. When they launched the General Agreement on Tariffs and Trade (GATT) in 1947 to liberalize and expand commerce, they also included "safeguard" provisions to protect countries from unfair trade practices and to assist those who were displaced. When they formed a European Common Market in 1957, they made sure that states would remain autonomous in the field of social policy.

In many ways, this global economic structure was a thing of beauty. It generated an unprecedented era of prosperity—at least among the major powers—and it also contributed to the long peace that mercifully characterized diplomatic relations among the leading military states in the postwar world. But its benefits within societies (not to mention industrial and developing worlds) have been less certain, as the gap between rich and poor widens. These developments are inevitably casting doubts on the continued viability of the postwar economic order.

WHITHER GLOBALIZATION?

Today, the international economy is spreading rapidly to new lands, and we hear in every country the cries of liberalization, deregulation, and privatization. Wherever we travel, we now find people fixing their gaze on stock prices and currency movements and asking how international capital markets are responding to the latest government policy measures. This integration of the world economy holds out the promise of a better life for millions, but it is also causing wrenching social and economic changes whose depths are still uncharted.

Tensions between the global market and domestic societies are already apparent throughout the world. In France, efforts to pare back the welfare state in response to European monetary union have been met by an almost continuous stream of strikes, leading in 1997 to a dramatic change in government with the election of the Socialist Party leader Lionel Jospin as prime minister; indeed, left-labor parties are now in power in the three major European states. In Eastern Europe and the former Soviet Union, the transition has been greeted with social protest and the rise of nationalist and xenophobic politicians, and in many cases the return to power of quasi-communist governments. In the United States, President Bill Clinton's effort to pass "fast-track" trade legislation in 1997 was defeated. And in Southeast Asia, the region's financial crisis has brought crowds into the streets, as rising food prices threaten displaced workers with starvation.

These developments lead us to probe deeper into the process of globalization. Are free trade and market liberalization inevitably associated with increasing income inequality? How far back must we cut social safety nets as states put their fiscal houses in order? What are the consequences of economic and technological change for the unskilled, the uneducated, and the poor? Can the advancement of market processes be made compatible with social demands for opportunity and a modicum of security or must these stand in opposition?

These are among the questions that I seek to address in this book. In so doing, I offer an argument as to why we should be vigilant in ensuring that our economic policies focus not solely on such criteria as efficiency and wealth creation but also on social welfare. Indeed, I argue that the search for economic justice—a distribution of resources and opportunities widely accepted as fair, coupled with a social safety net—is necessary if we seek to build a world characterized by political stability and economic growth.

The problem of achieving economic justice at home has grown more complex in a world where capital mobility is rapidly increasing. Building on a fundamental hypothesis of the public-finance literature, I argue that greater capital mobility makes it increasingly difficult for governments to adopt domestic policies of asset redistribution. This is because redistribution involves some form of taxation, and, all things being equal, mobile capital prefers less taxation to more. As the International Monetary Fund reports, "Globalization may be expected increasingly to constrain governments' choice of tax structures. . . . Internationally mobile factors of production . . . can more easily avoid taxes levied in particular countries. . . ."[8] As capital flees high-tax regimes, states thus are losing the ability to adopt policies that balance equity with efficiency concerns.

At this point, some readers may wish to applaud globalization for hastening the welfare state's demise. But I recommend a note of caution toward those who would adopt that position. Far from being an economic loss, the democratic welfare state has been at the cornerstone of our unprecedented era of peace and prosperity. Its demise should trouble all those who care about domestic stability and international security. At a minimum, we should be wondering about what, if anything, will assume its distributive functions as governments find it harder and harder to fulfill this function.

This is not to argue against reform of our welfare-state policies—unemployment insurance, pensions, aid to the poor, and health care must certainly be reexamined in such a way as to promote labor productivity and mobility. Yet few of us would wish to live in a world in which a rude strain of capitalistic social Darwinism reigns supreme; memories of "robber barons" on the one hand and "street urchins" on the other hold no charm for us either. Most of us want to enjoy the bounties that free markets bring, but we also seek to limit, if not eradicate, the misery that seems pervasive in our own countries and in distant lands.

Since work must be at the core of any public strategy to ensure economic security and social justice, the fate of labor is the major concern here.[9] Following the Harvard philosopher John Rawls, we will consider the argument that justice requires that societies do what is in their reasonable power to ensure that every individual, and particularly those who are least advantaged, have opportunities to realize his or her talents in the labor market. That represents a considerable challenge, for in many societies around the world, working people have little political voice, and their preferences and interests often go unheard.

In a global economy, however, more than domestic efforts may be needed for the achievement of economic justice; international action is required as well. After all, if international cooperation was viewed as critical to the making of the post–World War II order, why shouldn't it be seen as equally essential today, with the end of the Cold War and the rapid spread of globalization to lands that once sat in relative isolation from the West? Yet we might well ask how much voice labor has at the level of international institutions, and who represents it in this political setting.

In developing our economic policies, an emphasis on generating growth is certainly important for eliminating poverty and making resources available for redistribution, but growth on its own does not necessarily promote the opportunities of our least advantaged citizens. If the objective is to help those on the losing end of economic change, it must be done via some mechanism by which the economic "winners" in society take a percentage of their gains and transfer them to those who are identified as losers. Ideally, this mechanism would involve more than a simple income transfer, since ultimately we would like to see a profound transformation in which the losers can become winners themselves. That means offering all members of society the greatest possible opportunities for educational and professional advancement, as their talents permit.

Further, most of us recognize that some authoritative entity, such as the government, will normally have to take the lead in regulating and enforcing the process of redistribution. In all of the advanced capitalist countries, there is some degree of coerced transfer programs, principally through the progressive income tax and various kinds of welfare payments. This book reconsiders the case for redistributive policies, focusing on those that may be widely viewed as appropriate in a world of mobile capital.

The case must be made, too, that foreign aid, ever maligned, still has a role to play in shaping a more equitable global economy. Ever since the intense decolonization that followed the end of World War II, the leading industrial nations have provided foreign aid to developing countries for a variety of political, military, economic, and humanitarian reasons. Despite—or some might argue, because of—these policies, the plight of the poor has hardly been ameliorated. Should we care about this fact? Should we concern ourselves with the fate of the disadvantaged who live in distant lands? To pose the problem in another way, are territorial boundaries—nation-states—the appropriate unit of policy analysis if our objective is to redress large inequities in asset distribution, or must we take a broader, global view?

One answer to these questions would focus on the moral character of the international society in which we wish to live and raise our children. Individuals would ask themselves, as Rawls suggested, about the kind of society they would create if they worked from behind a "veil of ignorance." In such a world, most of us would seek the maximum degree of personal freedom consistent with not harming anyone else. We would wish, among other things, for equal opportunity, including the possibility of a job with a living wage for everyone who wanted one. We might certainly be willing to accept different income levels as rewards for different levels of educational attainment or expertise, or for the risks that people took in earning their wages. But most of us in building such a world would also seek to ensure that all people had access to the basic necessities of life, and we might well accept that in an increasingly complex society, those necessities grow more complex as well.

Today we might think that the *only* possible argument for economic justice is a moral one like that just sketched. Unlike the prewar period when Keynes was writing *The General Theory of Employment, Interest, and Money*, world politics now seems to be on a peaceful plane, with the threat of a major conflagration almost unimaginable. Democratic capitalism is spreading to countries that only a few years ago still lived under the bleak light of totalitarianism and communism. We seem to have entered an era of stability, with no threats at home or abroad.

Such a judgment is premature, for the real challenge to market economies may only now be appearing on the horizon. If growing numbers of people associate globalization with injustice, but the nation-state lacks the political will to respond, we will find ourselves in a dangerous situation. This book is designed to help guide our policies so that these shoals may be avoided. My warning is clear: To forget or leave aside those who are disadvantaged or struggling to find a toehold in the global economy can be fatal not just for domestic market economies but ultimately for the stability of the international system as a whole.

Now many if not most economists would argue that globalization has had only a small net impact on the fortunes of the world's workers, for either good or ill, and the appropriate place to cast blame or praise for their fate is on national governments.[10] If that is the case, why adopt an international perspective on labor outcomes at all? In response, I would make the following points: first, the jury is still out on the scale of the impact of globalization on the earnings and employment of domestic labor; second, no matter the size of the damage, polling data in the United States and Western Europe reveal a widespread perception that internationalization is "bad" for workers; third, governments have a responsibility to those who are hurt by the policy changes they have advocated; fourth, it will prove easy for demagogic politicians to use globalization as a scapegoat for a nation's economic problems, and to find willing supporters among the "losers." We have already seen this starting to happen in many countries around the world.

This book has been written, then, in an effort to defend globalization from its enemies, while saving it from those of its adherents who fail to recognize the damage it is bringing working people in its train. Economic institutions must be examined not just in terms of their contribution to efficiency but also with respect to their legitimacy. In sum, I seek to make the case that it is in our political, economic, and moral interest to ensure that globalization become associated with the spread of wealth and opportunity to all those who labor in its fields, factories, and office towers. If we do not, our best hopes for international economic integration—its promise of spreading peace and prosperity—will surely be disappointed.

2

MARKETS AND WORKERS IN HISTORICAL PERSPECTIVE

Our thesis is that the idea of a self-adjusting market implied a stark utopia. Such an institution could not exist for any length of time without annihilating the human and natural substance of society; it would have physically destroyed man and transformed his surroundings into a wilderness. Inevitably, society took measures to protect itself. . . .

— KARL POLANYI, 1944[1]

History has shown that economic distress and financial instability can threaten political stability and security.

— U.S. TREASURY SECRETARY ROBERT RUBIN,
21 JANUARY 1998

WHAT DIFFERENCE DOES IT MAKE TO the future of globalization if there are large gaps between rich and poor? Why should we care about whether or not the economic system is widely viewed by its participants as legitimate? Why should we endeavor to develop public policies that produce a more equitable distribution of resources and opportunities?

The answers begin with a short course in history, and an understanding of the social struggles that produced our current era. As we will see, World War I came on the heels of a century of political and economic liberalization, which had produced a golden age for trade and investment under the aegis of a hegemonic Great Britain. Accompanying that era of liberalization, however, was profound social disruption, leading to political instability across continental Europe. Ultimately, both international politics and the international economy would be destroyed, not to recover until after the Great Depression and a second world war.

Economic Deprivation and Political Instability

There are two necessary conditions for economic justice: first, our institutions should be structured in such a way as to enable every individual in society to realize his or her talents; second, the institutions should provide a safety net, a "social minimum," for times of need. Absent socioeconomic policies that are widely viewed as just, life is bound to become, in Thomas Hobbes's famous words, "solitary, poor, nasty, brutish and short."[2] Societies will become polarized and fearful, producing disruption and violence at home and conflict in international relations. If these seem like fabulous assertions, this chapter provides the theoretical and historical background to make us appreciate what is at stake.

In fact, the social-science literature regarding the relationship between economic well-being and political stability generally confirms what intuition would tell us. The hypothesis made famous by political scientist Ted Robert Gurr that "increasing men's opportunities decreases the potential for civil disorder"[3] helps to explain why governments have come to devote scarce resources to education and training programs. Flipping the coin, economists Alberto Alesina and Roberto Perotti have found that "income inequality increases social discontent and fuels social unrest,"[4] again reminding us why transfers of various kinds form such a large part of present-day government expenditures.

Gurr's now-classic work rested on the foundation of social and individual psychology. He suggested that "the potential for collective violence varies strongly with the intensity and scope of *relative deprivation* [italics added] among members of a collectivity."[5] From this follows the well-known dangers of "rising expectations" in a society where these expectations cannot be met! It is exactly this sort of problem that we face as income inequality suddenly worsens, even if absolute poverty levels are not increasing.

However, at some level of poverty, "absolute" deprivation may also prove sufficient to spark domestic rebellion. When survival itself is in question, people with nothing to lose take up violence as a last-ditch effort to get fed, clothed, and sheltered. As Keynes remarked in the context of the 1919 Versailles Treaty, which he knew would kill the German economy, "Men will not always die quietly."[6]

It is this fear that helps explain in part why the U.S. government and international organizations raced so quickly to East Asia's rescue in the wake of the 1997–98 financial collapse. As the World Bank's vice president for that region, Jean-Michel Severino has written of that crisis, "Many ordinary people are being hurt. . . . The social repercussions could be severe."[7] East Asia had been remarkably successful in raising its workers out of poverty; a generation of economic gain is now threatened, casting doubt on the continued utility of the regimes that brought about this state of affairs.

Economic deprivation is positively associated with political violence for the simple reason that the losers often feel that they have nothing more to lose.[8] But as social scientist Dipak Gupta reminds us, there is a profound difference between individual acts of violence and collective rebellion. Collective action of any kind requires the building of some group identification, such as "class consciousness." Later in this chapter, we will see that one of the motivating factors behind the development of "social democracy" and the "welfare state" in nineteenth-century Western Europe—and to a lesser degree in the United States—was the political and economic elites' fear of the growing Socialist Party movement, which appeared to be successful in shaping the "class" identity of workers and in providing them with an alternative model of political-economic organization.

Alberto Alesina and Roberto Perotti have provided us with further insights into the relationship between economic and political stability. Using data drawn from a large number of country cases, they show a strong correlation between income inequality and social unrest, and in turn on economic growth. The problem with inequality, they argue, is that it leads to social unrest, and as social unrest increases, investors become fearful for their investments. Not only do they fail to put new money in the country, but they'll withdraw money to the extent possible. As the level of investment falls, the economy inevitably slows, robbing the government of the resources needed for a sustained response. Countries thus become trapped in a vicious circle, with sub-Saharan Africa providing only the most obvious example.

It is important to emphasize that these sorts of economic and political theories are not just of academic interest but rather are fundamental to shaping our view of the role that governments ought to play in economic life, and the public policies that they should formulate in advancing the national interest in security and economic growth. After all, if we believe that poverty, inequality, and want lead to disruption and even war, we may wish to adopt policies to limit or even eradicate these social "diseases." However, if we believe only that poverty and want are morally bad, but not politically threatening, we may instead favor individual charity rather than public policy as the preferred response.

As this book will clearly demonstrate, by the end of World War II, political leaders in Europe and the United States had become convinced that economic instability and large-scale unemployment were the most important factors behind the social and political disruptions of the late nineteenth and early twentieth centuries—disruptions that produced World Wars I and II and the Russian Revolution. This elite drew a firm connection among economic deprivation, social conflict, revolution, and war, and they were determined to derail that causal train.

In tracing that history, we will see how responsibility for the economic "losers" in society has shifted over time from charitable organizations to the nation-state. But it did not rest there; welfare-state policies have also had a significant international dimension. International efforts to achieve economic justice—for example, through the creation of the International Labor Organization (ILO) following World War I—demonstrate that welfare policy could not stop at the frontier. These early projects would eventually lead to the sophisticated programs, policies, and institutions of the post–World War II era, including the Bretton Woods "twins," the International Monetary Fund and the World Bank, and to bilateral programs like those of the U.S. Agency for International Development (AID). Today, we can only expect an increase in the demand for international "solutions" to the social problems created by globalization.

MARKETS, STATES, AND SOCIAL DISRUPTION

Since the sixteenth century, the nation-state has played an ever-expanding role in the daily lives of most people. One of the most important fields for that expansion has been welfare policy, broadly defined. Whereas care of the poor, aged, unemployed, and infirm once rested with religious and charitable organizations, today the state and its institutions are ubiquitous providers of social insurance and welfare, and that is where the bulk of state spending is directed. Nearly 70 percent of all state spending in the industrial countries is devoted to transfers, subsidies, and interest payments on government debt, much of which has been incurred in the face of rising social spending.[9] This section traces that startling development.

A fundamental purpose of every government is to provide its citizens with physical security, which is why individuals in the mythical "state of nature" agree to give up some of their individual liberty and submit to the state and its laws. Threats to physical security could come from criminals and unruly bands roaming within a country, or it could come from the armies of other states. The challenge to provide security in these circumstances has not been an easy one, and throughout history states have failed in this basic task. Bruised by the experience of domestic revolt on the one hand and war on the other, governments over time have developed a wide range of foreign and domestic policies in response to the ever-present threat of violence. These have gone well beyond the establishment of professional police and armed forces to include a sophisticated array of social policies and programs.

It is often argued by social scientists that the modern welfare state is the evolutionary product of this history of violence, rising from the ashes of war and revolution. In 1971, the distinguished social historians Frances Fox Piven and Richard Cloward made the case that "western relief systems originated in the mass disturbances that erupted during the long transition from feudalism to capitalism."[10] To put this in another way, the welfare state has simply been one governmental response to the threat of social revolution.

Prior to the welfare state, the needy had no choice but to rely on charity, and it may well be that the world is turning again in that direction; who can forget President George Bush's image of the "thousand points of light"? Although Poor Laws had existed in Europe since the sixteenth century, responsibility for the destitute at that time fell largely on the Church and wealthy individuals. Almsgiving as an individual responsibility was certainly consistent with Christian doctrine, but charity also generated controversy, since it allegedly provided perverse incentives; at a time when workers were paid little more than subsistence wages to begin with, why work at all if charity was available?

Piven and Cloward suggest it was elite concern with the threat of mass civil disruption that ultimately overwhelmed any concerns about the perverse incentives that a broad-based charity program might generate. Thus, in Lyons, France, in 1534, following a decade of significant economic distress and constant food riots, "churchmen, notables, and merchants joined together to establish a centralized administration for disbursing aid. All charitable donations were consolidated under a central body, the 'Aumone-Générale,' whose responsibility was to 'nourish the poor forever.' A list of the needy was established by a house-to-house survey, and tickets for relief were issued to those who qualified. . . . Indeed, most features of modern welfare—from criteria to discriminate the worthy poor from the unworthy, to strict procedures for surveillance of recipients and measures for their rehabilitation—were present in Lyons' new relief administration." Soon, this system spread throughout France under the orders of King Francis I.[11]

During the sixteenth century, one European state after another saw poor relief shift from a charitable to a government-organized activity. In 1572, the famous Elizabethan Poor Laws were promulgated, establishing in England "a local tax, known as the poor rate, as the means for financing the care of paupers. . . ." Care for the poor, in turn, was handed over to local justices of the peace. This system of relief would remain the basis for English "welfare policy" for almost three centuries.[12]

Perhaps due to our reading Dickens at an impression-
able age, we tend to think that the great problems of social
dislocation and disruption that occurred in eighteenth- and nineteenth-century Europe were due primarily to the spread of industrialization and urbanization. Yet changes in the organization
of the agricultural sector, as graphically illustrated in such nineteenth-century English novels as *Middlemarch* and *Tess of the
D'Urbervilles*, were no less painful. In England, the enclosure
movement of the eighteenth and nineteenth centuries, which certainly contributed to increases in agricultural productivity, had a
rude effect on the smallholder, effectively transforming him into
a peasant. As G. M. Trevelyan has written, "The enclosures had
increased . . . the national wealth; but the increased wealth had
gone chiefly in rent to the landlord. . . . The lower middle class
had become poor, and the poor had become paupers. Agricultural
progress had been so handled as to bring disaster to the working
agriculturist. . . . The small yeoman or laborer . . . was left in
helpless dependence on the big farmer, who, just because the
rural proletariat had nothing now to live on but the farm wage,
was able to cut that wage down to the starvation rate."[13]

This concentration of land-holding would have widespread
social effects, among them a greater demand by the elite for
state protection. Adam Smith already recognized this in his
magisterial work of 1776, *The Wealth of Nations*, in which he
wrote: "Wherever there is great property, there is great inequality. For one very rich man, there must be at least five hundred poor, and the affluence of the few supposes the indigence
of the many." Indeed, for Smith, it was the acquisition of
property that gave rise to the demand for a "magistrate"
responsible for civil order, so that "the owner . . . can sleep in
security."[14]

As Smith's words suggest, the late eighteenth and early
nineteenth centuries became periods of tremendous social and
economic upheaval in Britain, where a sense of insecurity swept
a land that for centuries had known a highly regulated political

economy. The great historian E. J. Hobsbawm has written of this period of agricultural and industrial revolution that it destroyed "old ways of life without the substitution of anything the laboring poor could regard as a satisfactory equivalent." Accordingly, "waves of desperation broke time and again over the country: in 1811–13, in 1815–17, in 1819, in 1826, in 1829–35, in 1838–42, in 1843–44, in 1846–48. In the agricultural areas they were blind, spontaneous, and, so far as the objectives were at all defined, almost entirely economic. . . . In the industrial and urban areas after 1815 economic and social unrest were generally combined with a specific political ideology and program."[15] Overall, Hobsbawm asserts, "At no period in modern British history have the common people been so persistently, profoundly, and desperately dissatisfied. At no other period since the seventeenth century can we speak of large masses of them as revolutionary. . . ."[16]

These developments, of course, were hardly limited to Britain, and across the English Channel, they would be of even more dramatic political moment. In France, the Revolution of 1789 evolved in part "as a protest against the workings of the market that were producing untold misery. . . ."[17] The market quickly distinguished between large and small landholders, with increasing capital requirements favoring the former while driving the latter out of business.[18] A grain shortage soon resulted, as the large farmers saw an advantage in withholding their produce from the market in order to obtain higher prices. Grain scarcity, coupled with a generalized economic depression, caused bread riots in many parts of the country.

If the French bourgeoisie were ultimately successful in recapturing the Revolution from the violent mob of working people, and seeing Napoleon installed as emperor, they were less successful in stifling the ideas about the relationship between state and society that the turmoil had unleashed. Thus the early socialist Charles Babeuf—who would be executed for his ideas—proclaimed that, "Nature had given to every man an equal right to the enjoyment of every good," and, "The necessities of life were to be supplied by the government."[19] The promise of social improvement had been held out to the masses, and many of the ideas that we now associate with Karl Marx and his followers were released into the air, ready to be seized upon and brought into daily political life.

In Britain, socialist ideas famously captured the imagination of the utopian thinker Robert Owen, who by age twenty in 1791 was already a successful mill owner. His operation in New Lanark, Scotland, was a model for the industrial community, with good wages, secure employment, and exceptional educational and recreational facilities. Over time, Owen would "come to oppose the whole capitalistic profit system and to support all causes that promised to reduce the exploitation of workers."[20] Thus, by the early 1800s, he was agitating on behalf of the Factory Acts to improve working conditions, and he was an ardent supporter of the trade-union movement. In the United States, he established a nonprofit cooperative, New Harmony, Indiana, which would attract widespread attention.

Soon, Owen attempted to persuade British workers to make the spread of cooperatives the focal point of their political efforts. But union and working-class leaders had other ideas, seeking to achieve land reform and universal suffrage through the Chartist movement and waves of strikes. As a Chartist declared in 1848, upon their victory, they "would divide the land into small farms, and give every man an opportunity of getting his living by the sweat of his brow."[21] This was never achieved, but Parliament did respond to the social disruption by passing a number of acts aimed at improving the conditions workers faced in British factories and mines.[22]

Changes in the political economies of European countries were not simply the result of domestic developments. With the end of the Napoleonic wars, the world had witnessed the gradual establishment of a global economy, under the aegis of a triumphant Great Britain. That global economy, with its unforgiving gold standard, would place new pressures on national economies and societies, and in turn produce social tensions that would ultimately explode at the level of the international system.

BRITAIN AND THE INTERNATIONAL ECONOMY

Having defeated the French at Waterloo in 1815, Great Britain found itself in a position of economic and naval domination—*hegemonic power*—that would be unrivaled for much of the nineteenth century. With its unparalleled industrial and financial base, and its control of the sea lanes, Britain was in a position to shape international trade and investment flows in its interest. By 1860, when it was at its "peak," the United Kingdom produced half of the world's iron, coal, and lignite and bought almost half of all raw cotton.[23] Its Royal Navy was "probably as powerful as the next three or four navies. . . ."[24] British power, when coupled with the liberal ideologies propounded by Adam Smith and the father of modern free-trade doctrine, David Ricardo, heralded an era of globalization that would not be seen again until long after the end of World War II.

Britain's economic growth during this period was nothing short of phenomenal. Its international trade, which had risen by 30 percent between 1800 and 1830, multiplied *five times* between 1840 and 1870. During the early 1840s, Britain had accumulated about £160 million of credits abroad; by 1870, more than £1 billion. The effects of globalization were also felt in migration. Between 1800 and 1840, about one million Europeans left for the United States; between 1840 and 1870, almost seven million crossed the Atlantic.[25]

As a result of these developments, by the early twentieth century, in the famous words of John Maynard Keynes, "The inhabitant of London could order by telephone, sipping his morning tea in bed, the various products of the whole earth, in such quantity as he might see fit, and reasonably expect their early delivery upon his doorstep; he could at the same moment and by the same means adventure his wealth in the natural resources and new enterprises of any quarter of the world. . . ."[26] In other words, something resembling a global economy had been created.

There were, of course, significant differences between the Pax Britannica of the nineteenth century and the Pax Americana of the post–1945 period. For one thing, as just noted, migration was a critical part of the earlier process of globalization. Migrants and refugees confronted relatively open borders until at least the latter half of the nineteenth century. That difference with our current era cannot be overemphasized. Today, when we speak of globalization, we're really talking about trade, finance, and investment, but we conveniently exclude labor.

Further, while in fact many international institutions did arise during the nineteenth century to regulate commerce (such as the International Postal Union), the world was not "governed" by the sorts of rules and procedures that one finds associated with today's World Trade Organization and International Monetary Fund. And far from establishing a World Bank to help develop the poorer countries, Britain maintained—and expanded—a vast colonial system. In that world, as Karl Polanyi wrote, "Business success involved the wholesale bribing of backward administrations, and the use of all the underhand means of gaining ends familiar to the colonial and semi-colonial jungle."[27]

Nor was the world really characterized by free trade. Britain itself lowered domestic tariff barriers only with the greatest political difficulty, and many countries, prominently the United States, lowered them not at all. Germany opened itself to free trade for a few years before a coalition of economic and national-security special-interest groups pressured Chancellor Otto von Bismarck to adopt protectionist policies.

But in one arena, globalization was more advanced than it is today—monetary policy. Britain organized an international monetary system around the gold standard, and if countries wished to obtain investment capital from the City of London, they were encouraged to maintain their currencies against that standard. The gold standard in turn provided stability, encouraging the growth in trade and investment that fueled an era of tremendous prosperity. But it was ruthless in denying governments the monetary autonomy to respond to domestic problems, and therein lay its tragic flaw.[28]

The gold standard placed a premium on export-oriented strategies, encouraging globalization, but it placed high domestic adjustment costs on countries that sought to enter the system. In some countries, the results were tragic. Russia, for example, used tax policy to encourage farmers to export their grain. According to an official history of the International Monetary Fund, "In human terms, the costs of what would later be called an 'adjustment strategy' were quite terrifying. In the circumstances of the great Russian famine of 1891-92, in which millions died, this represented a call, not to export or die, but to export and die. The Finance Minister who began the process of adjustment, I. A. Vysnegradskii, indeed claimed that 'we must export though we die.' "[29] Russia's adoption of the international gold standard would be opposed by a broad spectrum of political groups, from conservatives to socialists.

It must be emphasized that the economic objective of the international gold standard was rather simple: It was monetary stability. Any domestic policy preferences had to be subordinated to that one goal. At a time when the social demands placed on the state were modest, the domestic effects were felt in prices of imports and exports rather than in the quality and quantity of state services. As the demand for greater social welfare increased alongside industrialization and internationalization, however, tensions within the gold-standard system began to mount.

That tension was at the core of Karl Polanyi's *The Great Transformation* (published, not coincidentally in 1944), which emphasized just how global the economy had become by the late nineteenth century, with all that implied for domestic polities. As he wrote, "By the fourth quarter of the nineteenth century, world commodity prices were the central reality in the lives of millions of Continental peasants; the repercussions of the London money market were daily noted by businessmen all over the world and governments discussed plans for the future in light of the situation on world capital markets. Only a madman would have doubted that the international economic system was the axis of the material existence of the race."[30]

But time and again, the gold standard proved a blunt instrument for transforming the global dictates of trade and finance into the demand for sound domestic policies. States adopted deflationary policies when their currency values got out of hand, but with the drastic domestic consequence of "a complete disorganization of business and mass unemployment. . . ."[31] When Europe suffered a prolonged depression, as in the period 1873–86, the great strains within the global market became apparent. By the end of that depression, "Germany had surrounded herself with protectionist tariffs, established a general cartel organization, set up an all-around social insurance system, and was practicing high-pressure colonial policies."[32] In essence, a race against the market was beginning, as state officials began to recognize that the international economy might be at odds with domestic politics.

The inflexibility of the gold standard and the exigencies of a free-trade regime gave governments very little room when it came to assisting those who found themselves on the losing end of economic change. By the mid-nineteenth century, these groups were beginning to rear their ugly heads, and the question was whether or not the capitalist state could control them before a general social explosion occurred.

THE SOCIALIST ALTERNATIVE

By the 1840s, the "market economy" was already under severe attack by its most significant challenger. With the publication of the *Communist Manifesto* in early 1848, the radical ideas of Marx and Engels about the political and economic organization of capitalist societies—combined with growing worker dissatisfaction in Europe—were poised to spread like wildfire. Marx and Engels called for nothing less than "the forcible overthrow of the whole extant social order," with its inequality at every level. It was the injustice of market outcomes and the commodification of labor—treating labor like grain or coal—that doomed capitalism as an economic system; it could not be saved by quick fixes on the margins.[33] As they wrote, capitalism had left no "bond between man and man than naked self-interest, than callous cash payment."[34]

Few published works have enjoyed better timing than the *Communist Manifesto*. After thirty years of economic (and population) expansion and relative peace following the defeat of Napoleon, Europe was now entering a period of bad harvests and economic depression. A crop disaster spread across the continent in 1845, as the potato blight destroyed the staple food of Europe's working people. The harvest of 1846, following a hot and dry summer, saw the lowest yields of the century. Prices soared and famine seemed inevitable. Across the continent, people rioted for bread and potatoes, and armies of beggars demanded charity.[35]

As the continent reached the year 1848, revolutions and revolts began to sprout like mushrooms from France to Prussia, catalyzed largely by the lack of food. In Paris, the July Monarchy was quickly overthrown, due mainly to the city's food shortages. Among the first acts of the newly proclaimed republic was to improve food supplies, out of a belief that continued economic distress would produce further social conflict. In a remarkable statement, the new government "proclaimed its belief in the right of all citizens to work."[36]

In Prussia, too, economic depression fueled rioting and political turmoil. The outcome would be the convening of a new National Parliament that drafted, among other things, a "Declaration of Fundamental Rights." But soon, the disparate groups that had joined to spark the revolution would become splintered, allowing the *ancien regime* to regain power. That would also be the fate of the revolution in France.

The "conservative recovery" of post–1848 Europe certainly emphasized repression of liberal political movements, but it was combined with some efforts at social policy as a way of sweetening the lot of workers and the poor. In the revolutionary aftermath, the elites developed a strategy that combined their shared fear of revolution with a more progressive agenda designed to instill conservative values among working people.[37] This attempt at social engineering took the form of increases in educational opportunities, Poor Laws that emphasized work instead of charity, and in some countries extensions of the suffrage. In pondering the willingness, if only grudgingly, of the English elite to adapt to some worker demands, E. H. Carr put it well in *The Twenty Years' Crisis* when he wrote that "those who profit most" from an established order "can in the long run only hope to maintain it by making sufficient concessions to make it tolerable to those who profit by it least. . . ."[38]

With the development of serious radical reform movements, especially the rise of socialist parties, nineteenth-century European governments would be pressured to do even more to ease the plight of working people—afflicted with low wages, poor working and living conditions, and high accident and mortality rates. The defeats of 1848 had not crushed the revolutionary ideas now planted in the continent's soil, and Marxian thought in particular would continue to sprout roots in many directions. One of the most prominent of these roots entered Germany and took the form of what we now call "social policy." To be sure, the call for social reform had been vigorous and influential in Britain, and British governance structures were slowly adapting to economic and social change through factory legislation and increasing suffrage. But, as historian Gustav Stolper has written, "In no other country had the idea of social reform taken hold of people's minds as thoroughly as in Germany, and nowhere else was it developed as comprehensively into a novel system of social thought. . . . In Germany more than in any other country it was the state that first adopted the philosophy of social reform and became active in the field. . . ."[39]

The reasons for this development are found in the political changes that accompanied German industrialization, and the rise of new interest groups that challenged laissez-faire economics. Germany's reaction against market forces was made manifest in two prominent ways: first, the rise of anti-free-trade ideology, and second, the growth of the Socialist Party. Protectionist forces, lodged in German business, were too much part of the elite for Chancellor Bismarck to ignore. By 1880, Germany had made a decisive break with free trade by reintroducing high tariffs on a wide range of agricultural and industrial goods.[40] That rejection of the market also established a precedent for labor-market policies and raised the question of whether or not labor should also be treated as an international commodity.

The Socialist Party, naturally, argued that economic policy must be designed to serve labor's interest. In its 1875 "Gotha Program," German socialists, led by Ferdinand Lassalle, married the Marxist critique of capitalism with a reform effort that had for its practical objectives such elements as universal suffrage and the introduction of a progressive income tax.[41] By the 1870s, the rapid growth of the Socialist Party threatened Bismarck, and in 1878 he put into place laws that essentially outlawed the party and its associations. The party's leaders were jailed and threatened, and many were sent into exile in Switzerland and elsewhere. In short, Bismarck's early anti-socialist tactics were purely coercive, and "every attempt was made to destroy the Socialist party utterly."[42]

But this effort to stomp out the socialist challenge would fail. Chameleon-like, the "party had rebuilt itself in camouflaged organizations such as glee clubs, bowling societies, and charity associations. . . ." By 1890, Bismarck would be dismissed, and Kaiser Wilhelm II allowed the anti-socialist laws to lapse.[43]

Indeed, Bismarck had recognized almost at the outset that his coercive measures were doomed to fail and would only result in a backlash against the government's authority. In his usual fashion, he thus changed gears, adopting a carrot-and-stick approach to the socialist movement. The carrot was in the form of offering workers some of the Socialist Party's most important ideas concerning worker protection. As a result, the anti-socialist laws coincided with the introduction over the next decade of health insurance, workers' compensation, and, in 1889, old age and disability insurance.[44] These programs in general were not truly distributive; that is, the wealthy were not taxed to pay for them, and the workers themselves bore most of the direct costs. Still, the German example demonstrates the increasingly important role the state was playing in organizing the social welfare of its citizens, and with that recognition, the outline of the modern welfare state was emerging.

The great question, of course, was whether the capitalist state could save itself by coming to terms with rising political demands for welfare. With their writings, Marx and Engels had convinced millions of people around the world that capitalism was not only an unjust system but, more problematic, an impossible one that must inevitably collapse. The exploitation of labor that was essential to industrialism, they had argued, could only result in endless cycles of consumption crises and economic depressions; capitalism literally was an economic system of boom and bust.

And the problems of capitalism could not be contained within national borders. As the English socialist John Hobson and the Russian Bolshevik Vladimir Illich Lenin would later teach in their respective books on imperialism, these domestic consumption crises forced capitalist states to expand abroad, adopting colonial policies to capture foreign markets. With every industrial state seeking to expand and export, the imperialist response was also doomed to failure; it had to lead to world war—as it did in 1914.

Marx and Engels did not believe that capitalists could make peace with their working class; revolution was inevitable. But despite war and crisis, most modern capitalist states have somehow avoided communist revolutions (although one could assert that in Germany and Italy, the responses to economic crisis would ultimately prove even more malign). A key to capitalism's survival has been the democratic welfare state.

THE WELFARE STATE

What is the welfare state? That question would seem deceptively simple to answer. Most of us live in states that seek to redistribute income from rich to poor and provide some level of public benefits to needy citizens. Don't these policies constitute the welfare state?

Certainly, coerced redistribution of assets and opportunities forms the hard core of welfare-state policies. But taking a larger view, we can conceptualize the welfare state as a vast regulatory mechanism; that is, a mechanism whose object is to regulate the "social realm." The historian George Steinmetz has written: "Regulation refers to all attempts to order collective forms of behavior. . . . It involves the use of formal and informal social arrangements, institutions, and norms to create or encourage orderly patterns of behavior."[45] In this sense, the evolution of the welfare state has represented an effort by capitalist states to

survive in a world where they are threatened by domestic revolution on the one hand and international war on the other.

To be sure, this view of the welfare state's history needs to
be supplemented by both economic and moral analysis. But as
the record suggests, elites in Western Europe—and to a lesser
degree in depression-era America—feared revolution and domestic violence and sought to develop policies that would prevent that outcome. They also feared war and needed to develop
programs that would motivate working people to fight for the
state; that is, they needed to hold out the promise to their sol-
diers of a better life upon their return. The welfare state would
serve to meet both these needs.

In building welfare-state institutions—social security, universal health care, unemployment benefits, a progressive income tax, public assistance, and the like—government officials
have had to confront both domestic and international challenges. Domestically, welfare programs would have to be
funded by tax revenues, and there was an effective political
limit to the state's taxation or revenue extraction capacity; after
a point, the government would face a taxpayer rebellion. Internationally, welfare programs could make the state less competitive economically, as enterprises faced higher charges than their
competitors abroad, which must result in higher prices for their
goods. Within these political and economic constraints, the
welfare state has been shaped.

As discussed in the previous section, Germany played a
leading role in the nineteenth century as an institutional inno-
vator in the area of social insurance, a role it would continue to
play in the early twentieth century. "Thus, the German Interior
Ministry mounted an exhibition at the 1904 St. Louis World's
Fair under the title, 'The German Worker Insurance as a Social
Instrumentality.' German officials pointed out that their pioneering effort had won not only worldwide attention, but also
widespread imitation."[46]

One British politician who took particular interest in these

German developments was Winston Churchill, "who in 1906 entered the Liberal cabinet to help prepare the initial British social insurance laws." Churchill spoke often at this time of "the left out millions" and contrasted them with the elite who were "more happy than any other . . . class have been in the whole history of the world." By 1911, Britain had passed a "National Insurance Act," which borrowed heavily from the German model.[47]

Curiously, one of the central elements of the modern welfare state—unemployment insurance—evolved slowly and, with some exceptions, did not become a responsibility of national governments until the 1930s and the Great Depression. Government officials in earlier economic downturns had certainly worried about unemployment as being socially and politically disruptive, but they did not yet conceive of the state as having direct responsibility for labor-market intervention and instead sought indirect methods for dealing with the problem.

In post–World War I England, for example, the government feared that unemployed veterans—and millions of young men had now been taught how to use firearms—might conceivably rise up in rebellion if they went jobless. It was this possibility—so ripe in light of the Russian Revolution—that prompted vigorous policy debate in the Cabinet. Officials argued, "Inflation is absolutely essential. . . . We have to keep up inflation." Economic historians Sean Glynn and Alan Booth explain that in this context, "Inflation consisted of encouraging private and public sector enterprises to borrow. It was essential because *inflation maintained employment in the short term* [italics added] at a time when the Cabinet was deeply suspicious of the revolutionary potential of ex-servicemen; Ministers feared the political consequences of rising unemployment."[48]

The very concept of unemployment is, of course, a relatively modern one. By some accounts, the equivalent term *chomage* first appeared in France in 1890, and the notion that the government had some responsibility for the fate of the unemployed came decades later. At first sight, the relatively slow development of this policy appears strange, but upon reflection we can understand this evolutionary process. The concepts of employment and unemployment reflect a relationship between individuals and their work life that is primarily industrial rather than rural. When workers were tied to the land, there was a relatively stable community that assisted the indigent to the best of its ability when times were hard, but with the Industrial Revolution, populations became more fluid and concentrated in large, impersonal cities. Social insurance accompanied this process of urbanization and industrialization, with the state taking on the role previously played by family and village. In an important sense, then, the welfare state substituted for the traditional social-economic relations that had once existed in agriculturally oriented communities.[49]

The United States government shared this initial indifference to the plight of the unemployed. During the depression year of 1894, for example, virtual armies of unemployed workers marched on Washington and demanded government action to create new jobs. The most famous of these armies was led by Ohio businessman Jacob Coxey, who had been inspired by the nineteenth-century "social-gospel" movement and its economic message that the well-being and dignity of the worker should be at the core of corporate and government policy. Despite growing political pressure, the federal government did virtually nothing at this time.[50]

In the United States, a broad array of social policies (e.g., unemployment insurance and pensions) would only emerge in the context of Franklin Roosevelt's New Deal and the subsequent wartime expansion of the federal government (with some important nineteenth-century exceptions, such as pensions for Civil War veterans). Prior to the Great Depression, the general problem of poor relief was left to charitable organizations, communities, and state governments. The idea of using deficit spending to increase the overall level of demand, and thus employment, only came later, with the publication and diffusion of Keynes's *General Theory of Employment, Interest, and Money*, in 1935. Thus, even when unemployment reached eight million in 1931, or nearly 20 percent of the working population, President Herbert Hoover could tell Congress, "I am opposed to any direct or indirect government dole."[51]

Why did policy change so sharply under Franklin Roosevelt? Undoubtedly he was shaped by ideas different from Hoover's, but Roosevelt also had growing fears about his country's political and social stability. During the Great Depression, organized groups of unemployed workers (often assembled by the Communist Party) descended on relief organizations and factories seeking money and work. In some cities, the ensuing riots became violent, and mayors and governors pleaded with Washington to provide more assistance. As New York Congressman Hamilton Fish, Jr.—certainly no liberal—told his colleagues, "If we don't give [security] under the existing system, the people will change the system. Make no mistake about that."[52]

It was not just communists who were posing a threat to the traditional American system. Demagogues ranging from Father Charles Coughlin to Louisiana Governor Huey Long stormed the radio waves and the political parties, and Coughlin sold his newspaper, *Social Justice*, outside Catholic churches on Sundays. While neither proved able to mobilize mass political movements, each influenced public debate about the relationship between the economy and society. Indeed, as the depression raged worldwide, the Catholic Church as a whole launched a dual-pronged attack on capitalism and the socialist alternative, seeking a middle ground known as "Catholic social action."[53]

If the experience of depression and the potential for mass disorder spurred the development of various social insurance programs as stopgap measures, the experience of nazism and World War II would hasten the full development of the welfare state. At the outset of the war, the German social insurance system was seen as an integral part of that country's military

preparations. As Edward Phelan of the International Labor Organization said in a 1941 speech:

> Germany prepared for war, not only militarily and indus-
> trially, but also socially. Its social machine, when placed at
> the service of military conquest, has been revised, lubri-
> cated and perfected in every part. . . . The Nazis, as soon
> as they came to power, while destroying the free organi-
> zation of the workers, took care to preserve the social in-
> surance scheme and the social services. In these they
> rightly saw an instrument for social preparedness.[54]

In time, the allies would also see the necessity to develop social insurance programs as part and parcel of the war effort with
Britain taking the lead. There, Sir William Beveridge chaired a
committee on Social Insurance and Allied Services, whose report
would bear his name. The *Beveridge Report* has gone into history
as a foundation document of the modern welfare state. It was in
wartime Britain that the term *welfare state* was first evoked,
when Archbishop of Canterbury William Temple "coined the
phrase in an attempt to characterize a polar contrast to the
'power' and 'warfare' state of the Nazis."[55] Beveridge noted in the
Report that some critics thought it inappropriate to worry about
social insurance programs during the war. He countered by stating "the purpose of victory is to live into a better world than the
old world; that each individual citizen is more likely to concentrate upon his war effort if he feels that his Government will be
ready in time with plans for that better world; that, if these
plans are to be ready in time, they must be made now."

The British commitment to universal welfare grew out of
the country's experience with World War I and the flawed peace
that followed—which, it was widely believed, had inevitably
produced World War II (more on this in the following section).
According to political scientist Stephen Blank, "The British
were convinced that the fundamental causes of the war were the

economic and social conditions of the interwar years. British economic commitments and policies in the postwar years were greatly influenced by the belief that it was necessary to avoid the recurrence of such conditions at almost any cost."[56]

Drawing from this belief, the objective of the Beveridge plan was nothing less than the "abolition of want." What the report proposed was "a scheme of social insurance against interruption and destruction of earning power. . . ." In all this, the state would have to play an essential role; indeed, "social security must be achieved by cooperation between the State and the individual."[57] The welfare state, with the displacement of charity by government policy at its core, had arrived.

The modern welfare state would also make another promise to workers: full employment. Again, elites in many of the industrial countries drew a causal link among high levels of unemployment, political instability, social conflict, and war. Thus, the British government produced a white paper in 1944 that began with the bold statement, "This Government accepts as one of their primary aims and responsibilities the maintenance of a high and stable level of employment after the war."[58] At the same time, Sir William Beveridge produced another report, *Full Employment in a Free Society*—which would also prove influential in the United States—that opened with the words of Charlotte Bronte, "Misery generates hate." Beveridge would go on to write: "The greatest evil of unemployment is not physical but moral, not the want which it may bring but the hatred and fear which it breeds."[59]

In the United States, the Truman administration would pass the GI Bill and the Employment Act of 1946, which declared it a responsibility of the federal government "to use all practicable means . . . to promote maximum employment, production, and purchasing power."[60] If this bill was less motivated by fears of domestic social conflict than similar European legislation, it was not because American leaders had dismissed the possibility of such conflict, but rather because they had faith in the ability of economic growth to restore public confidence in the industrial-capitalist system. As Harvard historian Charles Maier has written, America's "very emphasis on economic potential itself emerged from deeper divisions. The productivist view of America's postwar mission arose naturally out of the domestic modes of resolving social conflict, or, rather, the difficulty of resolving conflicts cleanly."[61]

Still, even in the American context, the memory of depression and the world wars, along with the threat posed by Soviet communism, shaped the domestic policy agenda. The postwar GI Bill was not simply a way of thanking American veterans for their military service, but a preventive measure aimed at keeping them under the democratic capitalist tent.[62] As in Britain, the American government recognized that the veteran must return to a better world if loyalties were to be maintained, and thus the war and its aftermath saw an expansive social agenda, as discussed fully in chapter 3.

As this capsule history suggests, the welfare state has grown out of conflicts, crises, and wars—events that were, at least in part, a product of the political failure to cope with economic change and its consequences for working people. When seen in that light, we recognize that distributive policies are not charity in a different form, but rather an essential function of modern states that must live with the threat of domestic violence and revolution on the one hand and war on the other.

But the equating of welfare-state functions with social conflict poses important challenges for those who would wish to maintain, if not expand, these institutions in the future. For with the collapse of the Soviet Union and the emergence of the United States as a hegemonic actor, the fear factor that has provided a cornerstone of these institutions may well be crumbling. As economic competition replaces military competition on the international scene, states may increasingly view their social safety nets as webs that entangle their enterprises rather than ones that strengthen their societies.

Yet there are good economic and moral reasons for welfare-state policies that go beyond political calculations, and these will be explored in later chapters. Further, notions of welfare provision will also have to go beyond the domestic realm to the international sphere in which, increasingly, debates about social policy are located. The following section explores the history of those international debates.

SOCIAL WELFARE AND INTERNATIONAL POLITICS

In fact, what we now call social or welfare policies have had an international dimension since the early days of the Industrial Revolution. Utopians like Robert Owen advocated for international social legislation on behalf of labor in order to establish some common floor so that workers would not be placed in a position of competing away their wages and benefits. These entrepreneurs, coupled with crusaders of varying political stripes, had already combined forces as early as 1802 to win passage of a Factory Act designed "to protect the health and morals of children employed in factories." Other laws dealing with women workers, the length of the workday, and workplace safety were also debated and passed at that time.[63]

But as national laws imposed additional costs on production, entrepreneurs soon confronted the problem of growing international trade and competitiveness issues, and the tensions between globalization and domestic social welfare could not be easily resolved. As State Department official Herbert Feis wrote in an early history of the problem, "Those interested in the improvement of industrial conditions in various countries had more than once found that a desired change in labor conditions was hindered by the possibility that the same industry in some other country might secure a competitive advantage as a result of the change. . . . The idea of resorting to joint international action is, therefore, natural in such contingencies."[64]

In addition to the nascent efforts by utopian industrialists to establish a level playing field for competition, international labor legislation would later receive strong support from the union movement, which was closely tied to the Socialist International. International unions of miners met alongside the Socialist International Congress of 1890, and metalworkers in 1893. The purpose of these international federations was to provide information about working conditions in different countries, give mutual support during strikes, and compare state policies and industrial approaches with respect to wages, factory laws, and training.[65]

Perhaps not surprisingly, the first major conference on international labor legislation was held in Berlin in 1890, quite literally over the dead political body of Chancellor Bismarck. Despite being an early pioneer of social insurance, Bismarck declared himself opposed to international labor legislation because of its strong socialist connection. It was this opposition that sealed his political fate, as he was summarily dismissed by the young German emperor Wilhelm II, who supported the conference.

The conference launched a process that would ultimately lead to the creation of the International Labor Organization in 1919. In its immediate wake, the International Association of Labor Legislation was formed by a diverse group of entrepreneurs, public officials, and trade unionists. This association chose two issues as immediate objectives of international legislation: a legal prohibition on night work by women, and an end to the use of highly flammable white phosphorous in factories. These two prohibitions were ultimately passed by international conventions early in the twentieth century.[66] Further, the American Association of Labor Legislation would spearhead the drive for a social insurance program in the United States.[67]

It was, however, the Great War that put international labor legislation firmly on the public agenda. At the instigation of the major international trade unions, whose members had fought and died during the conflict, the leaders who met at Versailles in 1919 were charged with ending destructive labor competition. The result would be the International Labor Organization (ILO).

The ILO—which, along with the League of Nations, was a direct artifact of the Treaty of Versailles—was a major component in the allies' efforts to put a definitive end to Europe's political troubles. Drawing from their historic memory of the nineteenth century, and, more important, the reality of the Russian Revolution, the postwar leaders drew a causal connection among worker dissatisfaction, agitation, revolution, and war. Thus, their challenge was to find a way to pacify worker concerns in the context of the capitalist order.

The Versailles treaty explicitly reflected these concerns. Its preamble stated: "Peace can be established only if it is based upon social justice; and . . . conditions of labor exist involving such injustice, hardship, and privation to large numbers of people as to produce unrest so great that the peace and harmony of the world are imperiled." The underlying thesis here was that economic inequality and insecurity were at the root cause of international conflict.

The ILO was a unique organization in many respects. First, it would not be composed solely of government representatives, but rather would take a tripartite form that included employers, workers, and public officials. Second, its membership would be "universal." Finally, there was a strong presumption that even though its recommendations would have to be passed into law via national legislation, its "conventions" would indeed be adopted. In fact, the Versailles treaty itself included the following labor principles and rights that would also form the basis for the ILO constitution:

1. Labor should not be regarded merely as a commodity or article of Commerce;

2. The right of association;
3. The payment of an adequate wage to maintain a reasonable standard of living;
4. An eight-hour day or forty-hour week;
5. A weekly rest of at least twenty-four hours;
6. Abolition of child labor;
7. Equal pay for equal work;
8. Equitable economic treatment for all workers in a country; and
9. An inspection system to ensure the enforcement of laws for worker protection.[68]

The "peacemakers" at Versailles who included such provisions were motivated not just by the lessons of the past, but equally by their fears of the future. In Russia, a communist revolution had just been completed, with the potential to spread far and wide. As Columbia University professor and Versailles delegate James Shotwell wrote of the treaty and the ILO it created:

> The Governments of Europe were nervous in the face of a rising industrial unrest, with unknown Bolshevist possibilities, with menacing fires of revolution in Germany, and with at least one or two of the governments represented at Paris daily in danger of being overthrown. . . . With this background, the Labor Commission of the Peace Conference settled down to over four months of steady work, framing the constitution of an organization that was to meet the challenge of socialism and communism and to prove to the workers of the world that the principles of social justice might be established under the capitalist system.[69]

Elsewhere, Shotwell would go even further, arguing that when the ILO "was conceived and set going, the revolutionary movement, triumphant in Russia, was threatening to overwhelm the whole tottering fabric of the state system of Europe."[70]

Paradoxically, the authors of the Treaty of Versailles would not apply their analysis to Germany, which would suffer, through territorial losses and heavy reparations payments, what British delegate John Maynard Keynes called a "Carthaginian Peace." Indeed, Keynes was so incensed by the proceedings that he resigned and went home to write *The Economic Consequences of the Peace*, a book that delivered a prophetic analysis of what lay ahead for a bankrupt and starved Germany and, as a consequence, for Europe. Drawing on the Russian Revolution, Keynes wrote of "how in the final catastrophe the malady of the body passes over into the malady of the mind. Economic privation proceeds by easy stages, and so long as men suffer it patiently the outside world cares little. . . . Then man shakes himself, and the bonds of custom are loosed. The power of ideas is sovereign, and he listens to whatever instruction of hope, illusion or revenge is carried to him on the air."[71]

The German delegates themselves eloquently expressed the impossible position in which Germany had been placed. The German financial delegates told their counterpart that as a result of the treaty,

> German democracy is thus annihilated at the very moment when the German people was about to build it up after a severe struggle—annihilated by the very persons who throughout the war never tired of maintaining that they sought to bring democracy to us. . . . Germany is no longer a people and a State, but becomes a mere trade concern placed by its creditors in the hands of a receiver . . . the German people under its regime would remain for decades to come shorn of all rights, and deprived, to a far greater extent than any people in the days of absolutism, of any independence of action, of any individual aspiration in its economic or even its ethical progress.[72]

And more powerful still were the words of Count Brock-dorff-Rantzau as he addressed the peace conference on how the treaty must affect the German population:

> We do not know, and indeed we doubt, whether the Delegates . . . realize the inevitable consequences which will take place if Germany, an industrial state, very thickly populated, closely bound up with the economic system of the world, and under the necessity of import-ing enormous quantities of raw material and foodstuffs, suddenly finds herself pushed back to the phase of her development, which corresponds to her economic con-ditions and the numbers of her population as they were half a century ago. *Those who sign this Treaty will sign the death sentence of many millions of German men, women, and children* [italics added].[73]

But the events toward which these words pointed were still in the future. Despite the bold statements made at Versailles, the treaty ultimately failed to serve the cause of social justice. It would take the Great Depression and another world war before the problems that confronted working people would again find their place on the international policy agenda.

CONCLUSIONS

Rapid economic change has been an important source of social disruption and political instability throughout modern history. The creation of social insurance schemes, and the subsequent expansion of the welfare state, cannot be explained as public acts of charity; these developments have been key elements in capitalism's survival strategy. The hypothesis that argues "states which adopt distributive policies are more stable," is not the product of the normative desires of woolly professors, or the wishful thinking of utopians, but rather has been borne out by both historical study and statistical analyses of country cases. Indeed, many of the founders of the welfare state—Bismarck among them—were conservative rulers who recognized that social safety nets had to be created, often over the opposition of powerful economic groups, if the state were to prevent domestic rebellion. That was also a key insight of Franklin D. Roosevelt, who was castigated by Wall Street for his "socialist" policies but who responded by saying he was saving the capitalists from themselves.

This chapter has also shown that matters of economic justice have not merely been embedded in domestic politics, but have been very much part of international relations since the early nineteenth century. Trade unionists, and visionaries like Robert Owen, feared that international competitive forces might prove capable of undermining domestic factory legislation, victimizing workers everywhere. These modest efforts provided the impetus for what would ultimately become the International Labor Organization. But the tensions between domestic economic policies and the international gold standard were never successfully resolved, and would not be resolved until the end of World War II, after mankind's most intense generation of bloodletting.

This historic record should, if nothing more, make us modest about our collective ability to reconcile economic change and social justice. Economic policy, with its utilitarian belief that more is always better, tends to overlook the distributive issues that are at the core of most political conflicts. But the way in which we distribute the economic gains that are associated with openness, liberalization, and technological development is not preordained; it is a matter of social choice. If those choices are made in a non-democratic fashion, "behind closed doors," or result in outcomes in which all the gains are concentrated in the hands of a few, they will not be accepted as just. That is a lesson that we will revisit again in future chapters.

LABOR AND THE
POSTWAR ORDER

> *. . . the twentieth century is likely to be known as the century
> of the worker. . . .*
>
> — FORMER U.S. SECRETARY OF LABOR
> JOHN DUNLOP, 1978[1]

THIS CHAPTER EXAMINES THE ROLE of labor in shaping the postwar economic order. The story is a puzzling one, for in the early years organized labor seemed to be gaining significant influence in agenda-setting, only to lose out over time to other interest groups and preoccupations. Today, the polling data taken in many countries suggest that unskilled workers increasingly perceive economic openness as a menace to their interests, rather than as a policy that spreads the wealth. This position was made plain by an American labor leader at the time of the North American Free Trade Agreement (NAFTA) debate; he said, "A U.S.-Mexican FTA poses a double threat: the loss of jobs for U.S. workers and even worse exploitation for Mexican workers."[2]

Labor's attitude toward globalization arises not just from the obvious fact that it is relatively immobile when compared to capital, but also because it seeks to be treated differently from other goods and services. For more than 100 years, working people have struggled to win recognition of their special economic position, and to have their dignity recognized and made part of the policymaking equation. Workers, they claim, should not be treated like a commodity. That, in turn, raises all sorts of complex questions about how labor is—and ought to be—treated that do not arise in the case of other economic inputs.

Yet it appears that these concerns are becoming increasingly marginalized. The position of labor in society now seems to take second place in economic policy decisionmaking, as countries give pride of place to the fight against inflation and budget deficits, the maintenance of stable exchange rates, privatization, and, in such corrupt cases as Russia or Indonesia, rent-seeking behavior (i.e., stealing from the government) by the rich. The postwar promise to place "full employment" and decent wages at the core of the economic policymaking has been forgotten. The story of that policy retreat is told in this chapter.

PLANNING THE POSTWAR ECONOMY

Meeting off the coast of Newfoundland in August 1941, just months before the surprise attack on Pearl Harbor, President Franklin Roosevelt and Prime Minister Winston Churchill laid the cornerstones of their wartime collaboration and postwar cooperation. In the Atlantic Charter, they pledged that at the war's end they would seek to secure "for all countries and peoples improved labor standards, economic advancement, and social security." They also vowed to end "freedom from fear or want."

Why were these statements made in the midst of war? According to Sir William Beveridge, such policies and programs were "a sign of the belief that the object of government in peace and war is not the glory of rulers or races, but the happiness of the common man."[3] Planning a postwar economy that somehow managed to reconcile the market's demand for efficiency with the political demand for equity became a major field of activity for policymakers.

The Atlantic Charter's words were inspired by the failure of the World War I settlement to achieve a "lasting peace," and the collapse of the world economy during the Great Depression, with its far-reaching political effects. By the time World War II erupted, people everywhere believed, as Harvard's Alvin Hansen wrote, "The great depression fanned the flames of a new world conflagration." Eliminating the possibility of a similar economic tragedy was the overriding objective of postwar planning.

We cannot exaggerate the degree to which the lessons of the past hung over these policymakers. They wanted to rebuild a global economy but recognized that international economic issues could not be treated in isolation from domestic social policy. As a League of Nations report stated in 1942, "Commercial policy cannot be considered by itself. . . . It must be considered as part of the more general constructive policies agreed among governments for the prevention of economic depressions and assurance of social stability."[4]

Yet in seeking the root cause of the Great Depression, analysts disagreed over whether its sources were to be found in the domestic or the international political economies. That is, was it the failure of individual nations to counter deflation and unemployment that led to the depression's global spread, or was it the failure of international cooperation to maintain open borders to trade and investment that turned domestic recessions into a global crisis? The likely answer was "some of both," and the postwar planners sought to build a structure in which the domestic and international economies operated in harmony rather than conflict.

In thinking about postwar reconstruction, western leaders were animated by several causal beliefs about the relationship between domestic economic performance and world politics. The first had its origins in the Treaty of Versailles, and it argued that by placing Germany in an economic straitjacket, impoverishing the country, the seeds of fascist rule and thus international conflict were planted. At the same time, they believed that the failure of international cooperation during the Great Depression caused the spread and prolongation of that economic crisis, with inevitably malign results for both domestic and international politics. These two beliefs led to the general theory that domestic economic instability and high levels of unemployment must produce internal conflict, regime change, and possibly international war. The lessons of history made plain that the postwar world would have to combine international economic cooperation on the one hand and the promotion of domestic full employment on the other, in the interest of political stability, sustained growth, and economic justice.

In building this new world order, the postwar leaders placed high hopes on an array of international organizations. The United Nations, International Monetary Fund, World Bank, and General Agreement on Tariffs and Trade were all designed to encourage nations to resolve their political and economic disputes in a peaceful manner. International financial resources—grants and low-interest loans—were made available to states in economic difficulties, so that they would not have to respond to their problems by adopting autarkic or beggar-thy-neighbor measures. Openness and autonomy would travel hand in hand rather than at cross-purposes.

International labor was excited by the promise of the new era. The wartime alliance between the western powers and the Soviet Union had muted the rifts within and between unions caused by communism, and in 1945 the World Federation of Trade Unions (WFTU) was founded, "which united unionists of almost all political loyalties from around the globe."[5] The

WFTU believed that it would play a crucial role in the governance of the emerging international organizations and help lead the nations of the world to a more peaceful plane. In the words of the great British trade unionist Walter Citrine, "The UN could not be a success without the support of the people . . . if the WFTU pulled out, the UN would collapse."[6] Union leaders now envisioned a corporatist world in which capital and labor would be equally represented in economic and political debates.[7]

Only a few years later, these hopes would be dashed. The Cold War again drove the communist stake into labor's heart, dividing and disrupting the movement within many countries and internationally; in 1949, the WFTU folded. Far from representing the interests of working people, the leading international institutions seemed to exclude them from their deliberations, while the International Labor Organization proved a thin reed for political support. These developments meant that labor had to find other ways to get its views on the policy agenda.

Naturally, the most important mechanism was through domestic politics, and here labor's prospects seemed more promising. After all, by 1945 Britain would have a Labour government, and across Europe labor parties would be part of the ruling coalitions that many states had formed. On the shop floor, too, there was hope for better relations with management, given the intense consumer demands that now existed, coupled with the severe labor shortage that was the war's grim outcome.

During the war, labor had begun to promote the central issue that it now sought to advance and turn into reality: full employment. As we saw in earlier chapters, full employment had been a distant dream of social reformers since the French Revolution, and now it seemed to be within labor's grasp. In one country after another, full employment would figure prominently in national debates about the postwar political economy.

That vision, however, would clash with another compelling

image: that of "free multilateralism," or global economic integration. Unlike the 1930s, the postwar era would usher in a period of trade and investment such as the world had not seen since the heyday of the British Empire. According to American officials, free trade would lead not just to global prosperity but also to world peace, since trading nations did not go to war with one another. But did free trade help or hurt the cause of full employment? Profound differences of opinion separated the allies on that question. Squaring full-employment and free-trade policies would prove one of the great challenges for the postwar order.

THE POLITICS OF FULL EMPLOYMENT

At the war's end, no political-economic objective became more crucial to the advanced industrial countries—with the partial and critical exception of the United States—than the achievement of "full employment." As Harvard's most influential Keynesian, Alvin Hansen, wrote in a survey of postwar planning, it was clear that "throughout the world, leaders in government and in industry are more and more committed to a program of sustained full employment."[8] During the war and its immediate aftermath, the governments of most allied countries would pledge themselves to adopt full-employment policies, something they had never done in the past.

The pacesetter in this development was Great Britain, operating under the sway of Keynesian ideas and bruised by the experience of a history that again and again pointed to the lesson that European peace depended above all on economic security. In 1944, the Churchill government unveiled its *White Paper on Employment*, which began with the now-famous words: "The Government accept as one of their primary aims and responsibilities the maintenance of a high and stable level of employment after the war." With those words, the welfare state took its place at the cornerstone of postwar economic planning. Again, British officials, recalling with terror the interwar years, were fearful that returning servicemen would not accept a jobless future peacefully.[9]

The establishment of full-employment policies was at the core of Britain's vision for the postwar world. If democratic governments failed, in the words of political scientist John Ikenberry, "to deliver the socioeconomic goods," the outcome might be the end of that regime type—and, after all, a powerful alternative now existed in the Soviet Union. Keynes himself argued that democracy was a fragile institution, and another depression "might easily mean the downfall of our present system of democratic government."[10]

But what was really meant by the term *full employment*? The concept's most influential advocate, Sir William Beveridge, defined it in the following terms: "Full employment . . . means always having more vacant jobs than unemployed men, not slightly fewer jobs. It means that the jobs are at fair wages, of such a kind, and so located that the unemployed men can reasonably be expected to take them; it means, by consequence, that the normal lag between losing one job and finding another will be very short."[11]

And how would full employment be achieved? This is the question that Keynes seemingly had answered in his *General Theory of Employment, Interest, and Money*. There Keynes argued that central governments must engage in active demand-side management through their manipulation of monetary and fiscal policy. According to Beveridge, full employment was the state's responsibility no less than its function "to defend citizens against attack from abroad and against robbery and violence at home." In short, job creation was now a fundamental task of every government.[12]

Britain was not alone in making this commitment to its workers, its veterans. At the war's end, Canada, Australia, New

Zealand, France, and other countries would also adopt similar declaratory policies, and Australia would prove to be a particularly vociferous advocate for that policy goal in international arenas. But one country would ultimately reject the concept of full employment as the beacon of its postwar economic policy— the United States.

In fact, the U.S. position was more complicated and ambiguous than that statement implies. During the war, the Roosevelt administration made several bows in the direction of full employment, both in its domestic and its international policies. This objective, however, faced significant opposition among congressional conservatives, who saw it as a first step on the dreaded road to economic planning, which must inevitably lead to socialism. Already, these same conservatives had fought the New Deal, saving the United States from the worst excesses of the Roosevelt administration. In the usual American style, a compromise would be reached on employment, which nonetheless, in tune with the times, placed a growing burden on the government for economic management.

As plans for the postwar world were debated and drafted, America's failure to declare full employment as its stated, explicit policy objective caused deep concern among its wartime allies. Countries feared that the United States would, at war's end, enter a period of depression, dragging the world economy down with it. As the world's largest economy, any decisions— or nondecisions—taken by the United States during that depression would necessarily reverberate worldwide. If Washington was unwilling to promise that it would adopt aggregate demand policies aimed at maintaining full employment, where did that leave smaller countries that would suffer as a result?

The defeat of full-employment legislation was surprising in that New Deal officials, like their British counterparts, had made it their central economic goal for the postwar period. As historian Alan Brinkley writes, "Full employment was necessary . . . not just to spare individuals the pain of joblessness, but also—and more important—to provide the nation with the largest possible body of consumers."[13] Naturally, the quest for full employment would involve government planning to ensure "the expansion of civilian consumption."[14] And it was exactly that aspect—the government as planner—that awakened the sensibilities of conservative critics.

The differing fates of full-employment policy in the United States and in Great Britain remind us of the importance of national political institutions in transforming ideas into legislation. After all, as in Britain, John Maynard Keynes had become a towering figure in American economic and official circles by the war's end, and it was he who animated the full-employment debate. Not only was he the most influential economist of the era, but he also had practical experience to bolster his theoretical claims. His *Economic Consequences of the Peace* had prophetically warned of the tragic flaws in the Versailles Treaty. If there was anyone who understood the intricate relationship between economic policy and political outcomes, it had to be Keynes.

Further, his adherents, such as Alvin Hansen and Seymour Harris of Harvard, were influential in the government, and Keynes himself was an able self-promoter. Brinkley reminds us that "Keynes devoted considerable attention to the United States throughout the war. He corresponded with sympathetic American policymakers and economists. He made periodic visits to Washington. . . . In the process, Keynes reinforced his allies and won new converts."[15]

But despite this firepower, the American Keynesians had to contend with a large, decentralized government bureaucracy, many parts of which were hostile to their ideas. Thus, the wartime National Resources Planning Board (NRPB), which had become a center for Keynesian ideas, was eliminated in 1943 by Congress, shortly after releasing a major report calling for extensive works programs and other government policies designed to ensure postwar full employment. In the wake of that decision, the Senate went so far as to convene its own committee on postwar planning, chaired by the conservative Walter George.[16]

The battle over full employment reached its peak following President Roosevelt's 1944 State of the Union address, in which he argued that political rights alone were "inadequate to assure us equality in the pursuit of happiness." "Economic security and independence," he said, were fundamental to human freedom. These words indicated that the president remained a committed New Dealer as he faced the postwar world.

Emboldened by the speech, a coalition of liberal groups, with intellectual support provided by academics like Alvin Hansen, pressed for the adoption of a Full Employment Bill. Finally, a bill of this title was introduced in early 1945 by Senator James Murray of Montana. It stated: "All Americans able to work and seeking work have the right to a useful and remunerative job. . . . It is essential that continuing full employment be maintained in the United States." Under the proposed bill, the president was required to prepare a national production and employment budget that would estimate "the number of jobs needed during the ensuing fiscal year or years to assure continuing full employment."[17]

With the death of President Roosevelt, the Full Employment Bill found its major champion in President Harry Truman. He called it a "middle way" between statism on the one hand and an unregulated marketplace on the other. But the bill's opponents saw it as the first step on a slippery slope to socialism. Its claim of a right to work could easily become the basis for an unprecedented peacetime expansion of government, with the power to order people to work.[18] It had no chance of passage in an increasingly conservative Congress. Ultimately, the United States would pass instead the 1946 Employment Act, which called upon the government "to use all practicable means . . . to foster and promote . . . conditions under which there will be afforded useful employment for those able, willing and seeking to work, and to promote maximum employment, production, and purchasing power."[19] And while many argued that the difference between these words and the phrase *full employment* was insignificant, still an uneasy gap between the United States and its alliance partners remained.

INTERNATIONAL FINANCE AND FULL EMPLOYMENT

As planning for the postwar international economy proceeded during the years 1944–47, a major issue that divided the United States from its allies was whether a policy of free multilateralism—openness to trade and investment flows—necessarily promoted national full-employment objectives. Americans held an evangelical belief that this was the case, but the British among others were less certain. This is somewhat ironic, given Britain's long experience with free trade, which the United States of course did not share. To the British, multilateralism might have much to recommend it in terms of efficiency goals, but advancing full employment was not necessarily among its attributes. In the event, London held that without the achievement of full employment, international economic cooperation simply could not be sustained; it was the price that must be paid to keep the peace, both at home and abroad.

Keynes had in fact devoted his wartime years to designing postwar institutions that could overcome these tensions. The principal way in which he proposed to link domestic full-employment policies to free multilateralism was through international financial cooperation. He had drawn from the history of the international gold standard that its tragic flaw was its inability to reconcile the domestic need for flexibility in economic policy and the international requirement for exchange-rate stability.

The problem with the gold standard was that, as countries ran trade deficits, their only option was to export gold to meet their payment requirements. This reduction in gold holdings, in turn, must eventually be met by an increase in domestic interest rates, in order to prevent further exports of the precious metal (gold, after all, was the only "reserve currency"). Higher interest rates would then cause a contraction in domestic economic activity, and consequently a decline in employment levels, producing the threat of social disruption and ultimately a rejection of the standard's legitimacy as an instrument for economic policy.

Thus, the gold standard exemplified the inherent conflict between "free" markets and civil society. The gold standard may have been a perfectly reasonable *economic* system—indeed, today we still find "goldbugs" around the world—but it could not be justified on political grounds. With demands on the state growing at a rapid pace during the nineteenth century, governments chafed under the system and its rigid constraints. Unfortunately, the world would not find alternatives to that system until the middle of the twentieth century.

The nineteenth-century international gold standard was the major economic casualty of World War I. During the war, countries had financed expenditures by issuing paper money and accumulating massive debt burdens, both national and international. Fears of domestic revolution—realized in Russia—made governments seek alternatives to the grim orthodoxy of the gold standard, which tied their hands in setting domestic economic policies. As a result, the war's aftermath saw inflation almost everywhere, reaching hyperinflation levels in Germany and Central Europe. Princeton historian Harold James writes of this period: "The story of the 1920s is a sad chronicle of attempts . . . to deal with the tangled financial legacy of the Great War."[20]

As we know, such efforts resulted in failure. The world's major creditor, the United States, adopted a set of monetary policies during the Great Depression that only contributed to the deepening and widening of the crisis. As countries faced global price deflation, competitive currency devaluation became the order of the day, leading to the infamous era of beggar-thy-neighbor policymaking. The ensuing international price collapse was first seen in commodities, but soon spread to financial markets. Banks fell in domino fashion around the world, and the meager efforts at international cooperation evaporated. In Italy and Germany, fascist governments came to power partly on the promise of restoring economic stability. By 1939, a world in depression was a world at war.

It was the Nazi minister of finance, Walther Funk, who, in 1940, made the first proposal for a "new economic order," providing an alternative to the international gold standard. He sketched a vision of a postwar Europe, under German aegis, that would be based on "an intelligent division of labor between the various European countries." European trade would be settled not through gold payments but through an exchange mechanism in which countries would establish fixed currency rates against the Reichsmark. In this way, the economy of a country would be limited not by its gold holdings but only by its available labor, resources, and technology.[21]

As part of its propaganda effort, the British government felt it necessary to counter Funk's proposal, and it immediately enlisted Keynes's support. He gladly took up the challenge, stating that he would propose "the same as what Dr. Funk offers, except that we shall do it better and more honestly. This is important. For a proposal to return to the blessings of 1920–1933 will not have much propaganda value."[22] Keynes, of course, recognized the failure of the gold system to meet the requirements of domestic economic stability, and indeed the matter would become pointed in the British case, as the country would certainly exhaust its gold holdings in fighting the war. Britain thus had as great an interest as any nation in developing an acceptable alternative.

Unlike Funk's proposal, which focused on trade financing, Keynes's goal was to establish an "international clearings union"

(ICU), which would provide countries with balance-of-payments financing so they could maintain full-employment policies in the event of temporary disequilibria in their external accounts. That is, countries confronting a temporary financial problem would not be faced with the immediate necessity of limiting their economic activity, producing unemployment in the process, but rather could borrow short-term funds from this ICU. That idea, when coupled with the American notion of a postwar "stabilization fund," ultimately provided the intellectual cornerstone of the postwar International Monetary Fund (IMF), founded in Bretton Woods, New Hampshire (along with its "twin," the World Bank), in 1944.

The postwar leaders who met at Bretton Woods, now influenced both by Keynesian economics and their personal experiences of war and depression, recognized that international markets for capital and trade, when left to their own devices, might not produce policy results consistent with world peace and prosperity. As the American architect of the IMF, Harry Dexter White, said in 1942, "The theoretical basis for the belief still so widely held, that interference with trade and with capital and gold movements, etc., are harmful, are hangovers from a nineteenth century creed, which held that international economic adjustments, if left alone, would work themselves out toward an 'equilibrium' with a minimum of harm to world trade and prosperity. It is doubtful whether that belief was ever sound."[23] The system they sought to build would not be automatic; it would be managed by governments acting in the interests of both prosperity and peace.

The bargain struck at Bretton Woods represented a preliminary effort at seeking a compromise between the economic dictates of free markets—particularly the logic of the international division of labor—with the need to create a "managed system" in the interests of domestic and international stability. In the famous phrase of political scientist John Ruggie, that postwar agreement represented "the embedded liberalism compromise:

unlike the economic nationalism of the thirties, it would be multilateral in character; unlike the liberalism of the gold standard and free trade, its multilateralism would be predicated upon domestic interventionism."[24]

At Bretton Woods, the postwar leaders sought to enjoy the benefits of free trade while maintaining the freedom to pursue domestic full-employment policies at the same time (though it should be noted that the IMF's Articles of Agreement did not speak of full employment but rather "high levels of employment"). Thus, the newly appointed executive directors of the IMF made it clear at their first meeting that countries pursuing full-employment policies, if facing balance-of-payments difficulties that threatened the advancement of that policy, could—without seeking IMF permission—"relieve the external pressure by a change in its exchange rate, even though the Fund might hold that a change in the internal policy could in the long run prove a more constructive solution."[25]

Unilateral currency devaluations were not, of course the IMF's preferred policy route, since they would open up the possibility of a return to a world of competitive devaluations and 1930s-style international economic chaos. The IMF was designed to avoid that outcome by providing countries with emergency loans. Still, it was prepared to accept sudden changes in exchange-rate parities in those cases where countries were "not prepared to deal boldly" with domestic economic problems.[26]

The solution adopted at Bretton Woods—of a world of convertible currencies with fixed exchange rates pegged to the dollar—would not long endure the postwar task of reconstruction. At the war's end, the world craved dollars—dollars needed to buy imports of food, coal, and machinery. Currency convertibility was impossible under these conditions of real scarcity. It was with the announcement of the Marshall Plan in June 1947 that the United States recognized its responsibility to provide the international economy with the liquidity it needed to operate.

TRADE AND LABOR

As the debate over the IMF suggests, a key issue in postwar planning concerned the role that domestic employment issues should be accorded in any international arrangements. For Britain and other countries, a national commitment to full employment seemed a basic requirement for any multilateral trade agreements. Countries that rejected the concept—chiefly the United States—were signaling a potential willingness to "export unemployment" during an economic downturn. That would inevitably lead to the sort of beggar-thy-neighbor policies that prolonged and expanded the Great Depression.

Given America's eventual rejection of full employment legislation, it is ironic that it was the United States that in 1943 called upon the International Labor Organization (ILO) to "hold a regular conference . . . for the purpose of making recommendations to the United Nations as to post-war labor policies."[27] Specifically, the ILO conference would address: "A. Labor policy in occupied territories. B. Social aims and economic policy. C. Labor provisions of the peace settlement. D. Minimum standards of security for workers demobilized from the armed forces and war industries, *including international machinery for the maintenance of full employment* [italics added]."[28]

The ILO conference that met in Philadelphia, Pennsylvania, from 20 April to 12 May 1944, and the declaration it issued, became the basis for tremendous hope about the role that labor questions would play in postwar planning. The Philadelphia declaration boldly stated: "All human beings, irrespective of race, creed or sex, have the right to pursue both their material well-being and their spiritual development in conditions of freedom and dignity, of economic security and equal opportunity." These words had tremendous resonance, providing the basis for similar statements in the United Nations Charter (article 55) and the

Universal Declaration of Human Rights (article 22). The declaration continued with the affirmation that the pursuit of this right should be central to economic planning; thus, "All national and international policies and measures, in particular those of an economic and financial character, should be judged in this light and accepted only in so far as they may be held to promote and not to hinder the achievement of this fundamental objective." These bold words meant that the only legitimate purpose of economic policy was to serve the cause of social justice.[29]

At Philadelphia, the ILO proclaimed that human rights should be at the core of economic policy, and that governments should use the national and international instruments at their disposal to advance those rights. Indeed, the ILO suggested that it had as one of its responsibilities the assessment of "all international economic and financial policies and measures" with respect to the declaration's objective. As Berkeley's Ernst Haas, a distinguished student of international organizations, has written, "If the Philadelphia Declaration had been taken literally by those who voted for it, the ILO would have developed into the master agency among the emerging family of functional international bodies. . . ."[30]

But that would not be the case, as the United States was certainly unprepared to give the ILO, with its tripartite representation from labor, business, and government, and its universal membership, a strong hand in international economic policy. Instead, the International Monetary Fund and the World Bank, and the planned-for International Trade Organization (ITO), would have pride of place. The first two of these organizations would not accord full employment a central focus in decision making, while the latter, which by charter was to be concerned with the relationship between trade and labor, ultimately died at the hands of the U.S. Congress—to be replaced by a narrower entity, the General Agreement on Tariffs and Trade (GATT).

The story of the ITO brings us to the heart of American ambivalence regarding the role that labor and full-employment policy ought to play in international economic planning. As part of its postwar architectural vision, the United States had sought to establish an International Trade Organization (ITO) alongside the IMF and the World Bank. In fact, it would be incorrect to say that this was purely an American scheme. Accompanying Keynes's notion of a clearings union, the British government had also sought the establishment of a "commercial union" whose purpose would be to promote free trade. For their part, the Australians had called upon the United States take the lead in holding a United Nations Conference on Trade and Employment. It would turn out, however, that the protagonists had very different ideas about what "free trade" really meant, and about its relationship to the goal of full employment.

For the United States, free multilateralism meant free trade and investment flows unencumbered by preferential blocs of any kind. The animator of this idea, Franklin Roosevelt's Secretary of State, Cordell Hull, had an evangelical belief in the free-trade religion. Recalling the breakdown of economic relations during the interwar period, he wrote in his memoirs that "unhampered trade dovetailed with peace; high tariffs, trade barriers, and unfair economic competition, with war."[31] Liberating trade from its political fetters was required not just for the sake of world prosperity, but also, by extension, for world peace.

Having experienced American idealism in the various proposals of Woodrow Wilson during and after World War I, Europeans were skeptical of any universalist schemes emanating from Washington. While nobody doubted that free trade theoretically produced a more efficient use of the world's scarce resources, its implementation at a time when economic power was so lopsided struck many as disingenuous. There were good reasons why the Europeans—and the British in particular—would wish to proceed slowly on the road to multilateralism. Specifically, at a time when the United States dominated the world economy, with Europe and its firms in ruins, it was unclear just how broadly distributed the gains from trade would be.[32] If free trade benefited the Americans and nobody else, how could that policy be justified?

Keynes, while no protectionist, was unsympathetic toward postwar American trade policy, which he viewed as dogmatic and detrimental to the British policy of full employment, at least over some relevant time horizon. He preferred to retain the imperial preferences system—trade preferences to Commonwealth countries—as a transition to freer trade, while agreeing that British action in removing preferences might be tied to the lowering of tariffs by the United States.[33]

Sir William Beveridge was also critical of the American position. He argued, "All nations which propose to have trade with one another should pursue full employment and economic stability."[34] That had to be the basis for any trade arrangements, he asserted, since only that domestic commitment would provide the partners with the confidence needed to build a multilateral system.

While Beveridge believed that multilateralism offered Britain—and the whole world—" the most desirable alternative," he was also wary of its risks, noting, "Multilateral trading spreads adversity as certainly and widely as it spreads prosperity."[35] For these reasons, each trading state must be clear in its commitment: "Full employment comes first." If the United States was unwilling to make that commitment, he was prepared to sacrifice free multilateralism as the basis for organizing the global economy. He suggested as a second-best step that Britain become the center "of a sterling full employment area," emphasizing trade among Commonwealth members and colonies. As we will see below, the British decision to maintain their discriminatory system of "imperial preferences" clashed with American views about the trade conditions that would best promote employment opportunities.

As ideas about the future trade order were being exchanged in 1945 and 1946, they were accompanied by fears that the United States would soon enter a postwar depression—one that could be much worse for the world than during the 1930s, given the immense task of reconstruction that now lay ahead. From Europe's perspective, the problem was that, in the event the United States slipped into a recession, its imports would fall and its exports would be pushed to third markets, to Europe's detriment. How, then, would Europe be able to earn the foreign exchange needed for reconstruction financing?[36]

Discussions between the United States and British architects of the postwar economic order foundered over the direction of the causal arrows relating trade and labor policy. The American delegation appeared to believe that the first emphasis in postwar planning ought to be put on trade liberalization, and they expressed the view that it was the contraction of trade that caused or prolonged the Great Depression, rather than domestic policies that then spread abroad. This was a peculiar view, given America's relative position of economic self-sufficiency.[37] The British, in contrast, argued that if full employment obtained, reductions in trade barriers would follow; everything had to start with the domestic employment situation.

Despite these differences, British and American planners could reach agreement on a number of general points. "They agreed that measures for the maintenance of employment should be taken in both the international and the domestic sphere. On the domestic side, nations should seek to maintain high levels of employment by measures appropriate to their political and economic institutions. These measures should be supplemented by action on the part of international agencies . . . ." Specifically, the officials considered the creation of an "advisory economic staff," possibly housed in the postwar United Nations, which would act to coordinate "domestic and international measures to promote employment" and which "might determine whether particular nations were pursuing policies designed to promote full employment internationally or policies involving the 'export' of unemployment."[38]

By 1946, having established the Bretton Woods twins and having held regular rounds of discussions on trade, the United States, Britain, and other participating countries were ready to move toward the drafting of a charter for the International Trade Organization (ITO), which they hoped to create. Thus, they met in London in the autumn to begin the arduous writing process, with the hope of producing a draft that could be refined into a final document in a following round of discussions. In fact, the United States and its allies were pursuing a "two-track" trade policy at this time. On a separate track, negotiators were working on the General Agreement on Tariffs and Trade (GATT), whose simple purpose was to achieve multilateral agreement on trade-barrier reductions. This was meant to be a temporary instrument, and upon its establishment, the ITO would subsume the GATT's functions, as well as tackle the broader issue of trade and employment.[39]

One issue most certainly did *not* arise in deliberations over the ITO, and that concerned international labor migration. Unlike nineteenth-century globalization, the free movement of persons across borders was now severely constrained by states through the use of visas and border controls. As a study by the Brookings Institution pointed out, "Migration from lands of lesser opportunity to lands of greater opportunity has been given relatively little emphasis as an equilibrator in the international economy."[40] At the very outset of the postwar order, then, labor was prevented from exercising the sort of freedom that the planners had ensured for capital and, to a lesser extent, for trade.

In London, two issues stood between the countries as they developed their bargaining positions: employment and quantitative trade restrictions. The latter issue concerned Britain's desire to maintain free trade for its exports while retaining the privilege of imposing quantitative restrictions on its imports in case of balance-of-payments difficulties. Ultimately, the draft ITO charter contained a reasonably liberal provision allowing for discrimination while calling for its "earliest possible elimination. . . ."

With respect to the labor issue, Great Britain and several other countries wanted to ensure that the commitment to something like full-employment policy was universal among the ITO's future members. As a result, the ITO's drafters now had to come up with precise language regarding the trade–labor relationship. The differences between the Americans and their British counterparts were clear at the outset. The American delegation proposed that the ITO charter's first principle read: "That existing barriers to international trade should be substantially reduced, so that the volume of such trade may be large." The British, in turn, suggested that the ITO's objective should be to "achieve an agreement as to the manner in which the nations can cooperate for the promotion of the highest level of employment and the maintenance of demand and bring some degree of regulation into world trade and commerce."[41]

The position of the United States was that "the reduction of trade barriers was something a government could effectively promise to accomplish; the maintenance of full employment was not."[42] Further, governments might legitimately differ on the weight placed on employment as opposed to other economic policy objectives, such as growth in per capita income and the gross national product. It seemed that countries had every right to pursue their own economic policy objectives within their own borders. The purpose of international economic cooperation was not to erase the differences in national policymaking, but rather to find and develop those areas where policy interests were convergent.

The British came to the ITO negotiations with another perspective. As one of the great students of the postwar economic order, Richard Gardner, tells it, the delegation arrived "with the intent of achieving a substantial expansion of the employment obligations. In so doing they appear to have been under considerable pressure from domestic opinion. The literature on foreign economic policy was now fairly saturated with the subject of full employment. It was widely predicted that a serious American depression would develop. . . ." For the British, a full-employment pledge by the American side represented a commitment to combat and contain that downturn.[43]

The British were quite vehement in maintaining their stance, advancing a proposal that made full-employment policy an *international* obligation and calling for international cooperation to realize that objective. Further, they suggested that countries pursuing full-employment policies should have "safeguards" to protect themselves against governments (i.e., the United States) that adopted deflationary measures. As a British memorandum stated, the maintenance of full employment was "a duty which each government owes not merely to its own nationals, but to the world as a whole. Accordingly, it must be a basic element in any international employment policy to secure from governments—particularly the governments of the main trading nations—an unambiguous recognition of their international responsibility in this regard." They went so far as to argue that "if all important countries" adopted full-employment policies, "no international depression need ever develop."[44]

The final document that emerged from the London conference in 1946 reflected the pulling and pushing not just of the American and British delegations but also domestic politics within each country. Thus, the United States acted to preserve domestic subsidies for agriculture in the charter, while outlawing the use of export subsidies. As a historian of the agreement has written, "The London draft of the ITO now codified exceptions to the rules of trade, rather than codifying the rules of trade."[45]

The year 1947 would not prove a propitious time for the United States to advance its cherished multilateral agenda. The Bretton Woods system was suffocating from a lack of dollars in the international economy, while the British economy was tumbling into crisis—despite the fact that the United States had floated a large loan to the country only a year earlier. The Marshall Plan would be announced in June that year, effectively signaling an end to the brief era of global dreams. It was now obvious that America was the only country in the world prepared to advance the multilateral agenda, leaving it with an empty dance card. Thus, the chances of winning broad congressional support for the ITO at such a time were minute.

Nonetheless, in 1948, delegations from around the world proceeded to Havana, Cuba, with the intention of drafting a final ITO charter. Before departing, the American delegation assured Congress that the British system of imperial preferences would be dropped as a condition of the agreement. Further, a number of special-interest groups (especially agriculture) had already mobilized their forces and been assured that their particular concerns would be taken into account.

At the end of the day, however, the ITO was not to be. Britain, given its growing economic difficulties, was determined to hold on to its sterling-area trading bloc. It also insisted that the various employment provisions be retained in the ITO charter. These positions were unlikely to be accepted by Congress.

For its part, congressional support for free multilateralism had largely evaporated. The Cold War was now in full gear, dividing the world into two separate economic and political spheres of influence. The Marshall Plan was America's major economic tool in the fight against communism, to be supported in later years by the Point Four assistance program for developing nations. (It took its name from being the fourth point in President Harry Truman's 1949 inaugural address.) Indeed, economic policy was increasingly couched in the Manichaean terms of the capitalist/communist struggle. In attacking the ITO charter, for example, the National Foreign Trade Council, a Washington-based lobbying group, asserted that its economic provisions "would operate inexorably to transform the free enterprise system of this country into a system of planned economy, with consequent initiative-destroying regimentation, reduction in productive output and standards of living, and threat to the free institutions and liberties of the American people."[49]

By 1950, realizing that the ITO would not pass, the Truman administration withdrew the charter from congressional consideration. Instead, the narrower GATT agreement—whose sole purpose was the reduction of trade barriers—would be relied upon to advance America's free-trade objectives. No new trade organization would be established until 1994, when the World Trade Organization (WTO) emerged out of the Uruguay Round of multilateral trade negotiations. Like the GATT, however, the WTO would also seek to avoid linking trade with employment issues.

The failure to create the ITO thus meant that issues of trade and employment would not be formally joined at the level of international institutions. Instead, labor would have to rely upon the International Labor Organization to advance its objectives in multilateral discussions. Given the relative inefficacy of that organization, the practical result was that labor's voice was effectively stilled in discussion and debate over international economic policy.

CONCLUSIONS

At the end of World War II, the United States and its allies faced the immense task of rebuilding the international economy. They did so with energy and imagination, driven by the fundamental belief that economic instability caused social disruption and bitter conflict within and between countries. All efforts at postwar economic policy focused on removing the domestic tensions that could lead to capitalism's downfall.

Yet there were differences among the allies as to how that postwar goal of economic security could best be achieved—differences that had their roots in domestic political economy. Great Britain—scarred by war, animated by Keynesianism, and fearful of its future—devoted itself to the advancement of full employment at home as its number one policy priority. The United States—with its overwhelming power on the one hand and its internal divisions over economic "planning" on the other—instead focused its efforts on the construction of a multilateral order with free trade at the core.

Because the world's leading power ultimately failed to advance the cause of full employment at the international level, the link between trade and labor, forged in the ITO charter and elsewhere, was ultimately broken. Instead, labor would rely on the obligations made by each nation-state to combat unemployment. As Robert Asher of the Brookings Institution wrote in a review of international economic policy, "Despite much talk, and many studies, the international community therefore remains almost entirely dependent on nationally devised and nationally executed safeguards against recession."[47] How labor has fared under that postwar regime is the topic of the next chapter.

HOW HAS LABOR FARED?

Inequality is harmful for growth.
— TORSTEN PERSSON AND GUIDO TABELLINI, 1994[1]

HOW HAS LABOR FARED WITHIN THE economic order established by the great powers after World War II? That is the question we address in this chapter. We will see that, after two golden decades of rising wages and low levels of unemployment, the situation for unskilled workers in the industrial world has deteriorated since the 1970s. Today, despite low levels of unemployment, American workers face shrinking wages and benefits and heightened job insecurity, while in Western Europe, double-digit levels of unemployment prevail. Explaining these developments has become a major preoccupation of economists, while reversing them is one of the toughest problems facing policy makers.

The situation is even more dire in the so-called emerging markets of the developing world, which have been buffeted by a series of financial crises during the 1990s. There, workers are facing massive unemployment—and this within countries that lack any social safety net outside the family structure. In the post-communist transition economies, too, unemployment and widespread poverty have tragically become associated with the advent of capitalism. In short, the benefits of globalization have yet to be experienced by millions of working people, and in that fact lie grave risks for the future.

It is not just the possibility of an anti-globalization back-lash that should cause us concern about labor's worsening economic position. In addition, there is a growing body of academic and policy literature that draws a causal connection between rising levels of income inequality and lower rates of economic growth. Simply stated, far from being inimical to a country's growth trajectory, appropriately targeted distributive policies, which make available greater resources and opportunities to unskilled workers and the poor, may benefit rather than retard a country's—and by extension, the world's—economic performance. On one level, this is nothing more than common sense; after all, the more intensive the use of existing resources, the more productive the overall economy. The challenge, then, is to develop policies that put that theory into practice.

LABOR'S ROAD FROM FREE TRADE
TO PROTECTIONISM

Since labor had no assigned seat at the table as the global economic architecture was being designed by such organizations as the IMF and the GATT from the 1950s onward, it had to rely on others to advance its interests. Those "others" were naturally national governments, which were—and still are—responsible for the well-being of their citizens. How successful has the post-war order, which combined globalization with the welfare state, been at delivering prosperity to the world's workers?

On one level, the international economy built after World War II has been a tremendous success. Trade has grown at a faster rate than gross national product in almost all developed and developing countries, fully realizing the promise of the GATT and its successor, the World Trade Organization (WTO). Between 1950 and 1993, world merchandise exports increased from 7 percent of global output to more than 17 percent. [2] Indeed, for the first three postwar decades, the world enjoyed both a gradual reduction in barriers to trade and investment *and* full employment, vindicating the postwar order that the allies had built. At the same time, incomes and consumption rose steadily, while, no less important, new opportunities for education and advancement become available to workers and their children. The American dream and its European equivalents seemed within reach for more people than at any previous time in history.

As a result, working people, as represented by their unions, were generally free traders for much of the postwar period. This was the case not only in the United States, but also in most industrial countries, and indeed unions in Western Europe were generally early supporters of postwar policies aimed at creating a Common Market. From the perspective of present-day electoral politics, it is of interest to note that for much of the postwar period, free trade found its natural home in the Democratic Party in the United States, and in left–labor parties in Western Europe.[3]

For example, when the Kennedy administration decided to reform U.S. trade policy with the Trade Expansion Act (TEA) of 1962, it relied heavily on labor support. The president of the AFL-CIO, George Meany, was often consulted by the administration as the bill was prepared, and the outcome would look "very similar" to the foreign-trade resolution passed by the AFL-CIO at its annual convention in December 1961.[4] The Trade Expansion Act, which made possible broad tariff cuts within the context of GATT negotiations and established the Office of the Special Trade Representative (USTR), replaced the Reciprocal Trade Agreements Act (RTAA), which had governed U.S. trade policy since 1934.

During congressional hearings over the bill's passage, Meany made the case for the Trade Expansion Act, despite the fact that increased imports would necessarily bring about some job losses. "Why," he asked rhetorically, should unions support the Act? "Because we, and the nation . . . will gain far more than we lose." He had reason to be positive, since the economy was growing rapidly (by 7.4 percent between 1961 and 1962), the trade balance was positive by some $5.5 billion, and the unemployment rate, which had climbed to 6.7 percent in 1961, was down to 5.5 percent in 1962 (unemployment among white males, Meany's core constituency, fell from 5.7 percent to 4.6 percent during this period).

Still, labor's support for the Trade Expansion Act was made conditional on congressional support for trade adjustment assistance (TAA)—a combination of extended unemployment insurance, coupled with training and relocation benefits for workers displaced by rising imports. As Meany said in his testimony, " . . . a trade adjustment assistance program is absolutely essential to a foreign trade policy, and, as we have said repeatedly, it is indispensable to our support of that policy." The Trade Expansion Act, along with trade adjustment assistance, passed the Congress in 1962, providing the cornerstone for modern trade policy. (It established the Office of the Special Trade Representative and enabled the president to negotiate across-the-board tariff reductions.)

Unfortunately, trade adjustment assistance never lived up to its promise. The legislation's phrasing made it nearly impossible for workers to qualify for benefits. Over time, changes in the policy would be made, but only a small percentage of trade-displaced workers would be assisted, and the compensation they received hardly made up for the job and income losses they suffered.[5] As a result, workers began to believe they had received a sucker's payoff for their early support for free trade (critics, on the other hand, wondered why "trade-displaced" workers had any special claims to adjustment assistance at all).

At the same time, during the late 1960s, the economy began to lose its Kennedy-era momentum. Growth in gross national product fell from more than 6 percent in 1965 and 1966 to 3 percent in 1969 and 0 percent in 1970. Unemployment rose from 3.8 percent in 1966 to 4.9 percent in 1970. The trade surplus was now vanishing, plummeting from $7 billion in 1964 to $607 million in 1970. In short, the economy was failing to live up to its Keynesian promise of growth, stability, and full employment.

This failure played a major role in causing organized labor to change its position on free trade. Whereas George Meany had publicly defended the TEA, by the late 1960s he had moved over to the protectionist camp. Further, union power was shrinking as corporations moved their plants to nonunion states and overseas, and as the economy shifted towards services and away from manufacturing. All told, the 1960s and 1970s saw growing labor disillusionment with the postwar order.[6]

Thus, by the early 1970s, organized labor was again calling for quotas on imports. Union leaders dismissed trade adjustment assistance as "burial insurance" and wanted good old protection instead. TAA had failed displaced workers, who found new jobs only at lower pay and benefit levels. But now, as unions and northern-state Democrats leaned toward protectionism, Republicans took up the mantle of free trade and open markets. The Nixon and Ford administrations easily passed their trade bills through Congress, albeit at the political cost of making it easier for workers to obtain TAA benefits.

As the 1980s saw a surge in U.S. imports under the aegis of a strong dollar, industrial workers became increasingly hostile to American trade policy. But at the same time, U.S.-based multinationals and consumers became strong advocates of open markets. The multinationals feared that protectionism in the United States would be met by higher tariffs and quotas abroad, particularly in a European Community that seemed bent on supporting the continent's enterprises in international competition. And consumers became increasingly appreciative of the wider range of products—often high-quality products—at low prices that imports made possible. During the 1980s and early 1990s, then, it became increasingly difficult for organized labor to build political coalitions, and the profound weakness of the union movement was made apparent early in the presidency of Ronald Reagan, when an air-controllers' strike resulted in nothing less than their union's destruction. Similar developments had already emerged in Margaret Thatcher's England, where union activity was largely crushed by strong government action.

As recent debates over the North American Free Trade Agreement (NAFTA) and fast-track trade legislation made clear, labor was not about to quit in its opposition to free trade. And by the late 1990s, there was some evidence that the pendulum might be swinging back in the unions' direction. President Bill Clinton's effort to extend fast-track trade legislation in 1997 went down to defeat, so the chances of extending NAFTA southward to Chile during his administration disappeared. In a 1998 poll, some 58 percent of Americans held that trade agreements between the United States and other countries were "bad for the economy."[7] Union support for Democratic Party candidates was still a factor that congressmen had to consider in casting their legislative votes.

Nor was this opposition to trade limited to Americans. In France, more than 60 percent of industrial workers polled by the SOFRES organization in 1997 thought that globalization was bad—and this in a country that has been running substantial trade surpluses! The far-right National Front Party, which consistently wins some 15 percent of the vote in French parliamentary elections, and which has had considerable success in winning local and regional races, runs on an anti-globalization, anti-immigration platform. A shift of labor votes from left- to right-leaning parties in countries around the world would be one of the more troubling developments in international politics, and it makes plain that economic interdependence is still far from winning the hearts and minds of working people.

HOW HAS LABOR FARED?

Perceptions are one thing, but what do the data tell us about the employment and wages of working people? Overall, the numbers demonstrate that labor's position—and particularly that of the unskilled—in the world economy has grown increasingly precarious. To begin with, the numbers point to an increase in unemployment, which is only recently being offset in the United States, but not yet in Western Europe. In the United States, unemployment averaged around 5 percent between 1949 and 1970. The 1970s saw an increase to 5.8 percent, while during the 1980s, it shot up to 7.1 percent. Between 1990 and 1997, it fell back to 6 percent, with the number declining in 1997 to 5 percent.

While the figures indicate strong job growth in the American economy during the late 1990s, this has been accompanied by record layoffs. According to Federal Reserve Bank Chairman Alan Greenspan, the United States loses about 300,000 jobs per week, creating a "very major set of churning forces."[8] It is perhaps for this reason that, according to the U.S. Council of Economic Advisers, job insecurity—defined as the percentage of workers who believe they are likely to lose their jobs—is now as high as it was during the Reagan years, which had much higher unemployment.[9] Indeed, this perception seems to be generalized across the industrial countries. According to the Paris-based Organization for Economic Cooperation and Development (OECD), "A widespread and, in some countries, very sharp increase in the number of individuals perceiving unemployment insecurity took place between the 1980s and 1990s."[10]

That finding is certainly understandable in the European

case, given its high levels of unemployment. But coming from Americans, it is puzzling, since it is likely that a displaced worker will quickly find a new job in an environment of high economic growth. The reason for this growing insecurity is that when a worker is displaced, he or she is likely to find the next position only at lower pay and benefit levels. In a recent study of displaced workers in Massachusetts, for example, the Federal Reserve Bank of Boston found that "in general, displaced workers experienced noticeable wage losses. Many . . . ended up finding jobs either without medical insurance or pension benefits. Most displaced workers experienced an extended period of joblessness. . . ." The mean wage loss for these workers was nearly 13 percent.[11] Similarly, a study of displaced workers in Pennsylvania placed the average value of lost lifetime earnings at $80,000.[12] These are not trivial sums.

At the same time, unionization rates have dropped sharply in the United States. In 1970, trade union membership constituted about 30 percent of the total workforce. That number fell to 15 percent by 1990. Beyond such changes as the general shift from manufacturing to service jobs, and the increase in moves by companies to non-union states, international capital mobility has also had a chilling effect on the American labor movement. Cornell University economist Kate Bronfenbrenner has demonstrated that the threat of moving production to Mexico effectively squashed unionization drives throughout the United States in a variety of sectors. Such threats, in turn, also place downward pressures on wage demands; indeed, globalization may partly explain why the United States has enjoyed high growth, low inflation, *and* rising inequality throughout the 1990s.[13] While that development has brought obvious benefits to many consumers, it also demonstrates vividly the lopsided position in which relatively immobile labor finds itself when confronted by mobile capital.

If the major concern of American workers today is compensation rather than unemployment, in many countries joblessness remains the central economic problem. In Western Europe, the unemployment figures have reached near-epidemic proportions. Whereas joblessness was insignificant during the early postwar years, standing at between 1 and 2 percent of the working population in 1960, it has now climbed to more than 10 percent. Of this number, more than 50 percent are characterized as being "long-term unemployed." Particularly hard hit have been European youth, who are twice as likely as adults to be unemployed. All told, there were fewer people employed in Europe in the late 1990s than there were at the beginning of the decade.[14]

Widespread unemployment is also beginning to reach places around the world that, unlike the United States or Europe, have little in the way of safety nets to buffer the shock. In East Asia, jobless rates have trebled from 2 to 6 percent of the working population, in the wake of the financial crises of 1997-98. Between October 1997 and March 1998, unemployment climbed in South Korea from 2.3 percent to 6.7 percent. During the same period, unemployment in Indonesia climbed to nearly 9 percent of the population, and it would reach some 20 million people, nearly a quarter of the workforce, in 1999. China's jobless rate in 1998 was estimated at 10 percent of the workforce. According to the *Economist* magazine, "These figures may well understate unemployment."[15]

Similar shocks have occurred to the labor force in the postcommunist transition economies. During the communist era, unemployment was basically illegal, so societies had no need to prepare safety nets for that eventuality. Today, unemployment stands at nearly 20 percent in Bulgaria and more than 10 percent in Hungary, Poland, Russia, and Slovakia. The International Labor Organization reports that unemployment has particularly struck women, youth, and the unskilled. It concludes: "Six years into the transition process, the shortfall from full employment remains enormous."[16]

Accompanying the changes in employment for unskilled

workers have been changes in income. The average weekly earnings of American workers in the private sector fell (in 1982 dollars) from a level of $260.86 in 1959 to $255.90 in 1995. To be sure, the cost of employer-provided benefits increased during this period, but this hardly offsets the earnings stagnation. Further, over the years more and more workers have seen reductions or complete losses in their benefit packages. Thus, the percentage of full-time private-sector workers covered by employer-provided health insurance fell from 71 to 64 percent between 1979 and 1993, while those with pension coverage fell from 48 to 45 percent.[17]

As compensation has fallen for the unskilled worker, it has increased mightily for highly educated workers; the result is increasing income inequality. According to the President's Council of Economic Advisers, in 1979 male workers with a college degree earned on average about 50 percent more than unskilled workers; by 1993 that difference was nearly 90 percent.[18] To put the inequality problem in its starkest terms, between 1979 and 1994 the upper 5 percent of American families captured 99 *percent* of the nation's per capita gains in gross domestic product! That is, with a mean family gain over this period of $4,419, $4,365 went to the upper 5 percent.[19]

Looking at these figures in another way, in 1982 the top 10 percent of American workers averaged $24.80 per hour, about four times what workers in the bottom tenth of the scale earned. By 1996, workers on the top were getting almost $26 per hour, or five times what workers on the bottom were earning. When benefits are counted, the gap is even larger, owing to the growing number of bottom-end workers who have no medical insurance, pension plans, or vacation pay.[20]

These numbers suggest the "have/have not" nature of contemporary American society. Those who possess education, skill, and investment capital have witnessed a tremendous increase in income growth over the past two decades, while the unskilled are being left far behind. This development has led

Harvard labor economist Richard Freeman to assert that the United States is moving "toward an apartheid economy."[21] That situation is troubling for several reasons, including its impacts on social stability, democracy, and, as I discuss in more detail below, long-term economic growth.

While the divergence in earnings is most acute in the United States, other industrial countries—including Australia, Canada, Sweden, and the United Kingdom—are experiencing a similar phenomenon. This story can also be told for many developing and transition economies. Throughout the post-Soviet world, unskilled workers have seen a sharp decline in wages, while skilled workers have suffered somewhat smaller losses.[22] And even in those countries—like Germany, where workers have enjoyed real wage gains since the 1980s—the raises were small in comparison with previous decades.[23]

One might hope that this problem, at least in part, will be taken care of by generational change. That is, the children of unskilled workers will recognize the need for education and prepare themselves accordingly. But in fact, social mobility is lower than most of us—especially Americans—would like to believe. If you are born poor (or rich), you are likely to remain so. Indeed, class or economic differences remain the single most powerful indicator of one's life chances, and social mobility is not much greater in the United States than in other industrial countries, despite popular myths to the contrary.[24]

Contributing to the change in income distribution has been a significant shift in tax policy. In both the United States and Europe, taxation is falling increasingly on labor's shoulders. This is what we would predict in a world of mobile capital, in which corporations can reduce their tax burden as they engage in a "race to the bottom" among states that seek investment; this has already occurred to a large degree within the United States, and some governors are now seeking help from Congress to put a floor to this process. As overall tax revenues decline, government programs that favor working people tend to be cut.

In the words of economist Dani Rodrik, "The evidence suggests three things: globalization reduces the ability of governments to spend resources on social programs, it makes it more difficult to tax capital, and labor now carries a growing share of the tax burden."[25]

It's important to emphasize that even if it is true that the rich are getting richer around the world, it does not necessarily follow that the poor are getting poorer. Too much public discussion has focused on the gains accruing to those at the top, with less attention being paid to what is happening to those living in poverty. If the rich are getting richer, but the poor are also getting richer, that puts a very different spin on the income-inequality debate.

Unfortunately, it is difficult to make a persuasive case for such a positive trend, at least from a global perspective. At best, the war on poverty is being fought to a draw. In the United States, according to the President's Council of Economic Advisers, the poverty rate fell sharply in the 1960s and early 1970s from 22.2 percent in 1960 to 11.1 percent in 1973, but it has increased since then. The poverty rate rose dramatically during the 1980s, and by 1995 some 36.4 million Americans were classified as living in poverty, or nearly 15 percent of the population.[26]

Most of the poor, it should be emphasized—and contrary to some popular myths—are *working poor*, and their numbers will certainly grow with the current policy shift from welfare to workfare.[27] Today, some 30 percent of American workers earn poverty-level wages, up from 24 percent in 1979. That is also the case around the world: the bulk of the poor are not indigent; they are workers.

Significant changes have also occurred among the American poor population since the mid-1960s. Specifically, the number of children as a percentage of the impoverished population has risen dramatically—from 14.4 percent in 1973 to 22.7 percent in 1993—while the numbers of elderly poor have fallen just as sharply.[28] In an important sense, "income" is being transferred in the United States from children to their grandparents! The fact that one in five American children still lives in poverty is nothing less than a national scandal.

According to statistics from the European Union, whose citizens generally pride themselves on their generous welfare states, some 57 million individuals were classified as living in poverty in the mid-1990s. Strikingly, some 17 percent of Western Europeans had incomes below the poverty line. Of these individuals, 13 million, nearly one-quarter, are children. It is of interest to note that while Portugal and Greece have the highest overall poverty rates in Europe, Britain and Ireland have the highest numbers of poor children.[29] When combined with the American numbers, the Anglo-Saxon countries might well be tempted to ask why their societies single out children in this way.

Throughout the developing world, poverty—defined by the World Bank as people living on less than $1 per day—continues to increase. East Asia, including China, was home to 446 million impoverished individuals, or one-third of the world's total, *before* the financial crisis of 1997-98. Since the crisis, that number has grown by several million. In Indonesia alone, some 96 million people would fall into poverty as a result of the crisis. In Latin America and the Caribbean, the number of poor rose from 91.2 million in 1987 to almost 110 million in 1993. In South Asia, the number has increased from 480 million to nearly 515 million, while in sub-Saharan Africa, the poor have swelled from 180 million to 220 million, or 39 percent of the population. Perhaps most dramatically, the post-communist transition in the former Soviet Union and in the countries of Eastern Europe has brought with it widespread income inequality and poverty. According to the World Bank, the number of poor increased in that region from 2.2 million in 1987 to 14.5 million in 1993.

These numbers signal a global economy that is characterized not just by trade and investment but also by widespread income inequality and poverty. As the World Bank has written, "Some inroads have been made in reducing poverty . . . since 1987, but overall the gains have been small."[30] Around the world, "50 million children are mentally or physically impaired because of inadequate nutrition, and 130 million children—80 percent of them girls—are denied the chance to go to school."[31] Put in crass, material terms, this is a terrible waste of resources, and it makes good economic sense to invest in that human capital today in order to enjoy its fruits tomorrow.[32]

WHY HAVE UNEMPLOYMENT AND INCOME INEQUALITY INCREASED?

It would take an entire book to describe in detail the different theories that have been offered to explain the troublesome rise in unemployment, income inequality, and global poverty. My purpose here is simply to sketch some of the most prominent hypotheses, in order to provide a flavor of the contending perspectives and the various policy implications associated with each. Although the focus is on the United States and Western Europe, reference must also be made to the developing and transition economies. After all, it is in those countries where unemployment and poverty have particularly severe human consequences, given the paucity of social-welfare programs. Indeed, it is possible that the anti-globalization forces will achieve their greatest success not in the old industrial and highly interdependent core of the world economy but in its developing periphery.

Explanations of trends within labor markets—e.g., changes in wages and employment levels—tend to focus on supply-side, demand-side, or institutional factors.[33] The first two factors can be thought of in terms of the simple models presented in any Econ 101 course taught to undergraduates. Using the familiar parlance, assume that we have two groups of workers, those who are *high-skilled* and those who are *low-skilled*. Imagine that the supply of low-skilled workers relative to high-skilled workers increases suddenly—perhaps due to immigration, imports from less-developed countries (these imports effectively substitute for low-skilled labor at home), or the entry into the labor market of large numbers of women, high school students, and others with little prior work experience. All these factors could combine to increase the supply of low-skilled workers relative to demand, lowering their wages.

Conversely, imagine any number of developments that increase the demand for high-skilled workers. These could include rapid technological development, increasing openness to trade (which creates export-oriented opportunities), or a surge in demand for professionals such as doctors, lawyers, and accountants—perhaps due to the aging of the population. The result of these developments could be a sharp increase in wages for those with the particular skills in demand. If all these factors are operating at the same time in the markets for high-and low-skilled labor, a surge in income inequality could occur.

In addition to these forces of supply and demand, institutional changes could also affect the distribution of income. A change in tax policy toward less income distribution, as occurred during the Reagan presidency, would be a clear example of such an institutional shift. A decline in rates of unionization, and with it the fall in the union "wage premium," could profoundly influence the earnings of working people. Finally, the fall in the real value of the minimum wage, or other policies designed to maintain earnings above a certain floor, could contribute to earnings inequality.

How do these supply, demand, and institutional factors influence unemployment levels as opposed to earnings? The villain we would seek in this story would be labor-market rigidities. Suppose, for example, that unions have the effect of maintaining wages at higher than market-clearing levels. Faced by this situation in the labor market, employers would hire fewer workers than otherwise, or would try not to fill vacancies when these occurred. Similarly, suppose that government policy required businesses to pay heavy benefits and social security taxes for their workers. Again, firms would then invest in labor-saving technology and other methods aimed at reducing the payroll. The result of these sorts of institutional factors is higher unemployment.

Many academics and public officials have argued in recent years that these labor-market rigidities explain the difference between employment outcomes in the United States and in Western Europe. The conventional wisdom has it that the United States has accepted lower wages as the price of full employment, while in Western Europe, unions have managed to preserve high wages for those who work, but these come at the cost of increasing joblessness.

There are, however, several difficulties inherent in that sort of analysis. First, for much of postwar history, Western Europe had less unemployment than the United States. Further, northern European countries, with the most rigid labor markets, have generally had less unemployment than southern European countries or Britain, where lower wages and more flexibility prevailed. What then explains the differences in unemployment across time and place?

Macroeconomic factors, of course, play a prominent role in the story. Countries with low growth, high inflation, or high interest rates are less likely to generate the investment needed to bolster employment than countries that enjoy a stable macroeconomic environment. Clearly, low growth in Western Europe since the 1980s has been a major factor in the continent's employment woes, and the same may be said of many post-communist transition economies. If there are no jobs to be had on the supply side, then demand-side changes won't amount to much.

But demand-side factors are also important. Specifically,

many Western European countries have adopted policies that provide the jobless with little incentive to seek work. Extended unemployment benefits, high taxes, and training that doesn't match work requirements are unlikely to promote job-seeking behavior. With extended benefits, the longer someone is unemployed, the more difficult it becomes to find new work; and in Western Europe, this issue of long-term unemployment is particularly acute. Tragically, it does not affect just middle-aged workers but also young workers who have only had a brief experience, at best, in the labor market.

It should be emphasized that high levels of unionization are *not* correlated with high rates of unemployment, nor are high levels of unemployment insurance. Both of these myths are frequently heard in American debates about the impediments to job creation, and they should be exploded. In fact, some labor-market rigidities are necessary not just for good economic performance but also for social stability! Overall, the Western European countries that do best like Holland, are providing generous insurance, but for relatively short periods of time, coupled with low tax rates that give both workers and employers the incentive to engage in productive activity.[34]

What about the problem of income inequality? As with unemployment, two factors that could contribute to changes for labor on the demand side have been under especially intense scrutiny in recent years: technological development and globalization. The two, of course, are not completely unrelated, since foreign direct investment results in technology transfer, while increasing competition could motivate firms to invest in new equipment. Indeed, the ways in which technology, capital mobility, and trade are interrelated is a topic deserving of much more study.

Technological development could worsen income distribution by favoring those workers who have a certain set of skills, while penalizing others who enter the job market without the requisite education and training. Technology, then, acts as a wedge in the labor market, dividing the world between those who possess and those who lack the needed skills for operating complex machinery or computers.

That trade could also influence the income received by different groups within a society has long been a part of received economic theory. The model that explains this outcome is surprisingly simple. It begins with the assumption of two trading partners, each of which possesses skilled and unskilled labor. Imagine that country A is relatively well endowed with skilled labor, while country B has plentiful supplies of unskilled labor; the specific examples I often use with students in this context are Sweden and China.

Now, when these countries trade with each other, they will adopt the principle of comparative advantage. Thus, country A (Sweden) will produce and export goods that make use of its skilled labor, while country B (China) will produce and export goods using unskilled labor. By opening its doors to foreign trade, country A basically increases the domestic supply of unskilled labor, forcing down the wages that these workers receive. Over time, the wages of the unskilled workers in both A and B will tend toward convergence.

This little model, published by the economist Paul Samuelson in 1948, has been at the center of tremendous controversy, as it could be used to challenge the benefits of adopting a free-trade policy. It suggests that unskilled workers in the industrial countries of the North will inevitably be harmed by trade with the developing countries of the South. Since rising income inequality in the North seems to be associated with the rapid increase in foreign trade flows that have occurred over the past two decades, economists have been busy testing whether or not the "factor price equalization" effect really explains the changes that have occurred in industrial-world labor markets. The answer remains in dispute.[35]

Most economists to date have argued that while trade may have contributed to some of the income inequality we observe, it has played a minor role when compared to technology. Paul Krugman, for example, has asserted that since trade with developing countries is a very small percentage of American gross national product—under 2 percent—it could not have a pervasive effect on the labor market.[36] But this is an incorrect inference. After all, a Middle East oil shock could have a profound impact on the American economy, even if oil imports constituted only a small share of GNP. The issue at stake is how much reverberation is felt throughout the economy as a result of the external impact.

Recent studies have been more circumspect in considering trade's influence on workers. In an important review of the literature, William Cline has argued that "the contribution of trade and immigration to rising US wage inequality has been somewhat larger than previously estimated in most of the literature." While not the sole villain in the inequality story, it is responsible for perhaps 25 percent of the change in earnings. He suggests that "the basic policy conclusion" stemming from this finding "is that a commitment to open trade needs to go hand in hand with a commitment to a whole array of domestic policies that help ensure that society evolves in an equitable rather than inequitable direction."[37] The question, addressed in a later chapter, is whether such domestic policy initiatives are still feasible in a world of balanced budgets, lower taxation, and increasing capital mobility.

As already suggested, trade is certainly not the only factor at work undermining workers' wages, and more studies must be done aimed at combining the trade and technology stories. One starting point would be a more detailed examination of the role of mobile capital, and particularly the multinational enterprise. The intuition behind the analysis goes as follows: First, globalization provides multinationals with the opportunity to move production to low-wage countries; second, this mobility promotes a "race to the bottom" among countries for investment dollars, in which they will act to lower wages, reduce taxes, overlook health and safety concerns, and break unions as part of that effort (so-called social dumping); third, as a result of this sectoral shift from high-wage, high-standard to low-wage, low-standard countries, unskilled workers in high-wage countries will be hurt. This sort of story seems plausible, say, in the case of the textile or electronic components industries.[38] (Parenthetically, we might note that this strategy might not be good for workers in the third world, either. As development economist Raphael Kaplinsky has argued, this strategy has trapped some Latin American countries into reliance on sectors that employ large pools of low-wage, unskilled labor. Because many countries are now similarly positioned in the international economy—producing textiles, toys, and commodity goods for exports—they must compete feverishly for investment by multinational producers. The result is an unending cycle of wage depression, decreasing benefits, and a lack of investment in education.)[39]

A recent staff study from the International Monetary Fund examined the effects of sectoral relocation on high-wage workers. Specifically, the IMF compared the welfare (defined in this case as *employment*) of industrial workers under autarchy (self-sufficiency) and globalization. It concluded, "*When the complete liberalization of trade and capital flows yields the relocation of the whole industry, autarchy is strictly better, on domestic welfare terms, than 'globalization* [italics added].' "[40] Like Cline, the authors draw from this finding the conclusion that pro-globalization policies must be accompanied by "strong structural and redistributive" measures. Again, a key issue for the next chapter, which focuses on policy remedies, concerns governmental capacity to influence labor market outcomes.

THE ECONOMIC CONSEQUENCES OF
INCOME INEQUALITY

The previous sections established the fragile position of un-skilled workers in the global economy. The issue we take up here is: Why should we care? Beyond the issues of political stability, discussed in earlier chapters, what are the consequences of these developments for economic performance?

Perhaps it will come as no surprise that it was John Maynard Keynes who helped launch the contemporary debate on this question. In his *Economic Consequences of the Peace*, Keynes argued that income inequality had played a useful role in providing financial resources for the Industrial Revolution and European economic development during the nineteenth century. He wrote: "It was precisely the *inequality* of the distribution of wealth which made possible those vast accumulations of fixed wealth and of capital improvements which distinguished that age from all others. Herein lay, in fact, the main justification of the Capitalist System. If the rich had spent their new wealth on their own enjoyments, the world would long ago have found such a regime intolerable. But like bees they saved and accumulated."[41] This, in essence, was a classic expression of the "trickle-down" model of economic growth. The wealthy saved and then invested in plant, equipment, mines, and infrastructure. That investment, in turn, produced jobs and income. That model has retained a powerful hold on the minds of many elites, and perhaps the public at large.

Underlying Keynes's model was an implicit social contract between rich and poor. Both classes were part of a single society, and they recognized the interdependent nature of their futures. This raises the question: Does such a social contract still exist within the context of a global economy?

In the event, nearly twenty years later, Keynes would adopt

a different line when faced with the Great Depression. In his most influential work, *The General Theory of Employment, Interest, and Money*, he argued: "*Measures for the redistribution of incomes in a way likely to raise the propensity to consume may prove positively favorable to the growth of capital* [italics added]."[42] To the extent that redistribution led to the creation of a broader base of consumers and more aggregate consumption, this would encourage investment and, in turn, economic growth. Keynes, of course, did not believe that markets would produce this outcome on their own, so he advocated an active role for government in the process.

Keynes, it should be emphasized, did not favor *equality* of incomes. He recognized that "money-making" provided a powerful incentive for economic activity and individual entrepreneurship, and that political efforts to equalize incomes would have disastrous effects. Recall his famous line, "It is better that a man should tyrannize over his bank balance than over his fellow citizens." After all, he knew about the Soviet system and, unlike many of his Cambridge University contemporaries, he did not find communism an attractive alternative to democratic capitalism.

What Keynes sought was moderation in the capitalist game, and he argued: "It is not necessary for the stimulation of these activities and the satisfaction of these proclivities that the game should be played for such high stakes as at present. Much lower stakes will serve the purpose equally well, as soon as the players are accustomed to it."[43] Thus, he drew a sharp distinction between distributive policies, which enabled more people to consume goods and services, and the complete eradication of income inequality.

Beyond the direct effects of income distribution on consumption, Yale political economists Charles Lindblom and Robert Dahl suggested that societies might adopt distributive policies in the interests of greater long-term productivity. Writing in 1953, they argued that it was useful "to consider distribution as an investment process. For any economy, the major resource is man himself. The United States has carried public education, scholarships, and technical training very far; even so, the existing distribution of income is inconsistent with as full a utilization of human resources as could reasonably be desired."[44] In short, to the extent that a society seeks to make full use of its available factors of production, especially labor, it will have to practice some redistribution of income and opportunity.

Not surprisingly, analyses of this sort have been heatedly disputed. The major claim made against distributive policies is that they generally hurt rather than benefit the truly needy. They do so because of the politics of distributive policies. Such policies are "captured" by powerful special-interest groups, such as unions, which then win measures that protect them and hurt the poor. Minimum wages and union protection laws, it is said, effectively exclude the poor and disadvantaged from the labor force.[45]

Now it is certainly true that, around the world, governments have often acted in ways that abuse the least-advantaged citizens. That should not surprise us, because the working poor generally have little political voice. At the same time, no mainstream economist has made the claim that markets acting on their own will deliver a social minimum to those in need, such as adequate food, shelter, clothing, and literacy. Surely the right route to take with respect to the disadvantaged is the one of more effective and accountable government policy, rather than no policy at all.

Indeed, in recent years, a new literature has developed that has caused academics and policymakers to revisit the relationship between income inequality and economic performance. Much of that literature has emerged in the context of studying the experience of the developing regions of the world, and especially the contrasting histories of Latin America and East Asia. Latin America has generally been characterized by some of the highest levels of income inequality in the world, and its economic performance has often been disastrous. Many East Asian countries, on the other hand, adopted relatively egalitarian policies as part of their development strategy, and they enjoyed rapid economic growth and rising living standards throughout most of the postwar era. Is there something to be learned from these examples about the benefits of redistributive policies?

At bottom, those economic approaches that favor greater income distribution do so out of the belief that extreme levels of inequality inevitably will hurt national economic performance. In support of this view, there is now a growing body of work demonstrating that distributive policies can have a positive effect on growth rates, and that there is no conflict between growth and the reduction of inequality. This literature contradicts a long-standing premise in economic-development theory that growth brings with it greater inequality.[46]

The classic position was expressed by Nobel Prize-winning economist Simon Kuznets in his 1954 presidential address to the American Economics Association. In addition to making the case that rising inequality invariably accompanied economic growth, he argued, as had Keynes, that such inequality could be *good* for economic growth. Focusing on the developing countries, Kuznets said it was necessary to produce a class of wealthy savers who would fuel investment, since "the poor simply could not save enough."[47] This, of course, assumed, as Keynes did, the existence of a group of wealth-holders who were willing to strike an implicit bargain with society, reinvesting their fortunes in their countries for the public good. Whether such a model held (or holds) in many developing and transition economies was (is) questionable at best, where the upper classes have often extracted wealth and then invested it in offshore banks and the industrial economies.

As noted above, in recent years a younger generation of scholars has come to dispute Kuznets's theory and findings. In perhaps the most influential article of this genre, the economists Torsten Persson and Guido Tabellini argued that inequality is harmful for growth. They base this assertion on the following logic: Economic growth depends upon the accumulation of capital and knowledge. People will invest in capital and knowledge to the extent they can appropriate the gains that accrue as a result. But in societies where distributional conflicts are rife, "political decisions are likely to result in policies that allow less private appropriation and therefore less accumulation and less growth."[48] What happens is that governments will have to allocate scarce resources—spend money—in order to quell social conflict, investing in such things as internal security (police and military forces). This, in turn, will require high levels of taxation, which provide a disincentive to investment. We might add that in a global economy, high taxation levels will also promote capital flight.

The appropriate policy answer, then, is to find the point where sufficient redistribution has occurred to prevent domestic turmoil, but where taxation remains low enough to encourage investment. Where that point may be found, of course, will differ across societies. The problem is that, in a global economy with mobile capital, states may be unable to engage in the very redistributive measures that are needed to promote political stability and, in turn, economic growth.

In a report for the World Bank, economist George Clarke has also found that "inequality is negatively associated with long-run growth."[49] Interestingly, this finding was independent of political regime type—whether or not the country was democratic. But Clarke was careful to state that his findings did not necessarily imply that governments should "soak the rich." As with other policy measures, the costs of so doing might outweigh the actual benefits.

This changed perception of the relationship between equality and growth is beginning to make a policy impact around the world. In a 1998 speech to the IMF, for example, U.S. Deputy Secretary of the Treasury Lawrence Summers argued: "Far from being the handmaiden of growth, certain kinds of inequalities can actively impede it." He stated: "The lessons about the links between equity and growth find deeper expression in the policies of the International Financial Institutions," and he noted that both the IMF and the World Bank are placing increased emphasis "on the needs of the poor in designing adjustment programs. . . ."[50]

For millions of people around the world, however, Summers's words will smack of "too little, too late." After all, the 1980s and 1990s have been the great decades of economic reform. In countries on every continent, the IMF and the World Bank told leaders to adopt macroeconomic and microeconomic policies conducive to stabilization, liberalization, and privatization. Human-development requirements have been placed at the bottom of the policy agenda. As a result, in almost all these cases, we have seen the rich get richer, the poor poorer.

In the post-Soviet transition economies, for example, great wealth is accumulating beside widespread poverty, with little evidence of a trickle-down effect; instead, the money is pouring out to safe havens. For the most part, the transition economies have seen both low growth and high levels of inequality.[51] In Latin America, some 40 million people have been added to the poverty rolls since the debt crisis of the 1980s.[52] Overall, one in three persons on the continent lives in poverty, which means that some 86 million people try to survive on less than $1 per day. At the same time, in many Latin countries, spending on health and education has been slashed in the name of fiscal responsibility. These austerity programs, however, have not hurt the rich. According to Nora Lustig of the Brookings Institution, "Perhaps the most important result of the economic crisis is that in country after country the income share of the top 10 percent increased, sometimes substantially."[53] We may reasonably speak of a "lost generation" of the disadvantaged who have borne the burden of economic reform.

COMBINING INCOME EQUALITY
AND GROWTH: THE CASE
OF TAIWAN

The greatest example of high rates of growth combined with relative income equality comes from several states in East Asia, including South Korea, Japan, and especially Taiwan. Not only did these countries manage their development in such a way as to promote income equality, but the policies that produced that result were probably critical to their growth trajectory.[54] While doubts may be cast on the ability of the "tigers" to sustain this record into the new century, especially in light of the financial crises of 1997–98, one should be equally skeptical about how far free markets for labor will penetrate these cultures.[55]

Among the distributive policies effected in East Asia, perhaps the most radical and openly coercive in the early days of postwar development was land reform. According to World Bank chief economist Joseph Stiglitz, land reform had three effects. It "increased rural productivity and income and resulted in increased savings; higher incomes provided the domestic demand that was important in these economies before export markets expanded; and the redistribution of income contributed to political stability, an important factor in creating a good environment for domestic and foreign investment."[56] Political stability has, of course, been more closely associated with Japan than Korea, Taiwan being somewhat of a special case in this regard, given its uncertain relationship to China.

With respect to the association between income equality and growth, the Taiwan experience provides a particularly useful case study. It exemplifies how public policy can play a crucial role in producing widely beneficial economic outcomes, driving a wedge between the market and society that causes neither to suffer unduly. Rather than adopt policies that simply resulted in the growth of national income, regardless of its distribution, Taiwan fashioned policies that provided many if not most of its citizens with opportunities for self-improvement. In the Taiwan case, economic growth and social concerns have gone hand in hand, making it an example worthy of closer analysis. We might also note that, of all the East Asian tigers, Taiwan has apparently been the least affected by the financial crises of the late 1990s.

In 1953, while Taiwan was still recovering from World War II, the island had a level of income inequality that was about the level found in *present-day* Latin America. Ten years later, it had dropped to the level *now found* in France. At the same time, growth rates in this period were on the order of 9 percent per annum. How did these developments coincide?

According to a definitive study, this outcome was due primarily to improved income distribution in Taiwan's agriculture sector.[57] This improvement, in turn, rested on a specific set of governmental policies, that focused in the first instance on agricultural reforms—especially land reform, infrastructure investment, and price reforms—coupled with a rapid proliferation of educational opportunities for Taiwanese students at all levels.

In terms of distributive measures, land reform was of greatest significance.[58] Postwar Taiwan was ripe for such reforms. The Japanese occupation had left the agricultural sector in a shambles. Further, "the loss of the mainland and the social unrest threatening in Taiwan made the redistribution of wealth a particularly important issue for the government."[59] And, as I have argued, political stability provides the first pillar of social justice.

The land-reform program was ambitious. In the first instance, the government called for a reduction in the rents paid by tenant farmers. This, in turn, lowered the price of farmland. The government then sold public land to tenant farmers at attractive prices. Finally, the government demanded that landlords sell to the state *all* the land they held over a certain limit, in return for bonds in newly privatized industrial companies.

As a result, landlords, who could no longer live off their holdings, were now forced to participate in their country's industrial projects.[60]

In addition to these policies, education played a central role in Taiwanese economic policy. The island made huge strides in increasing literacy rates, so that by the late 1970s, about 90 percent of the population was literate. Further, high levels of female education and labor-market participation led to reduced fertility, so Taiwan did not contend with the population pressures felt by many developing economies.

Economist Dani Rodrik points to another outcome of policies that promoted greater equality with high rates of growth: good governance. He suggests that equality could lead to better government policymaking (e.g., less corruption) for several different reasons. First, by breaking the power of the large landholders, the government became relatively insulated from pressure-group politics. This, in turn, permitted the bureaucracy to focus on national economic development as opposed to the promotion of special interests. Bureaucracies, he observes, are usually the target of capture by the very actors they are supposed to supervise, and in so doing they adopt policies that block entrepreneurship.[61] These points are supported by a recent World Bank study, which argues, not surprisingly, that "countries with good economic policies and stronger institutional capability grow faster."[62] Note how the Taiwanese experience contrasts with, say, the development of post-communist Russia, in which powerful financial-industrial groups captured the transition process, and particularly the privatization of state companies.

The Taiwan case teaches that growth and equality can be joined for the overall benefit of society. Far from being inimical, they were mutually supportive. Growth promoted equality and equality promoted growth. That lesson is quite different from the one economists traditionally had drawn from the development process. Kuznets's work in particular had led a generation of scholars to believe that growth necessarily produced inequality, and that inequality generated the wealth needed for investment and future growth.[63]

Will this model endure in light of the financial crisis of 1997–98? Certainly, the widespread unemployment generated by that shock will have severe repercussions in terms of income inequality and poverty. But even here, some East Asian countries may end up providing important lessons with respect to social dialogue during periods of profound economic stress. In South Korea, for example, which has witnessed a fair share of labor strife since the outset of the crisis, substantial efforts have also been made in fashioning agreements among unions, management, and government aimed at lessening the burdens of the current economic adjustments on working people. A tripartite commission was formed on 15 January 1998, and a tripartite social accord was signed on 6 February, outlining the policies that would be advanced to contain the costs associated with worker layoffs.

Specifically, the tripartite social accord calls for further promotion of the freedom of association of workers, greater management transparency in its business decisions, reforms of the social security system, and wage stabilization in the context of greater labor-market flexibility. A wage fund has also been created to provide workers with severance pay equal to the last three months of wages, with contributions made both by employers and by workers. These may seem like small steps by the standards of the advanced welfare states of Western Europe, and they may ultimately prove inadequate, but they were developed in a remarkably short time span in a crisis-ridden South Korea, and in a relatively cooperative manner following the initial wave of labor action in 1997. This experience suggests the hypothesis that states with a highly developed level of social dialogue will emerge from crises more readily than those countries, like Indonesia, where greater divisions exist among the major economic agents.[64]

CONCLUSIONS

Around the world, workers are struggling in the face of unemployment, job insecurity, poverty, and income inequality. Of all these data, rising income inequality is especially puzzling. Unlike unemployment, rising income inequality seems to be a phenomenon occurring almost everywhere, from the industrial North to the developing South, and encompassing the postcommunist transition economies.

That trend should concern us not only for political and moral reasons but also for its potential impact on economic performance. In the past, policy elites tended to support distributive policies either out of fear that inequality would produce social conflict, or out of a sense of obligation to working people. Politics and morality thus formed the main pillars of economic justice, as exemplified by welfare-state policies and programs.

But to the extent that redistribution promotes economic growth, there should be a broad societal interest in seeing that such policies are adopted. That inequality is harmful for growth is an economic finding of tremendous policy significance. It is a lesson that is now finding its way into the programs of the major international financial institutions and bilateral assistance programs.

The policy implications of this research, however, remain contested. Policies that soak the rich will only promote capital flight, and never more so than today, with the tremendous increase in capital mobility. Instead, policies will have to be designed that not only promote equality and growth but also entice capital to stay at home. The World Bank, for example, argues in favor of policies that augment the capabilities of the disadvantaged and "expand their opportunities. Policies that build up the human capital of the poor, such as public investment in primary and secondary education, basic health care, and water and sanitation, are examples of the first. Policies leading to more equal land distribution and public provision of rural infrastructure enlarge their opportunities."[65] The objective everywhere should be to bring the disadvantaged up rather than to drag the wealthy down.

One of the most troubling aspects of the distributive policies that were adopted in such East Asian countries as Taiwan was their highly coercive nature. To be sure, states by definition are coercive entities. But they can only go so far in coercing their citizens while still preserving their democratic legitimacy. States can only act in the narrow policy space where redistribution is consistent with legitimacy.

That, of course, will differ from one country to the next, but some generalizations can be made. The economic evidence presented in this chapter suggests that every country should have a broad interest in ensuring that the poor and least advantaged have the opportunity to become productive members of society. Policies that contribute to that goal are likely to generate growth, and all members of society surely can applaud that outcome.

SHARING THE
WEALTH

There is no reason to think that justice and efficiency come to the same thing.

— JOHN RAWLS[1]

THE LAST CHAPTER MADE THE CASE that the world provides an unkind environment for millions of its working people, and especially for the unskilled. Unemployment, income inequality, job insecurity, and poverty are widespread. This book argues that such labor-market outcomes are politically dangerous, economically unproductive, and morally bankrupt. The question remains: What is to be done?

As we contemplate the adoption of alternative policy measures, we would do well to use as beacons the promises made by our postwar leaders. It is they who sought to rebuild a global economy in the interests of peace and prosperity, and they recognized that these goals could only be achieved if workers believed that the economic and social policies being adopted by national governments and international institutions were in their long-run interests. Thus, in the Charter of the United Nations, article 55 states: "With a view to the creation of conditions of stability and well-being which are necessary for peaceful and friendly relations among nations . . . the United Nations shall promote: Higher standards of living, full employment, and conditions of economic and social progress and development. . . ." And article 23 of the Universal Declaration of Human Rights proclaims, "Everyone has the right to work, to free choice of employment, to just and favorable conditions of work and to protection against unemployment." The declaration also banned slavery and servitude, stating: "Everyone has the right to life, liberty, and the security of person."

These declarations suggested that the new international economy would represent a decisive break from the old, in which labor had been subject to the full power of market forces and human suffering was often justified in Darwinian terms. Now, fundamental human rights were recognized by signatory nations from every continent, holding out the promise of a better life for all working people.

The question of what can be done to assist working people realize their talents and ambitions is one that takes on special importance in this post–Cold War era, this era of the global free market. To the extent that governments were motivated in past decades to expand opportunities and provide safety nets for their workers out of fear—fear of domestic turmoil on the one hand and international war on the other—they may now lack the political will to continue that quest, as the communist and fascist threats become dim memories. Further, as globalization proceeds, officials may believe that their countries will be penalized by mobile capital markets for adopting costly social-welfare measures, which must be financed out of tax revenues.

This problem of how to create and maintain socioeconomic institutions that distribute assets and opportunities goes well beyond the advanced industrial economies. Today, as a growing number of developing countries seek to internationalize and become competitive, their governments are feeling the systemic pressure to liberalize, privatize, deregulate, and balance their budgets, while at the same time their societies have all sorts of unmet demands. Increasingly, public officials around the world are wondering if their economic and social objectives are locked in an irreconcilable conflict.[2]

To preview this chapter's argument, I will suggest that such concepts as human freedom, individual liberty, and democracy—popular in free-market rhetoric—are basically empty for people who are prevented from exercising their talents. If we really seek to build a democratic market economy, we must make a commitment to open it to as many players as possible, and on terms that are as near-equal as possible. This means that, in addition to ensuring that people have access to the basic necessities of life, they should also be able to gain education and training and thus compete for positions on the basis of personal ability. This line of argument is hardly radical; it is fully consistent with the kind of liberal internationalism our postwar leaders sought to promote.

The policies recommended in this chapter must be advanced at three different levels of social organization: at the associational level, which draws together individuals—increasingly on a trans-national basis—who share common interests and concerns; at the level of national governments, which is still the site of most welfare-state policies; and at the level of regional and international institutions, which are becoming increasingly important overseers of the global economy. Indeed, it may be that the first and third of these elements deserve particular emphasis in the current environment. That is not to deny the continuing strength of the nation-state, but it is to argue that new policy mechanisms, making use of consumer power on the one hand and international governance structures on the other, will probably have increasing roles to play in the years ahead.

Before the policy recommendations, however, comes a discussion of policy evaluation. By what criteria should we judge public-policy decisions and outcomes? In recent years, the economic approach, focusing on cost-benefit calculations and efficiency gains, has been the privileged methodology. But as the chapter's epigraph from Harvard philosopher John Rawls suggests, there is no reason to believe that justice and efficiency amount to the same thing. If our objective is to produce public policies that are widely viewed as legitimate, considerations of fairness must have a seat at the policy table alongside concerns about maximizing output.

JUSTICE VS. EFFICIENCY AS THE OBJECT OF PUBLIC POLICY

It is rare to hear economists discuss issues of justice or moral philosophy. For most of them, efficiency is the key policy objective, since other targets will likely result in losses for the economy as a whole. They take this approach not because they are heartless but rather because it is arguably simpler to reach agreement on which policy produces the most output than it is to decide which policy is "fair."

Probably the most influential methodology for dealing with questions of public policy is utilitarianism, initially formulated by Jeremy Bentham and his followers, the father-and-son team of James and John Stuart Mill, in the late eighteenth and early nineteenth centuries. Utilitarians advance a seemingly commonsense proposition: that public policies should be guided by the rule of advancing the greatest good for the greatest number. This calculation, still widely used today in "cost-benefit analysis" of policy alternatives (e.g., the decision to build a new highway or invest in mass transit), suggests that policy A should be preferred over policy B if policy A produces the most overall "utility" or "happiness" for a given population.

But it doesn't take much imagination to see that the formulation of the "greatest good for the greatest number" principle can quickly run into difficulty. To take a simple example, imagine a society with three persons, A, B, C, and two policies, I and II (see table 5-1). Under policy I, each member of society obtains three goods, for a total of nine goods. Under policy II, the distribution is different: A and B each receive two units, while C receives six, for a total of 10. Which policy is to be preferred?[3] Here we see that "the greatest good" and "the greatest number" are in conflict. Further, even if C could "compensate" A and B by giving each of them one unit—so that they now have 3 while C has 4—the policy shift could still be rejected by A and B, who now feel relatively worse off than before.

TABLE 5-1.

The Greatest Good or the Greatest Number?

	POLICY 1	POLICY 2
A	3	2
B	3	2
C	3	6
Total Goods	9	10

In resolving these sorts of problems, some modern-day utilitarians have simply dropped the greatest-number clause and instead argue that economists and policymakers should focus their efforts on determining which policy generates the greatest good. They do so because trying to achieve the greatest good for the greatest number implies the existence of a distributive principle (e.g., that we should strive for the highest *average* utility for each person, as in policy I), which may be impossible for a society to agree upon or achieve in many circumstances, or which may simply be so costly in efficiency terms that it renders the policy absurd. By choosing policy I over policy II, for example, we "lose" one good in the process.

Nobel Prize winner John Hicks had these concerns in mind when he wrote, "If measures making for efficiency are to have a fair chance, it is extremely desirable that they should be freed from distributive complications as much as possible. . . ."[4] That is, economists should worry more about producing the greatest amount of good, and less about how that good is distributed. But in a famous thought experiment, Arthur Okun of the Brookings Institution took a more subtle approach. He asked us to think about distributive policies as a leaky bucket, in which money and services were lost as transfers were made from rich to poor. He raised the question: How much leakage would society actually support as it advanced its distributive goals? The answer, he suggested, would be significantly more than zero but also considerably less than 100 percent.[5]

Since we can all think of countless examples where efficient outcomes come into conflict with our sense of justice, we must question the viability of utilitarian doctrines as a guiding principle for policymaking. We can, for the sake of argument, imagine a situation in which the institution of slavery produces the "greatest good for the greatest number," and we can assume that a majority of whites in the antebellum American South felt that way. But nobody today would consider adopting it as a labor policy, even if we could show that it produced the greatest economic good for the majority of citizens. The point is that our ideas about justice *do* make a difference to our economic arrangements.

Utilitarianism still holds a powerful hold on policymakers, especially when it comes to decisionmaking with respect to the global economy. Indeed, one can assert that international economics is a quintessentially utilitarian doctrine. As James Meade wrote of international economic analysis in his classic work *Trade and Welfare*, "We shall adopt very largely the old-fashioned utilitarian criterion of considering the total economic welfare of the community as made up of the sum of economic welfares of its individual citizens; and which shall attempt to judge all acts of policy from this point of view of their effects upon this total sum." Meade recognized the limitations of this approach, since "the statesmen cannot confine himself to the economic criterion. . . . There are other social and political criteria of which we need mention only two: freedom and equality."[6] The question is, how much attention have policy analysts paid to freedom and equality in their assessments of how globalization affects working people?

The failure of utilitarianism in dealing with basic questions of social justice prompted John Rawls to develop an alternative theoretical approach. In his monumental work A *Theory of Justice*, Rawls argues that our public institutions and policies should work to the benefit of the least advantaged among us. Basically, he asks each of us to imagine what policies and institutions we would build if we ourselves were disadvantaged. In so doing, he provides a fundamental challenge to those who would assert that we cannot find a central place for justice in our deliberations over economic policy, and, contra economists like John Hicks, Rawls argues that our search for justice must take precedence over our demand for efficiency.

In making this case, Rawls reminds us: "Justice is the first virtue of social institutions, as truth is of systems of thought. A theory however elegant and economical must be rejected or revised if it is untrue; likewise laws and institutions no matter how efficient and well-arranged must be reformed or abolished if they are unjust." This is because, under any liberal theory, "Each person possesses an inviolability founded on justice that even the welfare of society as a whole cannot override."[7] Rawls returns us to *individual* well-being as the fundamental unit of analysis of political theory, and he focuses on the role of institutions in shaping individual outcomes because their effects on our life chances "are so profound and present from the start." In short, Rawls defines justice as fairness.

Thus, a societal structure that institutionalizes discrimination against a particular group of individuals—that makes it more difficult or even impossible for certain people (perhaps because of race, creed, gender, or sexual orientation) to achieve the same goals as those who are in the favored group—must be considered unjust. We should evaluate institutions in terms of the inequalities they engender—of income, of life chances, of expectations for holding office, or of achieving one's goals.[8]

In making his claims, Rawls asks us to conduct a thought experiment. He posits an "original position" in which individuals must choose their constitutional principles—the principles that will guide their institutions and public policies—from behind a "veil of ignorance."[9] That is, in writing a constitution that will serve as the cornerstone of a society, each person must forget narrow self-interest and instead act as a "representative" member of their group. These individuals must forget their race, gender, economic background, and so forth, and choose principles of justice as if they did not know what their ultimate fate (or that of their families) would be—whether they would be privileged or disadvantaged, healthy or sick, brilliant or dim.

What principles of justice would we adopt if we were acting from behind this veil of ignorance? Rawls suggests two: First, that we would seek the most extensive set of individual liberties possible compatible with similar liberties for others; and second, that we would advance a "difference principle," which stipulates that social and economic institutions should be structured in such a way as to benefit the least advantaged among us.[10] This difference principle is founded upon the idea that the problem of social or distributive justice concerns the "differences in [an individual's] life prospects" that arise from institutional and societal factors. Discrimination against women or minorities in recruiting for certain jobs, or the decrease in opportunities for the child of a janitor rather than of a surgeon, would be examples of structural influences that place certain individuals in a disadvantage position, and that must be removed in the interest of justice.[11]

Now some might argue that, while Rawls provides a powerful theoretical line of argument, it is difficult to see how his ideas could be put into policy practice. For example, we might reasonably ask questions about "how far" the privileged members of a society must go in order to satisfy the resource claims made by the least advantaged (and that is, indeed, an important philosophical issue at the global level also, as in the case of foreign aid). Is it the case that, for Rawls, efficiency doesn't matter at all, and that he would have us transferring resources to the least advantaged to the point of equalization, no matter how much spills out from Okun's leaky bucket in the process? In proceeding from theory to policy, we must find more specific guidance than the claim that our institutions ought to remove any obstacles facing the disadvantaged—as useful as that general framework may be in shaping our overall approach.

We would argue as good liberals that we should strive to build free markets, removing impediments to any trades that rational individuals seek to make. Free markets satisfy our basic principles of justice to the extent that everyone is able to participate and exercise one's talents. In the *process* of building free markets, however, there will inevitably be scores of winners and losers along the way. Opening a country to free trade, for example, will produce such a distribution among the population. The economic and political transition now occurring in the post-communist countries represents another profound instance of a process that has transformed a population, producing new patterns of winners and losers. We cannot simply overlook these distributive effects. The *difference principle* suggests that any policy move, including the move to free markets, can be justified only when it works to everyone's benefit, and especially to that of the least advantaged among us.

In practice, what that may mean in many instances is that the winners from a given policy move will have to compensate the losers in the interest of justice. The underlying logic here from a liberal perspective is that no individual should be forced to accept a policy move that makes her worse off than she was before; to the contrary, following the famous argument of the economist Vilifredo Pareto, policy moves should only be made if someone is made better off and no one is made worse off.

In fact, this notion of providing economic compensation was advanced by one of the early utilitarian thinkers, John Stuart Mill, during the mid-nineteenth century. At that time, the political issue of how to evaluate public policies that produced both winners and losers became acute in Great Britain, as that country debated the dismantling of its long-standing Corn Laws, which protected domestic agriculture from foreign imports. In seeking to find a way to calculate the net societal benefits to the country from the increased wealth that free trade in agriculture would bring—taking into account the reduced welfare it would cause rural laborers and landowners—Mill argued for a "compensation principle." Mill suggested that if compensation were paid to those whose incomes fell after the abolition of the Corn Laws, nobody in Britain would be worse off, while the nation as a whole would be much better off. Free trade would increase national wealth, and, combined with compensation, it would improve national welfare also.[12]

Compensation, however, turns out to be one of those troublesome ideas that can be nicer in theory than practice, even though it is widely used in certain circumstances (think of liability awards as an example, or unemployment insurance). The problem is that it is difficult to calculate how much people actually lose as the result of a given policy move. How much of an earnings loss, for example, will a factory worker suffer when a country opens up to foreign competition? The worker may lose her job, but the ensuing economic growth could mean that she will get a better job in the future. Making *a priori* estimates of earnings losses is a difficult business. Further, if too much compensation is offered to potential losers, perverse incentives exist for people to come forward and identify themselves as such. Because of these informational and incentive difficulties, it is usually impossible to compensate people appropriately for the losses they have suffered.

Despite its inadequacies, it would seem that compensation represents the second-best world for most policymaking decisions that involve possible losses of an individual's future earnings and employment. Compensation alone, however, must be coupled with positive efforts aimed in the first instance at helping any losers become winners over a relevant time horizon. Such efforts recognize the real efficiency gains that particular policy moves—say, the move to free trade—can bring, while also making good on our moral obligations to those who may suffer as a result. Let me reiterate that our interest in establishing a moral foundation for the international economy is to ensure that the structure we are building is widely viewed as legitimate in the eyes of its participants, including its workers.

WORKER-ORIENTED ECONOMIC POLICIES

Thus far, I have tried to build a case for constructing economic policies that are sensitive to the growing concerns of working people for their future. Such policies, I have argued, are more conducive to political stability, economic growth, and "the good life" than those that prevent people from realizing their talents. I believe that these policies, far from being in conflict with the market, are market-enhancing.

With respect to the policy recommendations that I make here, clearly the specifics will have to be tailored to meet each individual national and regional case. For example, I do not hold an ideological position on whether education should be provided by the public or the private sector; in some cases, privatization may yield better outcomes for the society in question. My focus is on whether individual needs are being filled, and this suggests that there is at least one general principle, consistent with international norms with respect to human rights, that should inform the debate about policy reform everywhere. That principle is as follows: *Societies should seek to create an environment that enables each individual to realize his or her talents.*

It follows from this principle that: (1) Societies should remove discrimination; and (2) All members of society are entitled, by virtue of their humanity, to the basic necessities of life.

This principle, along with its corollaries, leads to the policy priorities discussed in this chapter.

POLICIES FOR INDIVIDUALS AND THEIR ASSOCIATIONS, INCLUDING ENTERPRISES AND UNIONS

A global economy that respects the interests of working people can be created only through political action. It is up to individuals, acting alone and in concert, to advance the ideas and objectives that they value. Indeed, to the extent we accept the argument that national governments are increasingly constrained in their capacity or willingness to advance social demands in the context of globalization, then we must accept that more of the burden will fall on the shoulders of individuals, subnational groups (including communities and charities), and transnational nongovernmental organizations (NGOs) to ensure that appropriate policy measures are taken around the world.

But what are the actual policies that people can implement in their homes or associations to promote economic justice? Some of the most promising steps that can be taken are discussed in the sections that follow.

INVEST IN AND BUY FROM SOCIALLY RESPONSIBLE FIRMS

Individuals and unions have potential clout in corporate affairs via the shares they hold in companies through pensions and savings plans. They should organize to use this influence more actively. One precedent for the exploitation of such leverage comes from the anti-apartheid movement of the 1970s and 1980s. During this period, for example, a large number of American universities sold off their shares in multinational corporations that continued to operate in or do business with South Africa. We can anticipate that the new millennium will bring with it a new era of shareholder activism, as groups concerned with human rights and the environment seek to place increasing pressure on the private sector.

In addition, individual investors now have the choice of placing their funds in "socially responsive portfolios," which are offered by such major investment firms as Neuberger and Berman and Merrill Lynch. According to Janet Prindle, manager of Neuberger and Berman's Socially Responsive Fund, "Our shareholders want to support companies that are creating equal opportunities, providing increased workplace benefits and safety, and improving the environment."[13] These funds provide an efficient way to join other investors who share similar social values.

According to comparative data, investors who place their money in such companies do not suffer as a result. Over the three years 1995–97, the Neuberger and Berman Socially Responsive Fund had average annual returns of 27 percent, compared to 31 percent for the Standard and Poor's 500 (made up of blue-chip companies) index on the one hand and 22.34 percent for the Russell 2000 (an index of smaller companies) on the other. The fund invests in such companies as the A. G. Edwards brokerage house, Warner-Lambert pharmaceuticals, Kimberly-Clark, and Core-States Financial, all of which, according to Prindle, are "standout companies . . . in such areas as environmental management and workplace policies. . . ."

Beyond their investments, all consumers vote on a daily basis with their pocketbooks. One of the most useful steps is to call for more precise labeling about the labor conditions under which the goods and services were made.[14] Consumers can demand that the big chain stores in which they shop, such as Wal-Mart and K Mart, refuse to buy items from wholesalers that do not provide full disclosure about the conditions under which clothing and consumer goods were manufactured. The role of consumer power in forcing companies to adopt higher labor standards has been powerfully demonstrated recently in such cases as Nike sportswear, which was sharply criticized for the low wages paid to its Asian workers.

It would be naïve, however, to expect too much from such a voluntaristic approach to advancing the social agenda. The problem is one of collective action. For example, while many individuals, when asked, may well respond that they place a high value on better wages for workers, any single consumer can only make a small difference in achieving that outcome. He or she might therefore choose the cheaper garment when shopping, since the potential impact on the world's workers from that individual choice is so small. If a large number of people adopt that logic, then consumerism loses much of its punch as a political force. For that reason, organizations with coercive power, meaning governments, must continue to play the major role in setting the social-policy agenda.

FORM DOMESTIC AND TRANSNATIONAL "ADVOCACY GROUPS"[15]

Philosopher-economist Amartya Sen likes to remind us that as individuals we have "plural affiliations" in our daily lives.[16] We are spouses, parents, workers, coaches, activists, and so forth. Increasingly, these activities are becoming transnational, as people commute across countries in their work lives and sometimes in their married ones as well! More relevant for our purposes, people are often engaged in associative activities that are transnational by nature, such as Amnesty International, or are becoming more so, such as unions and environmental groups. These transnational activities can serve as a cornerstone for promoting common sensibilities about such issues as labor standards and workers' rights.

Contemporary international politics is now replete with examples of nongovernmental organizations (NGOs) and advocacy groups exercising considerable influence over national and multilateral policymaking. In such issue areas as the environment and human rights, these groups have played leading roles in bringing problems to the public agenda and lobbying for an international policy response. Curiously, in recent years labor has been less successful in generating or participating in such transnational efforts.

To the contrary, time and again we have observed union efforts to form transnational links succumb to infighting over tactics, coupled with the divide-and-conquer strategies of multinational corporations. In Western Europe, labor solidarity both within and across nations has also been undermined by the various religious and political philosophies that underpin particular movements. But if unions are to be effective in advancing such objectives as labor standards and the working wage, they must work together and with other groups to form coalitions. In the distant past, unions partnered with religious and social organizations to advance their goals, and that tradition is in desperate need of rebuilding. Again, in a rapidly integrating Europe, the need for such cross-border coalitions that join labor with other groups would seem especially compelling.

Unfortunately, in many countries union corruption has provided a strong disincentive to any partnering arrangements with outside groups, in addition to giving unions a bad name. Corruption must be weeded out if unions are to play a leadership role in constructing a just global economy. Although the contemporary union movement, led by such officials as John Sweeney of the AFL-CIO, shows hopeful signs of getting the right message, it's still too early to tell whether it will overcome the seamier side of its past.

The erosion of union power around the world is one of the most disturbing trends confronting workers—and indeed confronting all those who care about human dignity. Unions have played a crucial role in improving the lives of working people by winning higher wages and benefits and workplace health and safety regulations. They were present at the creation of the postwar welfare state and helped to knit the social safety net that all citizens now enjoy. With millions of workers around the world still denied a life of dignity, unions in the industrial countries have a vital transnational role to play in trumpeting their cause. One need think only of the shipyard workers in Gdansk, Poland, organized under the name of *Solidarity*, to appreciate how central unions have been and must remain to the aspirations of working people everywhere.

Nor is it just workers who should have an interest in the fate of unions. Ironically, enterprises and national governments should promote the union cause as well. Around the world, the tripartite grouping of firms, governments, and unions working together has brought both economic growth and political stability. Today we see the benefits of such a tripartite organizational form in South Korea, which is weathering its current financial crisis with relatively little social disruption. The alternative to the union, with its *organization* of workers, is the crowd, and the shift from unions to crowds is one that should give us pause.

In promoting global worker solidarity, industrial world unions obviously have some hard political choices to make. Most difficult, obviously, is the choice between free trade and protectionism, as I will discuss in more detail below. Free trade may benefit workers in developing country A while hurting workers in industrial country B. Thus, country B's unions, which exist for the benefit of their workers, will naturally advocate a protectionist stance in such cases. A more promising approach for industrial workers would be to fight for better compensation packages in the context of any free-trade agreements—a subject also discussed in greater depth below.

At the same time, unions should focus their efforts on what might be considered less divisive goals: promoting freedom of association and organization in those countries where workers are denied basic rights, and advertising those cases where such rights are denied. Again, this area would seem ripe for joint action with human-rights organizations. Unions could also play a leading role in the labeling movement, as discussed earlier. By joining with other groups, and by emphasizing transnational issues, unions may enjoy a renaissance in the global setting, rather than being overwhelmed by it.

ADOPT CORPORATE CODES OF CONDUCT AND BEST PRACTICES

In recent years, Americans have been subjected to almost daily reports about corporate misbehavior. We have read about slave-labor sweatshops in New York and Los Angeles, the misdeeds of big tobacco companies, the forced pregnancy testing of textile workers in Latin American export processing zones, and the low wages of Nike workers in Asia, as made famous in *Doonesbury* cartoons. We have also read about companies that engage in mass layoffs with little in the way of advance notice for workers, and firms that use the threat of exit to a new, low-wage location as a way of preventing unionization. None of these actions help to advance the cause of the neoliberal economic model in the long run, and all of them suggest the need for more stringent codes of corporate conduct, developed in the first instance by the firms themselves with the assistance of nongovernmental organizations.

One example of such code-setting is provided by the Council on Economic Priorities, a nonprofit public-policy organization that each year evaluates the environmental practices of major corporations. In a recent study of oil companies, for example, it lauded Sun, Exxon, and Chevron for setting exemplary environmental standards. According to the *Wall Street Journal*, this recognition is beneficial to the firms, which are likely to see more activity at their gas pumps as a result.[17] There is no reason why firms could not join with their unions and other interested groups in coming up with such codes on their own, in the absence of further government-specified regulation.

These codes should cover such issues as labor standards, worker health and safety, and consumer and environmental protection. These firms should also adopt "best practices" with respect to their treatment of workers during layoffs, including the provision of advance notice, retraining, compensation, and job search assistance. In advocating such a proactive stance on the part of corporations, we should recognize that they may be properly considered as "moral persons"—meaning they should hold themselves to certain standards of decency in their behavior. Again, we should emphasize that such standard-setting is also likely to be good for business in a world where issues of social justice are again rising to the fore.

Further, in the quest for increasing worker productivity— and thus higher wages—it is the enterprises themselves that should be at the forefront of offering appropriate training and upskilling opportunities for all employees. They, rather than government agencies, are best suited to determining what works and what doesn't in improving the labor force. Enterprises can do a better job of promoting upward from within rather than slotting someone for life as a machine operator or secretary. They can also do more to ensure worker loyalty and performance through stock options and stock-purchase programs—benefits that give workers a direct stake in corporate earnings. One often hears that America is becoming a "stakeholder" society, and if so, that is all to the good. Unfortunately, the flip side for millions of working people is the image of a rootless and insecure society. The enterprise must play a central role in efforts to improve the lives of the least advantaged, and it should act out of a sense of enlightened self-interest rather than in response to government fiat.

POLICIES FOR NATIONAL GOVERNMENTS

While we may expect private associations and nongovernmental organizations to become increasingly active in labor politics around the world, citizens still look to their nation-state as the first line of defense for their welfare. In principle, governments that wish to assist their workers can influence either the demand side or the supply side of the employment equation. On the demand side, the classic Keynesian approach is to increase government spending in the interest of economic growth and full employment. An alternative demand-side measure is to seek changes in tax policy so that employers face reduced wage costs. This, for example, has been touted as a key to Holland's relative success in generating new jobs. On the supply side, in contrast, governments can seek to improve the match between labor-force qualifications and existing employment opportunities; such measures often are labeled "active labor market policies."

Given the problems of unemployment and inequality described in this book, it will come as no surprise that countries everywhere have been experimenting with any number of different policy measures aimed at stimulating job growth—from public works programs to the French call for a thirty-five-hour week. The fact that global employment rates vary suggests that countries still maintain significant capacity to influence labor-market outcomes. Several of the major policies for reducing unemployment and assisting unskilled and displaced workers are discussed in this section.[18]

The focus here will be on active labor-market policies— that is, public policies aimed directly at getting the unemployed back to work through training, employment subsidies, and the like. The reason for this emphasis is that economic growth, while absolutely crucial to job creation, does not seem to solve labor-market problems on its own. Between 1984 and 1994, for example, Western Europe saw an average annual growth rate in gross domestic product of some 2.3 percent, but its employment growth was only 0.6 percent per year. Even in the United States, employment growth was significantly lower than economic growth, and there remained questions about the *quality* of the jobs generated—the so-called McJobs problem.[19]

Many observers argue that the failure of economic growth to produce new jobs is due to labor-market rigidities, including minimum wage rates, unionization, generous unemployment benefits and employment protection legislation—leading to calls for increasing "flexibility" on the part of the working population.[20] Workers in many countries, perceiving this reaction as a code for seeking lower wages, have lobbied for alternatives aimed at increasing their productivity or protecting their jobs from foreign competition. Wage flexibility seems to work most effectively as a demand-side policy only in those cases, like Ireland and the Netherlands, where it has resulted from a tripartite agreement among trade unions, employers, and the state.

In terms of active measures aimed at assisting unskilled and displaced workers, governments have the following policy measures at their disposal: protectionism (used especially for large and politically well-organized groups like auto workers); expansion of education and training opportunities; adoption of public-works programs and labor subsidies of various types; and policies aimed at increasing labor mobility.[21] All of them entail costs, which must be paid for in one way or another, and in a world of mobile capital, the burden of social costs is falling on workers themselves. That raises equity concerns, which will undoubtedly become more charged as globalization proceeds. At the same time, a growing chorus is asking about state capacity in a global economy. Are nation-states still effective policy arenas, or is their scope for choice being reduced with the rapid increase in trade and capital flows?

As noted above, the variance in unemployment rates, even across the highly interdependent states of Western Europe, signifies that borders matter when it comes to labor policy. Still, there remains the issue of where the trend lines are headed, and it is certainly reasonable to assert that the policy effectiveness of governments is declining. Economic integration may undermine a nation's labor policies and institutions in several ways.[22] The previous chapter pointed out that workers in industrial countries who compete against labor in the developing world can face downward pressure on their wages and benefits. Within developing countries, international competition has helped the cause of politicians and industrialists who would ban unions, employ children, and maintain low health and safety standards—all in the interests of exploiting their comparative advantage in unskilled labor. And in countries around the world, free-trade agreements have generally moved in the direction of preventing states from using national standard-setting or preferential procurement policies in the effort to protect national industries.

For its part, capital mobility has probably had even more pervasive effects on national autonomy. The threat of exit by multinational firms may be used as a way of hammering down wages or preventing the formation of unions. Capital mobility also means that states will become less effective in using research and development (R&D) subsidies and other such programs as a means of bolstering national output. After all, a widget now developed by the R&D team of a multinational firm in country A can be easily shipped to its subsidiary in country B, with the net result that country A's imports will increase! Indeed, the bulk of world trade is carried out among the subsidiaries of multinational enterprises. Further, as already mentioned, capital mobility has profound effects on tax policy.

These constraints all point to the need for national policies that make states attractive places for investors. But how can social and labor policy fit that particular bill? Aren't living wages, reasonable benefits, and good working conditions anathema in a world of mobile capital? What could possibly draw investors to welfare states if other countries are willing to ban unions, accept low wages for their workers, and forgo social safety nets for losers? The following paragraphs discuss the policy options available to states, and their likely impact on labor. Overall, this section will argue that public spending must be reoriented to increase the working population's long-term productivity, while compensating and assisting those who find themselves on the losing end of economic change. These efforts should *complement* private-sector initiatives to produce a well-trained workforce. That argues for a priority on such areas as education, and it also means the need to redesign—but not abandon—welfare-state programs in such a way as to promote worker mobility, both upward in terms of career progression and outward in terms of capacity to move to new locations. Let's begin, however, by considering what might seem at first glance to be the most effective policy for helping the unskilled worker: protectionism.

PROTECTIONISM AND IMMIGRATION CONTROLS

Contemporary trade economists contend that the economic case for openness is unambiguous. They are wrong, and there are several instances in which protection might be a reasonable response to the international economic system that a state confronts. Free trade, for example, is only the "first-best" policy when there is no monopoly power in the trading system.[23] In the presence of a monopoly buyer of a country's exports, for example, free trade by definition doesn't exist at all, and the terms of trade may actually hurt the country's economy.

From a historical perspective, protectionism has long been respectable as a means for promoting domestic economic activity. In the "mercantilist" view of such statesmen as America's first Secretary of the Treasury, Alexander Hamilton, states had a legitimate role in protecting "infant industries" needed for national defense, and of course even Adam Smith had written that "defense is more important than opulence." For most of its history, the United States employed high tariff walls against foreign manufactured goods, lowering rates only after American industries were dominant on the world stage. In post–World War II Latin America, a "structuralist" economic literature arose that justified protectionism as the only way of enabling primary commodity exporters to diversify their economic base, thereby reducing earnings volatility.

Protectionism has received both renewed attention and scrutiny in recent years as political candidates around the world have used it in their campaign platforms. In the United States, the Republican presidential hopeful Patrick Buchanan, an avowed "economic nationalist," has asserted that he would place prohibitive tariffs on a range of imports in order to protect American jobs and wages. The underlying economic argument is that by protecting firms and workers in sectors exposed to foreign competition, those companies will remain in business and be able to pay decent wages for their unskilled labor. In France, the right-wing National Front party has placed "anti-globalization" at the center of its political platform.

The protectionist argument, however, is flawed in major respects. Whatever the benefits of protectionism for particular industries and their workers, the costs, also borne by workers, would likely outweigh them, and national income would certainly fall. Protectionism would lead to higher prices for all products, both foreign and domestic, resulting in lower consumption and an economic slowdown. Further, in the absence of foreign competition, firms will fail to innovate and may simply produce shoddy products that consumers no longer wish to purchase; this, for example, was the Soviet experience. At the same time, a country's trading partners could not be expected to sit on the sidelines passively while they were being victimized. They, too, would erect higher tariff barriers in response, eliminating markets for exports and the jobs that go with them. Since exports are now the fastest growing part of the economy in many countries, including the United States, policies that result in their restriction cannot be commended.

Beyond the economic arguments against protection are the political reasons. One problem with protectionism is that it resembles pregnancy; you can't adopt that condition "just a little bit." Thus, even if there were a sectoral case to be made for protection (e.g., in steel or shipbuilding), it would be hard for a government to limit its policy to that single case; other sectors, too, would clamor for similar treatment. And on the international level, we should not forget the Kantian argument, close to the heart of American officials, that "free trade dovetails with peace." To the extent that trade does promote the cause of peace, it should not be rejected too quickly.

In summation, then, protectionism is a remedy that is worse than the disease. It is an inefficient way of helping unskilled workers, and a backward foreign policy. But this does not mean that the case for free trade should go unchallenged. Like protection, free trade also produces winners and losers. The significant difference, however, is that it also generates greater wealth overall, and some of those gains can and should be used to help the losers. The American trade adjustment assistance (TAA) program, which provides trade-displaced workers with extended unemployment insurance and training benefits, represents one approach—though perhaps not the best—to the losers problem (indeed, the United States is among the few industrial countries with trade-specific adjustment assistance), although it has been of limited success in making up for income losses (that issue is taken up in a later paragraph).

A similar set of arguments about economic costs and benefits can be made for immigration controls, and this issue certainly will rise in salience as we enter the new millennium. On the one hand, falling unemployment rates in the United States mean that certain sectors, such as software manufacturers, have unfilled vacancies, so they are placing pressure on Washington to open the doors to those with the requisite skills. (In this context, it should be noted that the United States emphasizes family reunification over economic benefits in its immigration policies.) Further, aging populations in many European and Asian countries suggest the need for new cohorts of younger workers to help pay for underfunded pension programs. On the other hand, the fact that immigration—particularly illegal immigration—affects the employment and income of certain societal groups has caused a backlash against immigrants—and in places like France this sentiment has been tapped with some political success by parties like the National Front.

As with trade, most studies indicate that immigration generally represents a net economic blessing to the receiving country. Immigrants often engage in labor that is considered undesirable by many workers, and they stimulate job creation through their entrepreneurial activity. But that should not prevent us from recognizing that immigration can entail losses for certain groups of workers as well, and touting its benefits without recognizing its costs does not help those who would seek open rather than closed policies in this area. In the interests of maintaining relatively open immigration policies, the losers should be recognized and appropriately compensated through either new employment opportunities or income transfers.[24] Indeed, more research on exactly who those losers are should be a key undertaking of scholars who seek to maintain public support for an open-door policy.

EDUCATION AND TRAINING

Increased spending on education and training appears to be the only policy intervention that meets with universal approval across the political spectrum. The theory underlying this policy measure is that, over time, unskilled workers can be expected to respond to the economic signals of the marketplace and opt for (or at least encourage their children to do so) more education and training. Historical evidence suggests that this process occurs in most industrial countries undergoing significant economic change.[25]

As discussed in an earlier chapter, if there is one generalization that can be made about the life chances of a worker, it is that individual economic success is powerfully linked to educational attainment. Too often in these discussions, however, we tend to focus only on higher education. The real return, in contrast, may be in the primary grades, and this makes the elementary school teacher a critical actor in the economy—a fact that is rarely recognized in discussions of labor and economic policy. The World Bank finds: "Returns to education are especially high at the primary level, because universal basic literacy yields large externalities to society. Educating girls, for example, is linked to better health for women and their children. . . ."[26] One of a society's first responsibilities, then, is tending to the education of *all* of its youth, and in those places where parents have an incentive to put children to work at an early age, greater emphasis must be placed on the phrase *compulsory education*.

Unfortunately, in times of economic crisis, it is education that often feels the first hit of the budget ax. No less troubling, it is during crises when parents pull their children out of school. In Indonesia, for example, some 20 percent of the school-age children have been pulled from the classroom by desperate parents. This suggests the intergenerational effects of the current tragedy.[27] It also points to a possible positive role at such times for foreign assistance, as will be discussed in the next section of this chapter.

A second area in need of greater emphasis in many countries is vocational education. Traditionally, vocational schools have languished in the shadows of educational debate, cast as second-rate institutions with students who could not succeed in other programs. Instead, they should be viewed positively as institutions that help prepare nonacademically oriented students for the workforce. A potential model for these schools may be provided by the military, which in many countries does an excellent job of providing non-college-educated students with technical skills. In fact, the United States armed forces, as an example, have perhaps been too successful in this regard. With the ongoing economic expansion, thousands of these well-trained young adults are leaving the military after only a few years of service and heading for the civilian workforce, often for computer-related jobs. Stories like these should be used to help us determine what works and what doesn't with respect to vocational training, and several ongoing experiments in the industrial countries provide hopeful signs that a better understanding will soon exist. That work should receive widespread attention from senior education officials and scholars.[28]

It is difficult to argue that educational spending has been a high priority around the world. The richest industrial countries devoted 5.4 percent of gross national product to education in the 1990s, and the richest "developing countries" (e.g., Hong Kong, Singapore, Chile) spent 4.6 percent. But in Brazil, the government spent less than 2 percent of GNP on education, and in Turkey, only 3.3 percent. Indeed, Brazil and Turkey spent as much on defense as on education; at least in the former case, it is hard to define any threats to Brazil's national security.[29] These data suggest the need for a fundamental reorientation in public spending priorities. Removing the impediments to education for disadvantaged groups should be among every government's highest priorities. And to the extent that such a policy results in more productive workers, it should also be welcomed by a country's investors, who can play an active role in education by providing schools with needed technologies, equipment, and skills.

The experience with government-sponsored worker training and retraining programs, beyond those in the military, is less positive. Studies of training programs indicate any number of obstacles to success. In some cases, for example, displaced workers have faced prohibitive costs for the training programs that would likely lead to new jobs. In cases of capital market failure, where banks refuse to provide education and training loans, financial assistance and guarantees should be available. More frequently, workers have simply found a mismatch between training opportunities and projected new-job requirements. The fact is that the best training occurs within an organization that has already hired the worker, and this again speaks to the need for a sound basic education. Overall, as the World Bank and other organizations have concluded, results are mixed regarding the value of training in helping displaced workers find new jobs.

This does not mean training should be abandoned; as a matter of fairness, workers who seek training should have the opportunity to improve or change their skills. It may also be the case that some of the alleged failures of training programs are in fact due to a lack of supporting policy measures, such as those that would assist a worker in moving to a new location; more studies on the interaction between training and other measures would be useful in this regard. The mobility issue is particularly salient in Western Europe, where workers who receive good training may lack the appropriate incentives to move across borders. These issues will be discussed in greater detail in a later section.

But even if training were considered an *effective* means of improving the match between job and worker, the cost of providing it to all the unemployed would be prohibitive. There are now some 34 million unemployed persons in the industrial countries, and if the average cost of retraining each of these workers is on the order of $7,000, the total bill would be $238 billion. For the United States, with its seven million unemployed, the total would be $49 billion. Today, the U.S. government spends about $10 billion on work-related education and training. In the current fiscal environment, it is difficult to imagine that number rising to the required amount.

On the contrary, these programs are being cut back. Since 1992, funds for labor-market training and other "active" measures have fallen in such countries as Canada, Germany, Sweden, and the United States—the last being particularly ironic since it was a favorite of President Bill Clinton's first Secretary of Labor, Robert Reich (although he did, of course, have to contend with a Republican Congress). Such expenditures were cut by some 10 percent in the early 1990s in the United States as well as in Britain.

It is odd that training has become the "mom and apple pie" of economists and public officials across the political spectrum when it could, at best, provide only a partial response to the problems of unskilled and displaced workers—at least given present funding levels and our current knowledge base about "what works." Clearly, other measures will be needed, and these must be targeted more directly at the problems of employment and inequality. Some of the most promising alternatives are discussed in the following paragraphs.

PUBLIC JOBS AND WORKER-SUBSIDY PROGRAMS

When economists seek policy solutions to a given problem, they generally try to find the most efficient path available. In that context, it would seem that the most direct way of reducing unemployment and inequality, and compensating losers, would be for governments to create jobs and transfer incomes. Surprisingly, it is hard to find widespread support for many of the programs aimed at doing exactly that.

For example, of all the policy measures advocated to generate employment, it would be difficult to find one with fewer adherents in contemporary debate than public-job programs. In France, where such programs have a central place in Prime Minister Lionel Jospin's employment policy, they have been subject to widespread ridicule by the financial press. Governments, it is said, are incapable of creating meaningful employment, and to the extent that they launch such programs, they simply represent another burden for taxpayers.

Public jobs, however, should not be so quickly dismissed. We would do well to recall that President Franklin Roosevelt's New Deal policies were reasonably successful in creating jobs, reducing misery, and providing hope. As public employees, many American artists and writers produced vivid images of the Great Depression that form a significant part of our historical record, and the nation's environment and infrastructure were greatly improved by the public-works projects undertaken during the 1930s. In recent times, public-job programs have had positive results in a number of countries—including Ireland, the United Kingdom, and New Zealand—especially in helping minorities, youth, and the long-term unemployed enter the labor market.[30] Far from being wasteful, job creation represents a potentially efficient and socially productive way of removing the unemployed from the insurance rolls—or providing youth with first-time jobs—and it can be done fairly quickly.

This approach becomes all the more compelling in light of the sharp defense drawdowns among the member states of the North Atlantic Treaty Organization (NATO). In the United States, for example, the size of the armed forces has shrunk by nearly one million since 1986, closing a once-promising route to education, training, experience, and responsibility for thousands of young adults. France will soon end military conscription, and it already faces a severe problem in terms of youth unemployment. Alternative paths must be created to help this population enter the workforce, and in the absence of private-sector opportunities, public employment may be one worth following. Such programs, however, must be carefully targeted and structured to avoid the obvious pitfalls of producing dead-end jobs, creating public-sector jobs that compete with the private sector, or using these employees as a way of displacing existing workers.

With respect to direct wage and income support to workers or the employers who hire them, a growing number of labor-market observers are making the case that these represent perhaps the most efficient and equitable means of helping low-paid, unskilled workers. After all, other than finding a new job, the biggest problem facing a displaced worker is income loss.[31] Several methods of providing workers with a living wage are available, from subsidies to insurance, and it is certain that this general concept will become of increasing importance in labor policy debates.

Columbia University professor Edmund Phelps has been a particularly vigorous and influential proponent of what he calls an *employment subsidy*, or a monthly bonus for low-wage employees. Under Phelps's plan, the government would make a periodic disbursement "to each qualified enterprise for every low-wage worker in its employ. All employees having the same wage are to bring in the same subsidy to the employer. . . . The subsidy is thus like a matching grant rewarding the firm for as many workers as it employs. . . ." For example, imagine an individual earning $4 per hour; that is his "real" economic value to the enterprise. This amount would clearly make the individual a member of the working poor, and in the presence of other welfare schemes, it would hardly constitute an incentive to work. In such a case, the government would provide the firm a subsidy of $3 per hour, enabling the individual to earn $7, or something like a living wage. This amount represents the sum of the "private" value of the individual to the firm plus the "public" value of seeing that person participate in the labor force and receive a decent paycheck. Work, as Phelps reminds us, has social value that goes beyond the dollars it generates for the private employer.[32]

It should be emphasized that Phelps expresses preference for his plan over the earned-income tax credit (EITC) that is so popular as an income-transfer program in the United States. He observes that the EITC provides perverse incentives not to work, or to work only to the point where one hits the EITC income limit. He argues that "to this extent the program adds to the division of society between those who have ample incentive to work and those who do not."[33] Others, however, disagree, and instead have called for a significant expansion of the EITC program.[34]

The Phelps plan, with its emphasis on "rewarding work," is hardly pie in the sky. In Britain, the Labour government has already introduced a "working families' tax credit," which will provide in-work income benefits to those who qualify. Rather than receive a direct payment from the Inland Revenue (tax) Service at the year's end, as is the case with the U.S. EITC, the British plan provides workers with a direct "top up" in the weekly payment envelope. As Samuel Brittan of the *Financial Times* says of this plan, "It should even be of interest to financial markets if they wish to avoid an anti-globalization backlash leading to capital and currency controls."[35]

With respect to direct-compensation schemes for displaced workers, there are also several policy approaches that could be adopted in the interest of greater fairness to those who find themselves on the losing end of economic change. One of the most promising new policy ideas has been developed by economists at the Brookings Institution. They tout the concept of "earnings insurance" for workers. The idea is that if a displaced worker who was earning, say, $10 per hour at a factory finds that her next-best job opportunity is as a $7-per-hour salesperson, she would receive "insurance" for a given period that tops up the new pay to something approaching the old level. Since it is unlikely that a private insurance company would offer such a program—it would be subject to the "co-variance" problem in which many workers in a given community would be likely to need the insurance at the same time—this is the sort of policy measure that a national government should consider adopting or subsidizing.[36]

Still other compensatory schemes would be more proactive in assisting workers who are facing displacement. To date, most compensation programs go into effect only after a worker has received a layoff notice. Yet companies often know, many months before these notices are sent, that they will be reducing employment. They put off the day of reckoning with their workers until the last moment, often to avoid the "slacker" problem—workers who know they will be let go hurt the company's productivity by not showing up for work or by reducing their efforts. This slacker problem, however, must be balanced against questions of fairness to displaced workers, and it would seem that justice would move in the direction of generosity. Transfer payments, training schemes, and exposure to new job opportunities in different regions should begin *before* workers face unemployment, and not after the fact. It is well known that it is easier to find a new job while a worker is still employed than after she has been let go. Where displacement is likely and recalls are improbable, workers should be helped in the earliest stages of the retrenchment process.[37]

POLICIES FOR ENHANCING LABOR MOBILITY

Education and training and employment subsidies will be for naught if workers are unable or unwilling to take new jobs where they exist. Studies to date show that high-skilled workers are much more willing than the unskilled to move to a new location.[38] This would indicate that removal of the obstacles that block unskilled workers from moving has an important role in labor policy.

Some of these measures can be taken within a national context, but in integrated regions like Western Europe, multilateral efforts clearly will be needed. Specifically, workers should be given greater access to job opportunities in regions beyond their homes, and they should be provided with the kinds of financial options that make employment feasible in a new area. In this regard, issues such as housing take on special prominence. An International Monetary Fund study of the Spanish labor market, for example, found that "current arrangements in the housing market . . . contribute to limiting the geographic mobility of labor. In particular, the market for rental housing is relatively undeveloped and illiquid. . . ."[39] This is also a problem in many of the transition economies of Eastern Europe and the former Soviet Union, where workers are literally stuck in factory towns (which were often built for defense and economic-development reasons in desolate places like Siberia), unable to move to cities such as Moscow because of the housing shortage. (Moscow also has residency permits, further blocking labor mobility.) In the United States, insurance programs—sometimes provided by private-sector employers—that minimize any losses on housing sales have played a useful role in promoting labor mobility. The nation's highly developed capital markets, with relative ease of access to mortgages and other loans needed for making a move, also ease the dislocation burden. Further, the up-front costs associated with making moves could be subsidized through tax credits (indeed, a portion of moving costs can already be deducted for tax purposes in the United States) or funds used to offset moving expenses.

Increasing labor mobility can be expected to be a major issue within a Western Europe that is adopting a common currency. In that case, states will have less capacity to meet regional economic shocks through the use of financial transfers, and instead labor will have to move to find new employment, as is the case in the United States. Therefore, a premium should be placed on language training and the removal of other barriers that make cross-border employment unattractive. This means that job-search assistance will have to become European as opposed to national in scope. It will also mean changing unemployment insurance and other welfare schemes in order to promote rather than impede labor mobility.

Greater labor mobility, we should recognize, brings significant costs alongside the benefits. It leads to the disruption of communities and the possible decline of civic associations. It separates families and erodes their support systems. It suggests a kind of rootlessness that collides with many if not most people's values.

At the same time, labor mobility has long been part of the historical record. Workers have migrated from place to place not just as refugees from persecution but also in search of better opportunities for themselves and their children. The key to making policy with respect to labor mobility is to provide people with the possibility for *choice*. Leaving a given place may not be an option for some working people, but for those who seek new jobs in new regions, every reasonable effort should be made to assist that transition.

INTERNATIONAL-LEVEL POLICIES

In a world of increasing trade flows and capital mobility, even good policymaking aimed at improving the lives of working people is constrained by external economic forces. This naturally leads us to a consideration of the role that international institutions can play in shaping labor-market outcomes. Organizations such as the World Bank and the International

Monetary Fund loom large in the economies of several of their member countries, and their effect on the international economic system goes way beyond their capital base. Through the policy advice they articulate, and the signals they send about national economic performance, their influence ripples broadly throughout the world's capital markets, and in turn throughout labor markets.

It is ironic that these same organizations often make the claim that responsibility for social welfare rests squarely with the nation-state and its capacity for "good governance." Thus, the IMF states that a country's long-term per capita income levels are determined by its "own policies and resources." Yet at the same time, the Fund tells us that "globalization may be expected to increasingly constrain governments' choices of tax structures and tax rates. . . ."[40] If governments lack the power to shape tax policy, it is hard to see what sorts of powers they have over economic performance. These contradictions do not instill much confidence in its capacity for providing sound advice.

To claim that states alone are responsible for their fate in a global economy is disingenuous on several counts. First, it begs the question that if good national policy were enough to ensure good economic outcomes, why were international organizations ever needed, and why are they still needed today? Second, to the extent globalization undermines national policymaking capacity—as the IMF and the World Bank admit it does to some degree—then alternative methods obviously must be found for making good governance a reality. Third, since the benefits of globalization are not evenly distributed among nations, international mechanisms are needed to ensure that all players gain sufficiently to keep them in the game. Finally, since globalization requires international policy coordination and information-sharing with respect to the activities of both state and nonstate actors, efforts at international governance are needed by definition.

These points are not made in defense of an argument that

what we need is world government. International institutions, including the most advanced among them, such as the European Union, are fundamentally creatures of their member states. But member states can use these organizations in any number of ways. In some cases, state elites exploit international organizations as a way of escaping domestic political confrontations, claiming that the government's hands are tied on this or that issue. European leaders frequently make this argument with respect to Brussels, and of course they will use it about monetary policy as the European Central Bank and single currency become operational. Similarly, the International Monetary Fund serves this purpose for developing-country leaders who seek to make economic-policy reforms in the face of domestic opposition. In these cases, the international organization in question seems to be serving the policy goals of mobile capital rather than of immobile labor. For this reason, critics of international institutions frequently point to a democratic deficit between them and the citizens of their member countries.

It would be incorrect, however, to take the extreme position that international financial organizations have no concern with the fate of working people and only serve, say, the interests of multinational corporations and banks. If for nothing more than Real-politik concerns with political stability, organizations such as the IMF can go only so far in pushing for policy reform. Russia comes to mind as a good case study of a country that continued to receive significant IMF assistance largely because of its geostrategic importance—despite its failure to adopt economic reforms. In the European Union, too, the bureaucrats in Brussels can only adopt communitywide directives in light of what the political traffic will bear.

Still, the question remains as to whose interests are being served at the international level, and what the distribution of costs and benefits from given policy decisions looks like. The evidence in this book suggests that mobile capital is the big winner to date from policies aimed at promoting globalization, while unskilled workers are the losers. These economic outcomes are a reflection of relative political power, and the simple politics is that working people face a serious problem of collective action at the international level. This means that as policies are determined in arenas beyond the nation-state, it becomes increasingly difficult for workers to make their voices heard. As mentioned earlier, transnational union activity has been relatively weak during the postwar era, and international competition has been successfully used as a tool for dividing and conquering workers. This inability of labor to articulate common international goals means that it is harder for multilateral organizations to understand and respond to its concerns. Contrast this with the case of mobile capital, which can state with great clarity its demand for macroeconomic stability, balanced budgets, free-trade policies, and so forth.

This section therefore seeks to provide policy recommendations that give voice to the least advantaged. In a phrase, international organizations should play a more positive and active role in ensuring that fairness, no less than efficiency considerations, shapes global economic policies.[41] Such policies are in the long-run interests of all those who seek to advance the globalization experiment and believe in its contributions to world peace and prosperity. By helping the world's unskilled workers realize their talents and live in dignity, we all promote the causes of productivity, of stability, and of justice.

A BRETTON WOODS FOR WORKERS

As the allies began the liberation of Western Europe from Nazi terror in the summer of 1944, a group of international financial bureaucrats from the victorious powers met in Bretton Woods, New Hampshire, to shape the postwar economic order. While their grand design of free trade and financial stability would never be fully realized in a battle-scarred world that would soon enter the Cold War, they nonetheless gave the global economy its basic shape and vision. Simply put, that economy would combine the utilitarian, wealth-producing benefits of free multilateralism with the social benefits of the welfare state. It is a model that served industrial-world labor reasonably well for much of the postwar era, although we may question how well it has done by workers in the developing countries.

Today, the foundations of that structure are beginning to show their age. The world has learned to live with flexible exchange rates, but whether or not that has improved or impaired its health is a matter of some debate. While correlation is not causation, the shift from fixed to flexible rates that occurred in the 1970s also saw the beginning of much slower rates of industrial-world investment and growth, and higher unemployment and inequality, which have remained with us to the present day.[42] Tremendous capital mobility (threatened and real), never anticipated to such an extent by the postwar architects, is now emerging. Increasing trade flows are raising the specter of zero-sum international labor competition. With these developments, unskilled workers are becoming fearful of their futures—as well they might in the midst of unemployment, poverty, inequality, and insecurity.

If the great powers wish to restore confidence in the global economy, they would do well to consider a new Bretton Woods conference. The purpose of the meeting would be to address the sorts of questions raised in this book: How are workers doing, and what can be done to improve their lot? Is the current financial system consistent with growth and stability, or must a new order be contemplated? This latter issue would seem especially pertinent as Western Europe introduces its new common currency.

Among the most significant issues that a labor-oriented Bretton Woods conference would have to address is migration policy. As even the World Bank admits, while myriad international agreements have aimed at promoting capital mobility and free trade, "international migration of people in search of work is the laggard in this story."[43] People are no more free to migrate than they were a generation ago, and much less so in many cases than their grandparents. The role of labor mobility and migration in the global economy is an issue of the first order, and it must be treated in the interest of assuring working people the greatest possible set of opportunities. Again it must be emphasized that there is little point for an individual to invest in education, training, and self-improvement if no jobs are available. At the same time, he must recognize that societies may have legitimate reasons for limiting immigration.

Yet a second issue on which a new Bretton Woods should seek agreement is how to give workers a voice in existing international institutions. In the original postwar order, the planners had contemplated the creation of an International Trade Organization that would concern itself with both commercial and employment policies. With the failure to establish such an entity, trade and labor concerns went on separate paths, but workers have unfortunately stumbled into a dead end. Mechanisms for ensuring labor representation at the International Monetary Fund, the World Bank, and other such institutions would be one way to promote a more equitable global order, and a possible model might be found at the Organization for Economic Cooperation and Development, which has done perhaps the most of any multilateral organization to solicit labor input in its deliberations.

A third item for this meeting's agenda should be consideration of an international social minimum. This does not mean that we can expect agreement on a global minimum wage or anything of the sort. Instead, it means that each country should be responsible for defining what constitutes a decent standard of living for *all* citizens, including their access to education and health care, their working wages, and their entitlement to social safety nets. An international organization, perhaps the

World Bank, should be charged with producing an annual "social policy report," just as the International Monetary Fund produces studies of macroeconomic performance in its member countries. Gaps in providing the social minimum should be highlighted, to become targets for national economic reform efforts and international assistance.

One would hope that many of the suggestions in these pages would also prove useful to policymakers, labor leaders, and others responsible for planning such a meeting. But in thinking about a future Bretton Woods, we should recall that the last one only occurred following a generation of world conflict and depression that enveloped the major powers. Today, war and economic deprivation have, in large measure, been removed from the global economy's core countries, and instead they fester in the developing-world periphery, where, tragically, they draw less attention. What this means is that a sense of crisis is lacking in world capitals, making it unlikely that any bold initiatives will be forthcoming anytime soon. In the interests of political reality, then, the following paragraphs offer some recommendations that fall between a full-scale Bretton Woods-type conference on the one hand and the sort of marginal fixes now popular on the other.

LINK TRADE LIBERALIZATION WITH LABOR STANDARDS AND WORKER COMPENSATION PROGRAMS

In chapter 5, we saw that trade and labor policy have been on separate tracks since the end of World War II. The General Agreement on Tariffs and Trade, and its successor World Trade Organization, focused narrowly on reducing trade barriers, while the International Labor Organization was responsible for advancing the cause of core labor standards. That dualistic approach has now run its course, and it is time to join the issues.

The great fear that policymakers and economists usually express on this matter is that tying trade agreements to core labor standards (i.e., freedom of association, collective bargaining, removal of hiring discrimination, and the prohibition on using child and forced labor) will lead world trade down the slippery slope of trade protection. The failure of countries to achieve international labor standards, it is claimed, could be used as an excuse to halt trade with them, or it could raise their labor costs to the point where they are no longer competitive.

But these arguments are absurd for several reasons. First, a set of core international labor standards, promulgated by the International Labor Organization, *does* exist. Second, international trade is not a right but a privilege, and countries that seek to barter and truck with the community of nations should accept the common standards that exist. Third, the possibility of free trade and membership in the World Trade Organization *should* be held out as a carrot to those states that currently violate core labor standards; if it is not, what incentives can be offered?[44]

The international system has often responded with sanctions to countries exhibiting "bad behavior" of various kinds. India and Pakistan were slapped with trade sanctions by the United States following their nuclear tests in 1998. Iraq has been the target of a United Nations embargo since 1990, and Iran has enjoyed only limited access to world markets since its Islamic Revolution. Other countries that remain ostracized include Cuba, North Ko-rea, and Libya. In short, sanctions are widely used but for some reason have not been applied to states that violate core labor standards.

The world trading system can put great pressure on countries that fail to adopt these standards. Countries such as China would find their economic opportunities severely limited. But China is a case where the trading system seems to be basically operated by and for the large multinational corporations, which consistently reject tying trade agreements to labor rights.

We should note that the vigorous pursuit of core labor standards by the international community implies the acceptance of new, associated responsibilities. A country that is willing to abolish child labor, for example, may need foreign assistance to expand its school system. That is the sort of collective response that a world community bent on a just form of globalization should be willing and able to make.

At the same time that countries pursue free-trade agreements, they must also be sensitive to how trade will affect working people, and they will need to establish programs that assist displaced workers. Indeed, compensation should be another core labor standard. Traditionally, such compensation programs have been solely a national responsibility. But with a growing number of developing countries and transition economies entering the trading system, international assistance on this issue could be of tremendous value, and could help maintain political support for continued globalization. Again, it is important to emphasize that if the benefits of trade are so great, why not be generous to those on the losing end of this policy change?

ESTABLISH GREATER SUPERVISION OVER THE ACTIVITIES OF MULTINATIONAL ENTERPRISES AND BANKS

Trade and finance cross borders with relative ease, workers less so, and governments not at all. That tension is at the heart of all efforts aimed at greater international supervision over multinational activities. International policy coordination over multinational business has traditionally been an information-sharing exercise, but increasingly it is becoming a supervisory activity seeking to prevent international competition from sparking a destructive race to the bottom in which countries end up relieving themselves of all tax and regulatory authority. With the recent financial crisis in East Asia, the calls for tightened control over cross-border capital flows have grown in intensity and volume.

Already there is a significant amount of activity in this area. Banks and investment firms face the common standards set by the Basle Committee of Bank Supervisors and the International Organization of Securities Commissions with respect to capital adequacy, and the European Union is responsible for regional regulation over such areas as competition and antitrust policy.[45] The Organization for Economic Cooperation and Development (OECD) and the United Nations Conference on Trade and Development (UNCTAD) have also established codes of conduct for multinational enterprises regarding consumer protection and the like. Three issues of rising international importance, however, concern worker rights, capital controls, and international taxation.

Worker rights and labor standards have already been discussed in some detail in earlier sections. One additional point is that, in the absence of international agreements linking trade and labor standards, an alternative or complementary path would be to establish minimum codes of conduct regarding how multinationals treat their workers. These codes would include the core ILO labor standards and, it can be argued, provisions regarding a living wage and compensation in the event of worker displacement. Efforts have already been made along these lines by minority shareholders of some major corporations—almost always over the objections of the boards of directors—but they have generally failed to win the needed votes at shareholder meetings. Governments, nongovernmental organizations, and international organizations such as UNCTAD could thus play a useful role in shaping these standards, publicizing them, and monitoring enterprise performance. Indeed, in the absence of positive government action in this direction at the national level, code-setting could provide an interesting case of how NGOs and international organizations might form transnational alliances for the benefit of labor interests.

With respect to portfolio investment or "hot money" flows, it appears that governments and international organizations are again giving serious thought to capital controls of some type, through either tax policy or quantitative restrictions on inflows. With respect to tax policy, perhaps the most prominent idea is that of economist James Tobin, who suggests a tax on all cross-border financial transactions, in the hope of decreasing such flows and making them more manageable. Other approaches include graduated taxes according to the length of time in which an investor keeps his money inside a given country. The purpose of such graduated policies, which have been adopted with perhaps the greatest success in Chile, is to penalize short-term portfolio investors and reward long-term direct investment.

The national orientation of these measures, however, may mean that they will lose their effectiveness over time. States will be tempted to use differing policies on capital controls, including taxation, to the advantage of their domestic economies and financial institutions. Since large banks and investment firms tend to have significant voice in domestic policymaking, given their prominent role in economic activity and money creation, officials are sensitive to their competitive concerns and will develop regulatory policies that are in their interests.[46] In addition, monetary and financial policies tend to be obscure to many voters, and labor often has failed to understand how such policies will affect workers. Decisions over capital and labor markets thus become dissociated, often to labor's disadvantage.

These comments suggest that several problems associated with capital mobility must now be dealt with at the international level. One of the most prominent in light of the East Asian crisis concerns its destabilizing effects on national economies. And there is increasing discussion of international financial cooperation aimed at, for example, supervising or even limiting the cross-border loans made by banks and other financial institutions.[47] Since labor has been hit so hard by these destabilizing effects, its representatives should have a seat at the policy table while any decisions in this area are made. Unfortunately, the center of action in this debate has been the International Monetary Fund, which to date has hardly shown itself to be sensitive to workers' concerns or open to their participation in its deliberations.

A second and potentially more significant issue in terms of reshaping the international political economy concerns international taxation of mobile capital. As the public-finance literature shows, the effective tax rate on mobile capital is zero. And the data demonstrate that tax rates on mobile capital are falling. While tax competition has been used by states in the interest of attracting direct investment, it has had many negative effects as well, including declining revenues for government coffers. Tax competition can easily lead to a race to the bottom among states in which mobile capital gets away with paying virtually nothing to any government; that suggests a possible role for international coordination in this area.

Probably the leading advocate of a world tax organization has been IMF official Vito Tanzi. He argues that such an organization could perform the following functions: (1) identify the main trends in tax policy among its member countries; (2) compile cross-country tax statistics; (3) prepare an annual *World Tax Development Report*; (4) provide technical assistance in tax policy and tax administration; (5) develop basic principles and norms for tax policy; (6) create an international forum for discussion and debate on tax matters; (7) arbitrate frictions among countries with respect to their tax policies; and (8) survey tax developments and make policy recommendations.[48] Again, it's important to add that any such organization must give voice to labor concerns in its decisionmaking process.

Overall, the comments provided in this section all point to the growing gap between multinational enterprises and national economic institutions, including labor markets. Closing that gap will be a major item on the international agenda as we look toward the future. In shaping policies that aim to achieve that objective, the concerns of working people must be taken firmly into account. The current structure of our international institutions does not give sufficient voice to labor, and reforms in this direction are needed in the interest of legitimacy.

ENSURE THAT CONDITIONAL LENDING BY THE WORLD BANK AND THE IMF ARE SENSITIVE TO EQUITY CONSIDERATIONS

If we know one thing about the aftermath of an economic crisis, it is that the rich usually get richer and the poor get poorer. In the interests of macroeconomic stability, states often end up cutting those programs that benefit working people and the least advantaged. Further, it seems that interventions by such international organizations as the IMF and the World Bank do little to alter that outcome. To the contrary, the IMF has traditionally only suggested overall targets for budgetary spending; it generally avoids making recommendations with respect to which items should be cut or saved.

Given the economic and moral arguments made in this book, it follows that the Bank and the Fund should give greater thought to the distributional consequences of their policy-based lending. They should place more emphasis on the needs of the least advantaged and ensure that spending on education and social welfare programs receive adequate levels of funding. In this regard, the World Bank's announcement that it would seek to create seventy-five million jobs in East Asia through its post-financial-crisis project loans is welcome news indeed.[49]

The Bank also said it would give significant attention to poverty alleviation in its program of lending to this troubled region.

Similarly, the International Monetary Fund could take a more aggressive line in advocating for the poor and disadvantaged in its macroeconomic stabilization programs. Slowly, that recognition is dawning on policymakers. U.S. Deputy Secretary of the Treasury Lawrence Summers has said, "If most now agree that macroeconomic reforms took precedence over microeconomic . . . and reducing the size of government took precedence over improving its quality—then it is fair to say that education and other basic social investments were especially ill-served by these biases." He and others are now calling on the IMF and the World Bank to bolster their social-sector lending.[50] In so doing, they should consult with labor, nongovernmental organizations, and other interest groups.

Invest in Health Care and Public Health

Normally, when we think of international cooperation in health care, it is in terms of humanitarian assistance. That is all to the good, but in fact, good health care is a major contributor to economic performance as well. In the words of World Health Organization Director-General Gro Harlem Brundtland, new research "is making it increasingly clear that ill health leads to poverty in individuals, populations, and nations."[51] By recognizing its contributions to worker productivity and well-being, we can see that health care should be given significant attention by those who would promote the cause of globalization.

Unfortunately, that does not seem to be the case. Around the world, millions of people die each year from a variety of infectious diseases. More than one billion people do not have access to clean water, and nearly two billion lack proper sanitation facilities. At least 840 million people face the anguish of going hungry each day. As a result, in the developing world, nearly one-third of the population is not expected to reach the age of forty.[52] It is hard to develop an economy when large numbers of workers are dying in what should be the prime of life.

These facts seem far removed from the industrial countries, which have made great strides in disease and famine control, environmental protection, and in the provision of basic human needs. But even here, the gap between the haves and the have-nots is dramatic. In the United States, nearly fifty million people have no health insurance. Some urban slums are once again seeing the reemergence of diseases such as tuberculosis, stumping health-care experts who thought these particular enemies had been defeated. Indeed, many American slums have health-care statistics more typical of the third world than the first world.

In most of the post-communist transition economies, the health-care situation verges on the catastrophic. Soviet-style planning left a legacy of environmental devastation that has poisoned two generations, and it will take at least that long to clean up. Alcoholism, drug use, and poor nutrition further contribute to the deadly toll. On top of these problems, poorly paid doctors face a terrible shortage of medical equipment and drugs in outdated hospitals and clinics. Simply stated, living in Eastern Europe and the former Soviet Union is not good for one's health.

These public-health issues should be treated as economic problems for several reasons. First, an unsanitary and polluted environment is a major barrier to one's life chances. People living under these conditions are more likely to become ill and thus less capable of realizing their talents. The result is a waste of human resources. The more that people lose work or education days to illness, the more society as a whole suffers. Work and education represent important investments, and if people are incapacitated, that investment goes to waste.

Second, people and companies are more likely to invest in countries where the health risks are manageable. Where the threat of illness, epidemic, or famine looms large, investors understandably will wish to go elsewhere. Not surprisingly, a strong correlation exists between wealth and health.

Creating a healthy environment, then, would seem to make good economic sense, and this means it ought to receive greater consideration in debates over economic reform, alongside such standard measures as macroeconomic stabilization, privatization, and liberalization. Again, making this case could be the job for new transnational coalitions that join labor unions with health-care experts and environmentalists. Traditionally, health care has been the exclusive province of medical experts and their various national and international institutions, but the encouraging quote of WHO Director-General Gro Brundtland cited above (and it should be noted that Brundtland is both a medical doctor and former prime minister of Norway) suggests that the time may be ripe for new initiatives in this issue-area.

IMPROVE THE EFFECTIVENESS OF FOREIGN AID[53]

Few public expenditures seem to be more unpopular than foreign aid. In a recent poll, some 66 percent of Americans responded that "foreign aid spending is too high."[54] They may be right, as even the IMF has concluded that "development aid has not had a significant impact on growth in recipient countries." This is because it had little or no effect on a country's propensity to invest.[55]

Today, foreign aid occupies only a small fraction of both industrial-world and recipient-country budgets. According to the Paris-based Organization for Economic Cooperation and Development, official foreign aid in 1996 totaled just $59.9 billion, down nearly 6 percent from the previous year. Aid totaled no more than 0.25 percent of the combined gross domestic product of OECD member states. According to the OECD, this is "the lowest ratio recorded over the nearly thirty years since the United Nations established a goal of 0.70 percent." While it is true that private-sector investment flows to the developing world have increased during this time, these are not a direct substitute for foreign aid, which has poverty reduction as its focus.

The question then arises: What do governments do with the money they receive? In principle, they could do one of two things: invest it in projects of various kinds (these could range from education to health care to infrastructure), or transfer it to citizens through tax policy or cash payments. Since the IMF and other organizations have found no correlation between aid and investment, this suggests they transfer it. Then we must ask, to whom?

In a recent study, economist Peter Boone raised this very question. He found that, rather than transfer money to the poor, governments instead gave it to the regime's wealthy supporters. He found no evidence that aid was used in support of such human-development initiatives as health care or schooling; instead, it went to consumption by elites. This suggests that the problem with aid is that the donor institutions in practice do little to ensure that their funds are being used to help the neediest in target countries.[56]

Rather than abandon aid altogether, however, we should seek to improve its effectiveness. This means working closely with recipient countries to ensure that funds go to education, health care, and development of the social safety net. Contrary to the conventional wisdom, donor and recipient countries are capable of structuring assistance programs that make a material difference to the poor and the least advantaged.

CONCLUSIONS

The objective in this chapter has been to argue for public policies that balance efficiency considerations with concerns for justice as fairness. For too long, the first has been allowed to trump the second—and nowhere with greater force than in the global economy. As workers lose voice in economic policymaking, it follows that they garner fewer resources. Not surprisingly, they find themselves falling farther and farther behind those who control mobile capital.

Part of the answer for working people, then, must be found in international politics. Unions and other organizations that seek to represent interests of labor will have to form new coalitions and transnational associations. If they fail to do so, they will inevitably be divided and conquered by those who can speak with more authority and singleness of purpose in economic councils.

These comments should not be construed as a dismissal of the many serious dilemmas that policymakers face as they chart our economic course, or to suggest that their efforts are inevitably malign when it comes to working people. That is hardly the case, and both national governments and international institutions have any number of dedicated public officials who are struggling to reconcile globalization with social justice. But these good souls need help in their work, and they can get it only from their political surroundings. In crafting public policy, they face a great many forces, in both the domestic and external environments. Special-interest groups and lobbyists of all types feed information and money to the policy process. Yet ultimately our officials do act, for good or for ill. We must support them in making decisions that are consistent not only with some allegedly objective set of efficiency goals, but also with our shared sense of justice.

CONCLUSION:
IS AMERICA
"THE THIRD WAY"?

*I think that . . . it may be asserted that a slow and gradual rise
of wages is one of the general laws of democratic communities.*
— ALEXIS DE TOCQUEVILLE,
DEMOCRACY IN AMERICA, 1835

"WE'RE INHUMAN. WE LOVE rising unemployment,
declining interest rates. We love restructuring." So spoke investment banker J. Paul Horne in remarks to the *Wall Street
Journal*. These were the data points, he said, that he and his colleagues studied in making their judgments about future stock
market performance.[1] He encapsulates, of course, everything
that many people around the world love to hate about contemporary Anglo-Saxon capitalism.

Today, a growing number of intellectuals and public officials—perhaps best exemplified by British Prime Minister
Tony Blair—are seeking a "third way" between American economic liberalism and European statism.[2] Without specifying
what this third way actually means, they seem to be conceptu-

alizing a political and economic system that somehow combines America's raw dynamism with Western Europe's alleged social cohesion. And while the search for a "third way" might sound like a typical intellectual gimmick without policy substance, it is hardly limited to Chelsea or the Paris Left Bank; similar quests can also be found in East Asia and other regions where the benefits of the neoliberal economic model are increasingly viewed with skepticism.

This reconsideration of what the American model means for the world economy is of crucial importance today. With the end of the Cold War, the United States stands alone as a unipolar power with a unique mix of military, economic, ideological, and cultural capabilities. These concluding pages therefore consider the meaning of this state of affairs for the world economy and those who labor in it.

LIBERAL AMERICA AND THE WORLD ECONOMY

Compared to other great powers before it, the United States brings many notable attributes to the international policy agenda. America lacks territorial ambitions, at least in the sense of seeking to conquer or colonize other nation-states by military force, and that is no small distinction. It is a democratic state pledged to individual liberty, free and fair elections, the rule of law, and protection of minority rights. And it is an entrepreneurial economy, rewarding individual effort rather than inherited titles in a competitive market environment.

Yet beyond these characteristics, what *values* does the United States embody? This question has been asked by observers of American society at least since the time of Alexis de Tocqueville. He observed that Americans were "so practical, so confused, so excited, so active, that but little time remains to them for thought." He noted that they even eschewed religious guidance, which, given the separation of church and state, "carefully abstains from the daily turmoil of secular affairs. . . ."[3]

If the United States had any core value at all, it was probably "liberalism," or the belief that every American had been granted the liberty and opportunity to pursue his or her interests. While that condition only represented an "ideal type" that never really existed—minorities and women have had to fight for equality of opportunity every step of the way—it nonetheless provided the moral ground on which those battles for equal treatment could be fought. Unlike European aristocracies, where the playing field was tilted against the common man from birth, the United States could not hide its discriminatory practices behind a wall of tradition. Instead, its written constitution could be used as a vehicle for promoting equal rights within the national polity.

American liberalism, however, has never been defined in terms of "equality of income," and the notion that economic differences posed a barrier to achievement has historically been rejected. As de Tocqueville wrote, "I know of no country where . . . a profounder contempt is expressed for the theory of the permanent equality of property."[4] To the contrary, the great American heroes have always been those rugged individualists who "made it on their own."[5] It is perhaps for this reason that Americans, whether at the political fringes in the nineteenth-century social gospel movement or even at the seat of power in the New Deal, have had such a difficult time making the case that the exercise of personal freedom requires some minimal resource base.

This seems curious, for the fact is that social mobility has never been as great as Americans would like to believe. If you are born poor (or rich), you are most likely to remain in that economic condition. Indeed, sociologists have found that economic background or class remains the single most important determinant of an individual's life chances.[6] Nor, despite popular misconception, is social mobility in the United States markedly higher than in other industrial countries. Yet Americans have successfully avoided bringing these potentially divisive class or economic distinctions into their liberal rhetoric.

One more point needs to be made about American liberalism before consideration of its international implications, and that is its absolutism.[7] The United States has never considered alternatives to its form of liberal democratic capitalism, either at home or abroad. In each and every case, these alternatives posed challenges that had to be defeated. As Americans mythically believed that theirs was the only society in the world to overcome domestic class struggle, they were not prepared to consider any other political-economic system as capable of delivering real freedom. Those systems must lead to conflict, revolution, and war.

All this is not to argue that Americans systematically deny their own experience of social and economic strife. They recognize it on the historical margins but also believe that the country has managed to solve that fundamental problem with an approach that is almost cookie-cutter in its efficacy: sustained growth. As long as economic growth promised and produced increasing demands for labor—ultimately pressing into service women and minorities and the disadvantaged, and in turn holding out the promise of a better life for these workers and their children—the possibility of social conflict could be suppressed.[8] Sustained growth was and is absolutely central to the American political economy; it is at the core of the country's self-definition as an eternally dynamic power. And that is also the promise that the American system brings to the world: of growth leading inevitably to greater opportunity for all.

Now what do these observations suggest for the country's international economic policy? Following the path forged by such scholars as Louis Hartz and Robert Packenham, it's possible to assert that from this liberal self-definition a number of hypotheses have emerged about how the world *ought* to work. It is not so much that Americans believe their own experience to be "universal," for they likely recognize the uniqueness of their historical experience. Instead, as noted above, Americans are constitutionally incapable of considering the possibility that other modes of political economic organization could feasibly deliver its unique combination of personal freedom and social welfare.

The first of these liberal hypotheses is that "change and development are easy."[9] In its most simplistic formulation, Americans seem to believe that if only countries would adopt its market model through liberalization and privatization, economic growth would surely follow. For the United States, there is no mystery to sustained economic growth (equitable growth is hardly a concern); it is found in the adoption of free-market principles.

A powerful example of this worldview is found in the post-communist transition, surely the most challenging economic transformation of our time. As absurd as it may now seem, many western economists at the outset of the transition were optimistic that a rapid improvement would occur in the performance of former Soviet-bloc countries. The logic was drawn from market economics, and it began with the assumption that the communist countries had made inefficient use of their factors of production. With the transition, and adoption of market principles, these factors would effectively be "liberated" and channeled by the invisible hand to their best use. That belief in the uplifting power of market processes was so strong that MIT's Olivier Blanchard has recently asserted that explaining why that outcome did not occur, and why instead a major economic decline followed liberalization, "is the major theoretical challenge facing economists working on the transition."[10]

What was absent from this model, of course, was any appreciation of the other elements that go into building market structures—including, most important, a state capable of providing such public goods as legal and regulatory regimes. In their own storybook history, many Americans seem to overlook the active role the state played in promoting economic activity ranging from exploration (from Lewis and Clark to the space shuttle) to infrastructure development (from canals to highways) to education (from public schools to land-grant universities). Further, they seem to forget the crucial role played by the state in securing property rights and ensuring people law and order.

A second major hypothesis that flows from American liberalism is that "all good things go together."[11] As detailed in chapter 3, Washington policymakers after World War II held firm to the belief that "free multilateralism" would produce both peace and prosperity, which would then trickle down to all countries and all peoples; and they still cling to that belief today. The notion that free trade or technological change (good things) could lead to greater income inequality and social divisiveness (bad things) just didn't compute. Indeed, that particular causal link would not necessarily even be acknowledged by American policymakers, as income inequality was not necessarily a bad thing, and the risk of social divisiveness (at least of the regime-threatening kind) had been "solved" within the American political framework.

Yet a third hypothesis, emphasized by both Hartz and Packenham in their scholarly work, is that "alternatives to democratic capitalism are bad." American liberalism is so absolute in its value system that every alternative represents a challenge that can only lead countries down the wrong path. Historian Charles Maier has said of American politics that its cohesiveness "lay in the reluctance to suggest alternative questions."[12] It is difficult to conceive of an American president speaking of a "third way," because that would imply that other economic systems are valid. What many foreign observers fail to understand is that, to Americans, their political economy represents the first way, the second way, *and* the third way.

GLOBALIZATION AND THE
AMERICAN DREAM

The jury is still out on whether or not America's global vision of a liberal order, peaceful and prosperous for all, is being achieved. To date, postwar growth has certainly brought material improvements to the lives of millions around the world, but millions more, *most of whom are working*, remain in poverty. Growth has created opportunity, but it has failed to stem the rise in income inequality that is now a universal phenomenon—with the risks to social stability that this brings in its train. The net result is that, while the United States may have successfully suppressed its divisions at home, the international system, the global economy, is still rife with tension.

And that is the great puzzle for the American elite. Why is it, they wonder, that the rest of the world is resisting the adoption of our definition of liberal democratic capitalism? Perhaps it is due to the fact, as stressed throughout this book, that the United States has adopted a position toward labor that is fundamentally at odds with the historical experience of other societies. Because Americans have not acknowledged social turmoil in any deep way, they have failed to take seriously the argument that labor is different from other commodities and, in the interests of stability and economic justice, must be removed from market transactions.

Can America "overcome" its liberal tradition and recognize at a deep level the fundamental concern that so many working people around the world now express about their future? If so, does the nation possess the capacity for creative policy development, which recognizes that the demands of working people for a modicum of security and a living wage are consistent rather than in conflict with the advancement of the neoliberal economic agenda?

For his part, Hartz, writing in the early 1950s, was already pessimistic. Examining the interaction of American liberalism with the wider world, he suggested, "The question is not whether our history has given us something to 'export' but whether it has given us the right thing. And this question has to be answered in the negative." The inability of Americans to understand social struggle around the world, he argued, made it impossible for the country to formulate a foreign policy that was sensitive to countries and cultures that faced a domestically divisive political environment.[13]

There is, however, a more hopeful side to American history that might again be studied and celebrated with profit. From the nineteenth-century social gospel movement to the progressives of the 1900s to the New Deal, public policy has always been sensitive to popular movements and the ideas they espouse. It would be wrong to say that America had witnessed no progress over its history; the fact is it has become a fundamentally better place for millions of its citizens who, in the past, were excluded from its political economy by being denied freedom, political voice, or access to certain universities and jobs. During the late nineteenth-century, the great social gospel leader George Herron said, "The worst charge that can be made against a Christian is that he accepts the existing order." Millions of Americans have rejected the existing order and have labored to create a better country for their fellows.

Will the United States ever advance a progressive politics at the global level? Today, Washington has once again been given the opportunity to ask and answer the question about the interaction between its values and the world. It can formulate a response free of the political-military strictures created by the Cold War setting. In many ways, that makes it much more difficult to find the right words, but in others it opens a new door to generosity and creativity in policymaking.

At this writing, there are few entries on the positive side of the ledger to make us believe that the United States is now placing the quest for economic justice near the top of its international agenda. Instead, it has de-linked trade and human rights issues in China, blindly supported the interests of multinational corporations in the World Trade Organization while doing little to promote core labor standards, and continued to support corrupt regimes from Russia to Indonesia. It has reduced foreign aid spending to a pittance, and the vast bulk of those funds go to support military equipment transfers. It has done everything to protect mobile capital, little to support immobile labor. As the data show, working people everywhere are today facing job insecurity, falling wages and benefits, and, at least in Europe, double-digit unemployment. Poverty is rife, and still today we find millions of people, mostly women and children, who are malnourished.

To be sure, there is at present no apparent alternative to America's corporate neoliberalism. But one need not wait for a hostile power to arise to be concerned about the fate of the international economy. As even the *Wall Street Journal* has written, "No system that we are aware of has survived on a foundation of rank cynicism."[14]

It may well be that America's globalism will bring all good things to the world's working people, and that the magic of the market will shine on the least advantaged. History, however, rewards prudence, and it rewards wisdom. The United States must do more than take the market to the people; it must bring people to the market. And in order to do that, it will have to play a leadership role in investing in those necessities of life that will enable working people everywhere to seize the opportunities that democratic capitalism has to offer. If it does not, America's long-standing vision of a truly global economy, of a peaceful and prosperous world, will ultimately be revealed as nothing more than a mirage on a bleak road.

NOTES

PREFACE

1. Michael Phillips, "Globalization Comes to a Southern Town," *Wall Street Journal*, 12 February 1998.

CHAPTER 1

1. John Maynard Keynes, *The General Theory of Employment, Interest, and Money* (New York: Harcourt Brace, 1964; orig. 1936), p. 372.
2. United Nations Development Program (UNDP), *Human Development Report (HDR): 1997* (New York: Oxford University Press, 1997), p. 24.
3. This insight is owed to John Rawls, *A Theory of Justice* (Cambridge, MA: Harvard University Press, 1971).
4. John Stuart Mill, *Principles of Political Economy* (New York: Penguin, 1979; orig. 1848), book II, ch. 1, p. 350.
5. Sidney Fine, *Laissez-Faire and the General-Welfare State* (Ann Arbor: University of Michigan Press, 1956), p. 200.
6. This citation and much of this section are drawn from Ethan B. Kapstein, "Workers and the World Economy," *Foreign Affairs* (May/June 1996): 17–37.

7. John Ruggie, "International Regimes, Transactions, and Change: Embedded Liberalism in the Postwar Economic Order," *International Organization* 36 (Spring 1982): 195–231.

8. International Monetary Fund, *World Economic Outlook: May 1997* (Washington, DC: IMF, 1997), p. 70.

9. For an elaboration of this theme, see Edmund Phelps, *Rewarding Work* (Cambridge, MA: Harvard University Press, 1997).

10. See, for example, World Bank, *World Development Report: 1997* (New York: Oxford University Press, 1997).

CHAPTER 2

1. Karl Polanyi, *The Great Transformation* (Boston: Beacon Press, 1944), p. 3.

2. Thomas Hobbes, *Leviathan* (New York: Collier, 1962; orig. 1651), p. 100.

3. Ted Robert Gurr, *Why Men Rebel* (Princeton, NJ: Princeton University Press, 1970), p. 228.

4. Alberto Alesina and Roberto Perotti, "Income Distribution, Political Instability and Investment," *European Economic Review* 40 (1996): 1203–28, at 1204.

5. Gurr, *Why Men Rebel*, p. 24.

6. John Maynard Keynes, *The Economic Consequences of the Peace* (New York: Harcourt Brace, 1920), p. 228.

7. Jean-Michael Severino, "Toward a More Equitable and Caring East Asia," *International Herald Tribune*, 27 January 1998.

8. Dipak Gupta, *The Economics of Political Violence* (Westport, CT: Praeger, 1990), p. 253.

9. World Bank, *World Development Report: 1997* (New York: Oxford University Press, 1997), p. 23.

10. Frances Fox Piven and Richard Cloward, *Regulating the Poor* (New York: Vintage, 1971), pp. 10–11.

11. Piven and Cloward, *Regulating the Poor*, p. 11.
12. Piven and Cloward, *Regulating the Poor*, p. 15.
13. G. M. Trevelyan, *British History in the Nineteenth Century* (New York: Longmans, Green, 1930), p. 143.
14. Adam Smith, *The Nature and Causes of the Wealth of Nations* (New York: Oxford University Press, 1993; orig. 1776), p. 408.
15. E. J. Hobsbawm, *Industry and Empire* (New York: Penguin, 1969), p. 94.
16. Hobsbawm, *Industry and Empire*, p. 73.
17. Barrington Moore, *Social Origins of Democracy and Dictatorship* (Boston: Beacon Press, 1966), p. 102.
18. Theda Skocpol, *Social Revolutions in the Modern World* (New York: Cambridge University Press, 1994), p. 148.
19. Edmund Wilson, *To the Finland Station* (New York: Farrar, Straus and Giroux, 1972; orig. 1940), p. 86.
20. Gordon Craig, *Europe Since 1815* (New York: Holt, Rinehart and Winston, 1961), p. 116.
21. Cited in E. P. Thompson, *The Making of the English Working Class* (New York: Vintage, 1966), p. 295.
22. Craig, *Europe Since 1815*, p. 123.
23. Paul Kennedy, *The Rise and Fall of the Great Powers* (New York: Random House, 1987), p. 151.
24. Kennedy, *Rise and Fall*, p. 154.
25. Hobsbawm, *Industry and Empire*, p. 139.
26. Keynes, *Economic Consequences of the Peace*, p. 11.
27. Polanyi, *The Great Transformation*, p. 13.
28. Robert Gilpin, *The Political Economy of International Relations* (Princeton, NJ: Princeton University Press, 1987), p. 124.
29. Harold James, *International Monetary Cooperation Since Bretton Woods* (New York: Oxford University Press, 1996), p. 15.
30. Polanyi, *The Great Transformation*, p. 18.
31. Polanyi, *The Great Transformation*, p. 195.

32. Polanyi, *The Great Transformation*, p. 216.

33. Wilson, *To the Finland Station*, pp. 185–89.

34. Karl Marx and Friedrich Engels, *Manifesto of the Communist Party* (New York: International Publishers, 1948).

35. Jonathan Sperber, *The European Revolutions, 1848–1851* (New York: Cambridge University Press, 1994), p. 106.

36. Craig, *Europe Since 1815*, p. 133.

37. Roger Price, *The Revolutions of 1848* (Atlantic Highlands, NJ: Humanities Press, 1988), p. 100.

38. E. H. Carr, *The Twenty Years' Crisis* (New York: Harper and Row, 1964; orig. 1939), p. 169.

39. Gustav Stolper, *The German Economy: 1870 to the Present* (London: Weidenfeld and Nicolson, 1967), p. 44.

40. Stolper, *The German Economy*, p. 37.

41. Craig, *Europe Since 1815*, p. 387.

42. Craig, *Europe Since 1815*, p. 386.

43. Stolper, *The German Economy*, p. 45.

44. Stolper, *The German Economy*, p. 45.

45. George Steinmetz, *Regulating the Social* (Princeton, NJ: Princeton University Press, 1993), p. 2.

46. Peter Flora and Arnold J. Heidenheimer, "The Historical Core and Changing Boundaries of the Welfare State," in Flora and Heidenheimer, eds., *The Development of Welfare States in Europe and America* (New Brunswick, NJ: Transaction Publishers, 1984), p. 19.

47. Flora and Heidenheimer, "The Historical Core," p. 20.

48. Sean Glynn and Alan Booth, "Unemployment in Interwar Britain: A Case for Relearning the Lessons of the 1930s?" *Economic History Review*, 2nd series, 36 (August 1983): 329–48, at 339.

49. Michael Piore, "Historical Perspectives and the Interpretation of Unemployment," *Journal of Economic Literature* 25 (December 1987): 1834–50, at 1836.

50. Sidney Fine, *Laissez Faire and the General-Welfare State* (Ann Arbor: University of Michigan Press, 1956), p. 325.

51. Cited in Fox Piven and Cloward, *Regulating the Poor*, p. 53.
52. Cited in Fox Piven and Cloward, *Regulating the Poor*, p. 68.
53. Michael Kazin, *The Populist Persuasion* (New York: Basic Books, 1995), p. 116.
54. Edward Phelan, "Social Services and Defense," in *Proceedings of the National Conference of Social Work, 1941* (New York: Columbia University Press, 1941).
55. Flora and Heidenheimer, "The Historical Core," p. 19.
56. Stephen Blank, "Britain: The Politics of Foreign Economic Policy, the Domestic Economy, and the Problem of Pluralistic Stagnation," in Peter Katzenstein, ed., *Between Power and Plenty* (Madison: University of Wisconsin Press, 1978), p. 95.
57. Sir William Beveridge, *Social Insurance and Allied Services* (New York: Macmillan, 1942), p. 7.
58. Cited in Alan Booth, "The Keynesian Revolution in Economic Policy-Making," *Economic History Review*, 2nd series, 36 (February 1983): 103–23, at 114.
59. Beveridge, *Full Employment in a Free Society* (New York: Norton, 1945), p. 15.
60. Cited in Alan Brinkley, *The End of Reform* (New York: Vintage, 1995), p. 263.
61. See Charles Maier, "The Politics of Productivity," in Katzenstein, *Between Power and Plenty*, p. 27.
62. Walter Goodman, "A Way to Repay the GIs and Rebuild America," *New York Times*, 22 October 1997, B3.
63. Ernest Mahaim, "The Historical and Social Importance of International Labor Legislation," in James Shotwell, ed., *The Origins of the International Labor Organization* (New York: Columbia University Press, 1934), p. 13.
64. Herbert Feis, "International Labor Legislation in the Light of Economic Theory," in Werner Sengenberger and Duncan Campbell, eds., *International Labor Standards and Economic Interdependence* (Geneva, Switzerland: International Institute for Labor Studies, 1994): 29–55, at 35.

65. Denis Macshane, *International Labor and the Origins of the Cold War* (Oxford, UK: Clarendon Press, 1992), p. 16.
66. Mahaim, "Historical and Social Importance of International Labor Legislation," pp. 8–10.
67. Daniel Nelson, *Unemployment Insurance: The American Experience* (Madison: University of Wisconsin Press, 1969), pp. 10–17.
68. Antony Alcock, *History of the International Labor Organization* (London: Macmillan, 1971), p. 35.
69. James Shotwell, "The International Labor Organization as an Alternative to Violent Revolution," *The Annals* 166 (March 1933): 18–25, at 18.
70. Shotwell, *Origins of the International Labor Organization*, p. xxi.
71. Keynes, *Economic Consequences of the Peace*, p. 251.
72. Cited in Keynes, *Economic Consequences*, p. 217.
73. Keynes, *Economic Consequences*, p. 230.

CHAPTER 3

1. John Dunlop, "Introduction," in John Dunlop and Walter Galenson, eds., *Labor in the 20th Century* (New York: Academic Press, 1978), p. 1.
2. M. E. Nicols, "Unions and Transnational Boundaries," in Mario Bognano and Kathryn Ready, eds., *The North American Free Trade Agreement* (Westport, CT: Praeger, 1993), p. 194.
3. Sir William Beveridge, *Social Insurance and Allied Services* (New York: Macmillan, 1942), p. 171.
4. Cited in William Diebold, *The End of the ITO* (Princeton, NJ: Princeton Essays in International Finance no. 16, October 1952), p. 12.
5. Victor I. Silverman, *Stillbirth of a World Order: Union Internationalism from War to Cold War in the United States and Britain, 1939–1949*, Ph.D. diss., University of California, Berkeley, 1990, p. 13.

6. Silverman, *Stillbirth of a World Order*, p. 15.

7. Silverman, *Stillbirth of a World Order*, p. 17.

8. Alvin Hansen, *America's Role in the World Economy* (New York: Norton, 1945), p. 19.

9. Jim Tomlinson, *Employment Policy: The Crucial Years* (Oxford, UK: Clarendon Press, 1987), p. 59.

10. G. John Ikenberry, "Creating Yesterday's New Order: Keynesian 'New Thinking' and the Anglo-American Postwar Settlement," in Judith Goldstein and Robert Keohane, eds., *Ideas and Foreign Policy* (Ithaca, NY: Cornell University Press, 1993), p. 71.

11. Sir William Beveridge, *Full Employment in a Free Society* (New York: Norton, 1945), p. 18.

12. Beveridge, *Full Employment*, p. 29.

13. Alan Brinkley, *The End of Reform* (New York: Vintage, 1995), p. 229.

14. Brinkley, *End of Reform*, p. 231.

15. Brinkley, *End of Reform*, p. 232.

16. Margaret Weir, "Ideas and Politics: The Acceptance of Keynesianism in Britain and the United States," in Peter Hall, ed., *The Political Power of Economic Ideas: Keynesianism Across Nations* (Princeton, NJ: Princeton University Press, 1989), p. 71.

17. Brinkley, *End of Reform*, p. 261.

18. Brinkley, *End of Reform*, p. 262.

19. Brinkley, *End of Reform*, p. 262.

20. Harold James, *International Monetary Cooperation Since Bretton Woods* (New York: Oxford University Press, 1996), p. 18.

21. See Armand Van Dormael, *Bretton Woods: Birth of a Monetary System* (New York: Holmes and Meier, 1978), p. 6.

22. Cited in Van Dormael, *Bretton Woods*, p. 7.

23. Cited in Ikenberry, "Creating Yesterday's New Order," p. 70.

24. John Gerard Ruggie, "International Regimes, Transac-

tions, and Change, *International Organization* 36 (Spring 1982): 195–231, at 209.

25. Robert Asher, et al., *The United Nations and the Promotion of the General Welfare* (Washington, DC: Brookings Institution, 1957), p. 374.

26. Camille Gutt, "Exchange Rates and the International Monetary Fund," in Seymour Harris, ed., *Foreign Economic Policy for the United States* (Cambridge, MA: Harvard University Press, 1948), p. 225.

27. Secretary of State to US Embassy Moscow, 25 September 1943, in U.S. Department of State, *Foreign Relations of the United States* (hereafter *FRUS*) *1944*, v. II (Washington, DC: GPO, 1967), p. 1007.

28. Acting Secretary of State to US Embassy Moscow, 27 October 1943, *FRUS 1944*, p. 1010.

29. Antony Alcock, *History of the International Labor Organization* (London: Macmillan, 1971), p. 183.

30. Ernst Haas, *Beyond the Nation State* (Stanford, CA: Stanford University Press, 1964), p. 156.

31. Cited in Richard Gardner, *Sterling-Dollar Diplomacy* (New York: McGraw-Hill, 1969), p. 9.

32. Gardner, *Sterling-Dollar Diplomacy*, p. 14.

33. Susan Ariel Aaronson, *Trade and the American Dream* (Lexington: University Press of Kentucky, 1996), p. 30.

34. Beveridge, *Full Employment*, p. 234.

35. Beveridge, *Full Employment*, p. 210.

36. Asher, *The United Nations*, p. 375.

37. Gardner, *Sterling-Dollar Diplomacy*, p. 105.

38. Gardner, *Sterling-Dollar Diplomacy*, p. 106.

39. Aaronson, *Trade and the American Dream*, p. 62.

40. Asher, *The United Nations*, p. 377.

41. Gardner, *Sterling-Dollar Diplomacy*, p. 271.

42. Gardner, *Sterling-Dollar Diplomacy*, p. 271.

43. Gardner, *Sterling-Dollar Diplomacy*, p. 272.

44. Cited in Gardner, *Sterling-Dollar Diplomacy*, p. 275.

45. Aaronson, *Trade and the American Dream*, p. 68.
46. Cited in Gardner, *Sterling-Dollar Diplomacy*, p. 376.
47. Asher, *The United Nations*, p. 372.

CHAPTER 4

1. Torsten Persson and Guido Tabellini, "Is Inequality Harmful for Growth?" *American Economic Review* 84 (June 1994): 600–621, at 600.

2. Paul Krugman, "Growing World Trade: Causes and Consequences," *Brookings Papers on Economic Activity* 1 (1995): 327–62.

3. I. M. Destler, "Trade Politics and Labor Issues," in Susan Collins, ed., *Imports, Exports, and the American Worker* (Washington, DC: Brookings Institution, 1998), p. 389.

4. George Meany, "Statement," U.S. Congress. House of Representatives. Committee on Ways and Means. *Trade Expansion Act of 1962* (87th Congress, 2nd Session, 13 March 1962).

5. Destler, "Trade Politics," p. 391.

6. Patrick Renshaw, *American Labor and Consensus Capitalism, 1935–1990* (Jackson: University Press of Mississippi, 1991), p. 153.

7. Jackie Calmes, "Despite Buoyant Economic Times, Americans Don't Buy Free Trade," *Wall Street Journal*, 10 December 1998.

8. Michael Phillips, "Globalization Comes to a Southern Town," *Wall Street Journal*, 12 February 1998.

9. See U.S. President Council of Economic Advisers, *Economic Report of the President: 1997* (Washington, DC: GPO, 1997).

10. OECD, *Employment Outlook: July 1997* (Paris: OECD, 1997), p. 129.

11. Yolanda Kodrzycki, "Laid-Off Workers in a Time of Structural Change," *New England Economic Review* (July/August 1996): 4–26, at 22.

12. Louis Jacobson, "Compensation Programs," in Collins, ed., *Imports, Exports, and the American Worker*, p. 477.

13. Kate Bronfenbrenner, "The Effects of Plant Closing or Threat of Plant Closing on the Right of Workers to Organize," North American Commission for Labor Cooperation, September 30, 1996.

14. See European Commission, *Employment in Europe* (Brussels: European Communities, 1996), p. 7.

15. *Economist,* "Asia Goes on the Dole," 25 April 1998, p. 71.

16. International Labor Organization, *World Employment: 1996/97* (Geneva, Switzerland: ILO, 1996), p. 117.

17. Lawrence Mishel, Jared Bernstein, and John Schmitt, *The State of Working America* (Armonk, NY: M. E. Sharpe, 1997), pp. 159–60.

18. U.S. President, Council of Economic Advisers, *Economic Report of the President: 1997* (Washington, DC: February 1996), p. 191.

19. Richard Freeman, "The Facts about Rising Economic Disparity," in James Auerbach and Richard Belous, eds., *The Inequality Paradox: Growth of Income Disparity* (Washington, DC: National Policy Association, 1998), p. 19.

20. Peter Passell, "Benefits Dwindle Along with Wages for the Unskilled," *New York Times*, 14 June 1998, 1.

21. Richard Freeman, "Toward an Apartheid Economy," *Harvard Business Review* (September–October 1996):114–21.

22. Jan Rutkowski, "Changes in the Wage Structure During Economic Transition in Central and Eastern Europe," *World Bank Technical Paper no. 340*, 1996, pp. 9–10.

23. OECD, *The OECD Jobs Study: Evidence and Explanations* (Paris: OECD, 1994), pp. 18–22.

24. Robert Erikson and John Goldthorpe, *The Constant Flux: A Study of Class Mobility in Industrial Societies* (Oxford, UK: Clarendon Press, 1992).

25. Dani Rodrik, *Has Globalization Gone Too Far?* (Washington, DC: Institute for International Economics, 1997), p. 64.

26. Council of Economic Advisers, *Economic Report of the President: 1997*, pp. 178–79.

27. William Cline, *Trade and Income Distribution* (Washington, DC: Institute for International Economics, 1997), p. 254.

28. Council of Economic Advisers, *Economic Report of the President: 1997*, p. 179.

29. Eurostat, *Income Distribution and Poverty Levels in the EU*, p. 5.

30. World Bank, *Poverty Reduction, and the World Bank* (Washington, World Bank, 1996). p. 9.

31. World Bank, *Poverty Reduction*, p. 2.

32. Hollis Chenery et al., *Redistribution with Growth* (New York: Oxford University Press, 1974), p. 46.

33. Council of Economic Advisers, *Economic Report of the President*, p. 170.

34. For a useful overview, see Stephen Nickell, "Unemployment and Labor Market Rigidities: Europe versus North America," *Journal of Economic Perspectives* 11 (Summer 1997): 55–74.

35. Paul Samuelson, "International Trade and the Equalization of Factor Prices," *Economic Journal* 58 (June 1948): 163–84.

36. See Krugman, "Growing World Trade, 327–77.

37. Cline, *Trade and Income Distribution*, p. 275.

38. See Tito Cordell and Isabel Grilo, "Globalization and Relocation in a Vertically Differentiated Industry," *International Monetary Fund Working Paper* WP/98/48 (April 1998).

39. Raphael Kaplinsky, "Export Processing Zones in the Dominican Republic: Transforming Manufactures into Commodities," *World Development* 21 (1993): 1851–65.

40. Cordell and Grilo, "Globalization and Relocation," p. 5.

41. John Maynard Keynes, *The Economic Consequences of the Peace* (New York: Harcourt Brace, 1920), p. 19.

42. John Maynard Keynes, *The General Theory of Employment, Interest, and Money* (New York: Harcourt Brace, 1964; orig. 1936), p. 373.

43. Keynes, *General Theory*, p. 374.
44. Robert Dahl and Charles Lindblom, *Politics, Economics and Welfare* (New York: Harper and Row, 1953), p. 140.
45. For examples of this line of argumentation, see Mancur Olson, *The Rise and Decline of Nations* (New Haven, CT: Yale University Press, 1982), and P. T. Bauer, *Equality, The Third World, and Economic Delusion* (Cambridge, MA: Harvard University Press, 1981).
46. Roberto Chang, "Income Inequality and Economic Growth: Evidence and Recent Theories," *Federal Reserve Bank of Atlanta Economic Review* (July/August 1994):1–10, at 2.
47. Joseph Stiglitz, "Some Lessons from the East Asian Miracle," *World Bank Research Observer* 11 (August 1996): 151–77, at 167.
48. Persson and Tabellini, "Is Inequality Harmful for Growth?": 600.
49. George Clarke, "More Evidence on Income Distribution, and Growth," *World Bank Policy Research Working Papers*, 1064, December 1992.
50. Lawrence Summers, "Equity in a Global Economy," *Treasury News*, 8 June 1998.
51. Michael Bruno, Martin Ravaillon, and Lyn Squire, "Equity and Growth in Developing Countries," *World Bank Policy Research Working Papers*, no. 1563 (January 1996), p. 15.
52. Samuel Morley, *Poverty and Inequality in Latin America* (Baltimore: Johns Hopkins, 1995), p. 196.
53. Nora Lustig, "Introduction," in Lustig, ed., *Coping with Austerity: Poverty and Inequality in Latin America* (Washington, DC: Brookings Institution, 1995), p. 5.
54. Stiglitz, "Some Lessons," p. 167.
55. See Ronald Dore, *Taking Japan Seriously* (Stanford, CA: Stanford University Press, 1987).
56. Stiglitz, "Some Lessons," p. 167.
57. Shirley Kuo, Gustav Ranis, and John Fei, "Rapid Growth

with Improved Income Distribution: The Taiwan Success Story," in Mitchell Seligson, *The Gap Between Rich and Poor*, (Boulder, CO: Westview Press, 1984), p. 383.

58. Kuo, Ranis, and Fei, "Rapid Growth," p. 384.

59. Kuo, Ranis, and Fei, "Rapid Growth," p. 385.

60. Kuo, Ranis, and Fei, "Rapid Growth," p. 386.

61. Dani Rodrik, "Understanding Economic Policy Reform," *Journal of Economic Literature* 34 (March 1996): 9–41, at 21.

62. World Bank, *World Development Report: 1997* (New York: Oxford University Press, 1997), p. 13.

63. Stiglitz, "Some Lessons," p. 169.

64. International Labor Organization Regional Office for Asia and the Pacific, "The Social Impact of the Asian Financial Crisis," Bangkok, 22–24 April 1998.

65. Vinod Ahuja, et al., *Everyone's Miracle?* (Washington, DC: World Bank, 1997).

CHAPTER 5

1. John Rawls, "Distributive Justice," in Edmund Phelps, ed., *Economic Justice* (Baltimore: Penguin, 1973), p. 327.

2. For a study that analyzes the dilemmas in the post-communist states, see Ethan B. Kapstein and Michael Mandelbaum, eds., *Sustaining the Transition: The Social Safety Net in Post-Communist Europe* (New York: Council on Foreign Relations Press, 1997).

3. The example is drawn from Nicholas Rescher, *Distributive Justice* (New York: Bobbs-Merrill, 1966), p. 26.

4. Daniel Hausman and Michael McPherson, *Economic Analysis and Moral Philosophy* (New York: Cambridge University Press, 1996), pp. 95–96.

5. Arthur Okun, *Equality and Efficiency: The Big Tradeoff* (Washington, DC: Brookings Institution, 1973), pp. 91–95.

6. James Meade, *Trade and Welfare* (Oxford: Oxford University Press, 1955), p. 5.

7. John Rawls, *A Theory of Justice* (Cambridge, MA: Harvard University Press, 1971), p. 3.

8. Rawls, *Theory of Justice*, p. 7.

9. Rawls, "Distributive Justice," p. 321.

10. Rawls, *Theory of Justice*, p. 60.

11. Rawls, "Distributive Justice," p. 328.

12. Douglas Irwin, *Against the Tide* (Princeton, NJ: Princeton University Press, 1996), p. 183.

13. Neuberger and Berman, "Socially Responsive Portfolio Manager," www.nbfunds.com/funds/socman.html.

14. This argument is developed by Richard Freeman in "International Labor Standards and World Trade: Friends or Foes?" in Jeffrey Schott, ed., *Challenges to the International Trading System* (Washington, DC: Institute for International Economics, 1996), pp. 87–112.

15. This discussion is drawn from Margaret Keck and Kathryn Sikkink, *Activists Beyond Borders: Transnational Advocacy Networks in International Politics* (Ithaca, NY: Cornell University Press, 1998).

16. Amartya Sen, "International Equity vs. Global Justice: Concepts and Agencies," paper presented to the United Nations Development Program Conference on "Global Housekeeping," New York, 22 June 1998.

17. "Business Bulletin," *Wall Street Journal*, 12 February 1998, 1.

18. For an overview of industrial-country efforts, see OECD, *Implementing the OECD Jobs Strategy: Member Countries' Experience* (Paris: OECD, 1997).

19. See OECD, *Employment Outlook: July 1997* (Paris: OECD, 1997), pp. 2–3.

20. See, for example, Horst Siebert, "Labor Market Rigidities: At the Root of Unemployment in Europe," *Journal of Economic Perspectives* 11 (Summer 1997): 37–54.

21. For a comprehensive review of the options, see Adrian Wood, *North-South Trade, Employment, and Inequality* (Oxford, UK: Clarendon Press, 1994); see also OECD, *Implementing the OECD Jobs Strategy: Member Countries' Experiences* (Paris: OECD, 1997).

22. For an excellent review of the issues, see Deutsches Institut für Wirtschaftsforschung, *Employment and Social Policies under International Constraints* (Gravenhage, Netherlands: Vuga, November 1996).

23. Ronald Findlay and Stanislaw Wellisz, "Endogenous Tariffs, the Political Economy of Trade Restrictions, and Welfare," in Jagdish Bhagwati, ed., *Import Competition and Response* (Chicago: University of Chicago Press, 1982), pp. 223–33.

24. For a useful discussion, see Steven Camarota and Mark Krikorian, "The Impact of Immigration on the U.S. Labor Market," Center for Immigration Studies, n.d.

25. Jeffrey G. Williamson, *Inequality, Poverty and History* (Cambridge, MA: Blackwell, 1991).

26. World Bank, *World Development Report: 1997* (New York: Oxford University Press, 1997), p. 52.

27. Michael Richardson, "Indonesia's Debacle Pulls Children Out of Schools," *International Herald Tribune*, 21 July 1998, p. 1.

28. OECD, *Implementing the Jobs Strategy*, pp. 95–96.

29. UNDP, *Human Development Report (HDR): 1997* (New York: Oxford University Press, 1997), assorted tables.

30. See World Bank, *World Development Report: 1995* (New York: Oxford University Press, 1995), p. 109, and OECD, *Implementing the Jobs Strategy*, p. 86.

31. See Louis Jacobson, "Compensation Programs," in Susan Col-lins, ed., *Imports, Exports, and the American Worker* (Washington, DC: Brookings Institution, 1998), pp. 514–16.

32. Edmund Phelps, *Rewarding Work* (Cambridge, MA: Harvard University Press, 1997), p. 106.

33. Phelps, *Rewarding Work*, p. 134.
34. See OECD, *Implementing the Jobs Strategy*, for discussions on tax policy and the labor market.
35. Samuel Brittan, "How to Make Work Pay," *Financial Times*, 22 January 1998, p. 12.
36. See Martin Baily, Robert Litan, and Robert Lawrence, *Growth with Equity* (Washington, DC: Brookings Institution, 1994).
37. For an elaboration of these arguments, see Louis Jacobson, "Compensation Programs," pp. 473–537.
38. Paolo Mauro and Antonio Spilimbergo, "How Do the Skilled and the Unskilled Respond to Regional Shocks? The Case of Spain," International Monetary Fund Working Paper WP/98/77, May 1998, p. 23.
39. Mauro and Spilimbergo, p. 19.
40. International Monetary Fund, *World Economic Outlook: May 1997* (Washington, DC: IMF, 1997), pp. 70, 80.
41. For a similar argument in the European context, see Fritz Scharpf, "Economic Integration, Democracy and the Welfare State," unpublished manuscript, 1996.
42. Paul Davidson, "Post Keynesian Employment Analysis and the Macroeconomics of OECD Unemployment," *The Economic Journal* 108 (May 1998): 817–31, at 819.
43. World Bank, *World Development Report: 1997*, p. 134.
44. For an excellent overview of the labor standards debate, see OECD, *Trade, Employment and Labor Standards* (Paris: OECD, 1996).
45. See Ethan B. Kapstein, *Governing the Global Economy: International Finance and the State* (Cambridge, MA: Harvard University Press, 1994).
46. See Kapstein, *Governing the Global Economy*.
47. For an overview, see Barry Eichengreen, "International Financial Cooperation: Lessons and Questions from the Asian Crisis," paper presented at the Meeting on Global Public Goods, United Nations Development Program, 22 June 1998.

48. Vito Tanzi, "Is There a Need for a World Tax Organization?" paper presented at the International Institute of Public Finance, Tel Aviv, Israel, 26–29 August 1996.

49. Jay Solomon, "World Bank Says It Was Wrong on Indonesia," *Wall Street Journal*, 5 February 1998, A17.

50. Lawrence Summers, "Equity in a Global Economy," *Treasury News*, 8 June 1998.

51. Lawrence K. Altman, "Next WHO Chief Will Brave Politics in Name of Science," *New York Times*, 3 February 1998, B10.

52. UNDP, *HDR 1997*, p. 5.

53. This section is drawn from World Bank, *World Development Report: 1997*, p. 140.

54. Robert J. Blendon, et al., "Bridging the Gap Between the Public's and Economists' Views of the Economy," *Journal of Economic Perspectives* 11 (Summer 1997): 105–18, at 113.

55. Tsidi Tsikata, "Aid Effectiveness: A Survey of the Recent Empirical Literature," IMF Paper on Policy Analysis and Assessment, March 1998, p. 1.

56. For an elaboration of this approach to foreign aid, see Peter Boone, "Politics and the Effectiveness of Foreign Aid," *European Economic Review* 40 (1996): 290–329.

CHAPTER 6

1. Cited in Sara Calian and Silvia Ascarelli, "Playing with Pain," *Wall Street Journal Europe*, 17 February 1997, 1.

2. Thomas Edsall, "Clinton and Blair Seek New New Left," *International Herald Tribune*, 29 June 1998, 1.

3. Alexis de Tocqueville, *Democracy in America*, v.2 (New York: Vintage, 1990; orig. 1832), p. 51.

4. de Tocqueville, *Democracy in America*, v.1, p. 51.

5. Louis Hartz, *The Liberal Tradition in America* (New York: Harvest, 1952).

6. See Robert Erikson and John Goldthorpe, *The Constant Flux: A Study of Class Mobility* (Oxford, UK: Clarendon Press, 1992).

7. This point was brilliantly made in Hartz, *The Liberal Tradition*.

8. For an elaboration of this argument, see Maier, "The Politics of Productivity," in Peter Katzenstein, ed., *Between Power and Plenty* (Madison: University of Wisconsin Press, 1978).

9. See Robert Packenham, *Liberal America and the Third World* (Princeton, NJ: Princeton University Press, 1973), p. 287.

10. Oliver Blanchard, "Theoretical Aspects of Transition," *American Economic Review* 86 (May 1996): 117–22, at 117.

11. Packenham, *Liberal America*, p. 288.

12. Maier, "The Politics of Productivity," p. 49.

13. Hartz, *The Liberal Tradition*, p. 305.

14. "A Refresher Course," *Wall Street Journal*, 12 February 1998, A22.

SELECTED
BIBLIOGRAPHY

Aaronson, Susan Ariel. *Trade and the American Dream.* Lexington, KY: University Press of Kentucky, 1996.

Alcock, Antony. *History of the International Labor Organization.* London: Macmillan, 1971.

Alesina, Alberto, and Roberto Perotti. "Income Distribution, Political Instability and Investment." *European Economic Review*, No. 40 (1996): 1203–28, at 1204.

Asher, Robert et al., eds. *The United Nations and the Promotion of the General Welfare.* Washington, DC: Brookings Institution, 1957.

Auerbach, James, and Richard Belous, eds. *The Inequality Paradox: Growth of Income Disparity.* Washington, DC: National Policy Association, 1998.

Bauer, P. T. *Equality, The Third World, and Economic Delusion.* Cambridge, MA: Harvard University Press, 1981.

Beveridge, Sir William. *Social Insurance and Allied Services.* New York: Macmillan, 1942.

Beveridge, Sir William. *Full Employment in a Free Society.* New York: Norton, 1975.

Bhagwati, Jagdish, ed. *Import Competition and Response.* Chicago: University of Chicago Press, 1982.

Bognano, Mario, and Kathryn Ready, eds. *The North American Free Trade Agreement*. Westport, CT: Praeger Press, 1993.

Brinkley, Alan. *The End of Reform*. New York: Vintage, 1995.

Bronfenbrenner, Kate. "The Effects of Plant Change or Threat of Plant Closing on the Right of Workers to Organize." *North American Commission for Labor Cooperation*, September 30 (1996).

Bruno, Michael, Martin Ravaillon, and Lyn Squire. "Equity and Growth in Developing Countries." *World Bank Policy Research Working Papers* 1563, January (1996).

Carr, E. H. *The Twenty Years' Crisis*. 1964 ed. New York: Harper and Row, 1939.

Chang, Roberto. "Income Inequality and Economic Growth: Evidence and Recent Theories." *Federal Reserve Bank of Atlanta Economic Review,* July/August (1994).

Cline, William. *Trade and Income Distribution*. Washington, DC: Institute for International Economics, 1997.

Collins, Susan, ed. *Imports, Exports, and the American Worker*. Washington, DC: Brookings Institution, 1998.

Cordell, Tito, and Isabel Grilo. "Globalization and Relocation in a Vertically Differentiated Industry." *International Monetary Fund Working Paper* WP/98/48, April (1998).

Davidson, Paul. "Post Keynesian Employment Analysis and the Macroeconomics of OECD Unemployment." *The Economic Journal* 108, May (1998).

de Tocqueville, Alexis. *Democracy in America*. Vol. 2. 1990 ed. New York: Vintage, 1832.

Diebold, William. *The End of the ITO*. Vol. 16, October, Princeton Essays in International Finance. Princeton, NJ, 1952.

Dunlop, John, and Walter Galenson, eds. *Labor in the 20th Century*. New York: Academic Press, 1978.

Erikson, Robert, and John Goldthorpe. *The Constant Flux: A Study of Class Mobility in Industrial Societies*. Oxford, UK: Clarendon Press, 1992.

European Commission. *Employment in Europe*. Brussels: European Communities, 1996.

Fine, Sidney. *Laissez Faire and the General-Welfare State*. Ann Arbor: University of Michigan Press, 1956.

Flora, Peter, and Arnold J. Heidenheimer, eds. *The Development of Welfare States in Europe and America,* New Brunswick, NJ: Transaction Publishers, 1984.

Freeman, Richard. "Toward an Apartheid Economy." *Harvard Business Review,* September/October (1996).

Gardner, Richard. *Sterling-Dollar Diplomacy*. New York: McGraw-Hill, 1969.

Gilpin, Robert. *The Political Economy of International Relations*. Princeton, NJ: Princeton University Press, 1987.

Glynn, Sean, and Alan Booth. "Unemployment in Interwar Britain: A Case for Relearning the Lessons of the 1930s?" *Economic History Review* 2nd series, 36, August (1983): 329–48.

Goldstein, Judith, and Robert Keohane, eds. *Ideas and Foreign Policy*. Ithaca, NY: Cornell University Press, 1993.

Gupta, Dipak. *The Economics of Political Violence*. New York: Praeger, 1990.

Gurr, Red Robert. *Why Men Rebel*. Princeton, NJ: Princeton University Press, 1970.

Haas, Ernst. *Beyond the Nation State*. Stanford, CA: Stanford University Press, 1964.

Hall, Peter, ed. *The Political Power of Economic Ideas: Keynesianism Across Nations*. Princeton, NJ: Princeton University Press, 1989.

Hansen, Alvin. *America's Role in the World Economy*. New York: Norton, 1945.

Harris, Seymour, ed. *Foreign Economic Policy for the United States*. Cambridge, MA: Harvard University Press, 1948.

Hartz, Louis. *The Liberal Tradition in America*. New York: Harvest, 1952.

Hausman, Daniel, and Michael McPherson. *Economic Analysis*

and Moral Philosophy. New York: Cambridge University Press, 1996.

Hobsbawm, E. J. *Industry and Empire*. New York: Penguin, 1969.

International Labor Organization. *World Employment: 1996/97*. Geneva, Switzerland: ILO, 1996.

International Monetary Fund. *World Economic Outlook: May 1997*. Washington, DC: International Monetary Fund, 1997.

Irwin, Douglas. *Against the Tide*. Princeton, NJ: Princeton University Press, 1996.

James, Harold. *International Monetary Cooperation Since Bretton Woods*. New York: Oxford University Press, 1996.

Kaplinsky, Raphael. "Export Processing Zones in the Dominican Republic: Transforming Manufactures into Commodities." *World Development*, no. 21 (1993): 1851–65.

Kapstein, Ethan B. *Governing the Global Economy: International Finance and the State*. Cambridge, MA: Harvard University Press, 1994.

Kapstein, Ethan. "Workers and the World Economy." *Foreign Affairs*, May/June (1996).

Kapstein, Ethan B., and Michael Mandelbaum, eds. *Sustaining the Transition: The Social Safety Net in Post-Communist Europe*. New York: Council on Foreign Relations Press, 1997.

Kazin, Michael. *The Populist Persuasion*. New York: Basic Books, 1995.

Keck, Margaret, and Kathryn Sikkink. *Activists Beyond Borders: Transnational Advocacy Networks in International Politics*. Ithaca, NY: Cornell University Press, 1998.

Kennedy, Paul. *The Rise and Fall of the Great Powers*. New York: Random House, 1987.

Keynes, John Maynard. *The Economic Consequences of the Peace*. New York: Harcourt Brace, 1920.

Keynes, John Maynard. *The General Theory of Employment, Interest, and Money*. 1964 ed. New York: Harcourt Brace, 1936.

Kodrzycki, Yolanda. "Laid-Off Workers in a Time of Structural Change." *New England Economic Review*, July/August (1996).

Krugman, Paul. "Growing World Trade: Causes and Consequences." *Brookings Papers on Economic Activity* 1 (1995).

Lustig, Nora, ed. *Coping with Austerity: Poverty and Inequality in Latin America*. Washington, DC: Brookings Institution, 1995.

Macshane, Denis. *International Labor and the Origins of the Cold War*. Oxford: Clarendon Press, 1992.

Marx, Karl, and Friedrich Engels. *Manifesto of the Communist Party*. New York: international Publishers, 1948.

Meade, James. *Trade and Welfare*. Oxford, UK: Oxford University Press, 1955.

Mill, John Stuart. *Principles of Political Economy*. 1979 ed. New York: Penguin, 1848.

Mishel, Lawrence, Jared Bernstein, and John Schmitt. *The State of Working America*. Armonk, NY: M. E. Sharpe, 1997.

Moore, Barrington. *Social Origins of Democracy and Dictatorship*. Boston: Beacon Press, 1966.

Nelson, Daniel. *Unemployment Insurance: The American Experience*. Madison, WI: University of Wisconsin Press, 1969.

Nickell, Stephen. "Unemployment and Labor Market Rigidities: Europe versus North America." *Journal of Economic Perspectives* 11, Summer (1997).

OECD. *The OECD Jobs Study: Evidence and Explanations*. Paris: OECD, 1994.

OECD. *Trade, Employment and Labor Standards*. Paris: OECD, 1996.

Okun, Arthur. *Equality and Efficiency: The Big Tradeoff*. Washington, DC: Brookings Institution, 1973.

Olson, Mancur. *The Rise and Decline of Nations*. New Haven, CT: Yale University Press, 1982.

Packenham, Robert. *Liberal America and the Third World*. Princeton, NJ: Princeton University Press, 1973.

Persson, Torsten, and Guido Tabellini. "Is Inequality Harmful for Growth?" *American Economic Review* 84, June (1994).

Phelps, Edmund. *Rewarding Work*. Cambridge, MA: Harvard University Press, 1997.

Piore, Michael. "Historical Perspectives and the Interpretation of Unemployment." *Journal of Economic Literature* 25, December (1987): 1834–50.

Piven, Frances Fox, and Richard Cloward. *Regulating the Poor*. New York: Vintage, 1971.

Polanyi, Karl. *The Great Transformation*. Boston: Beacon Press, 1944.

Price, Roger. *The Revolutions of 1848*. Atlantic Highlands, NJ: Humanities Press, 1988.

Rawls, John. *A Theory of Justice*. Cambridge, MA: Harvard University Press, 1971.

Renshaw, Patrick. *American Labor and Consensus Capitalism, 1935–1990*. Jackson, MS: University Press of Mississippi, 1991.

Rodrik, Dani. "Understanding Economic Policy Reform." *Journal of Economic Literature* 34, March (1996).

Rodrik, Dani. *Has Globalization Gone Too Far?* Washington, DC: Institute for International Economics, 1997.

Ruggie, John. "International Regimes, Transactions, and Change: Embedded Liberalism in the Postwar Economic Order." *International Organization* 36, Spring (1982).

Sen, Amartya. *On Ethics and Economics*. New York: Blackwell, 1987.

Sengenberger, Werner, and Duncan Campbell, eds. *International Labor Standards and Economic Interdependence*. Geneva, Switzerland: International Institute for Labor Studies, 1994.

Shotwell, James, ed. *The Origins of the International Labor Organization*. New York: Columbia University Press, 1934.

Siebert, Horst. "Labor Market Rigidities: At the Root of Unemployment in Europe." *Journal of Economic Perspectives* 11, Summer (1997).

Skocpol, Theda. *Social Revolutions in the Modern World*. New York: Cambridge University Press, 1994.

Smith, Adam. *The Nature and Causes of the Wealth of Nations*. 1993 ed. New York: Oxford University Press, 1776.

Sperber, Jonathan. *The European Revolutions*. New York: Cambridge University Press, 1994.

Steinmetz, George. *Regulating the Social*. Princeton, NJ: Princeton University Press, 1993.

Stiglitz, Joseph. "Some Lessons from the East Asian Miracle." *World Bank Research Observer* 11, August (1996).

Stolper, Gustav. *The German Economy: 1870 to the Present*. London: Weidenfeld and Nicolson, 1967.

Tevelyan, G. M. *British History in the 19th Century*. New York: Longmans, Green, 1930.

Thompson, E. P. *The Making of the English Working Class*. New York: Vintage, 1966.

Tomlinson, Jim. *Employment Policy: The Crucial Years*. Oxford, UK: Clarendon Press, 1987.

United Nations Development Program (UNDP). *Human Development Report (HDR): 1997*. New York: Oxford University Press, 1997.

U.S. President, Council of Economic Advisers. *Economic Report of the President*, 1997.

Weir, Margaret. *Politics and Jobs*. Princeton, NJ: Princeton University Press, 1992.

Williamson, Jeffrey G. *Inequality, Poverty and History*. Cambridge, MA: Blackwell, 1991.

Wilson, Edmund. *To the Finland Station*. New York: Farrar, Straus and Giroux, 1940.

Wood, Adrian. *North-South Trade, Employment, and Inequality*. Oxford, UK: Clarendon Press, 1994.

World Bank. *World Development Report: 1997*. New York: Oxford University Press, 1997.

INDEX

PRAISE FOR *GIVE*

"Nicholas is the total package when it comes to Facebook advertising. He's an industry leader at both campaign targeting and writing great ads that convert. Lots of experts are good at one, but few combine true expertise in both of these critical areas. Nicholas can, and he has the playbook and results to prove it."

– Ryan Deiss
Founder and CEO of DigitalMarketer.com

"How many people would you trust with your credit card to spend $10,000+ per day to get you customers and make you money? I trust Nicholas because he's made me hundreds of thousands. In business, results matter, and Kusmich delivers."

– Todd Herman
Leading High-Performance Coach and Founder of the 90 Day Year

"I've worked with Nicholas exclusively for the past three years to run all of my lead generation, which has resulted in over seven figures of revenue directly from his efforts. He is my secret weapon, my Facebook ninja."

– Giovanni Marsico
Founder of Archangel Academy Inc.

"Unlike most 'marketers'…Nic is in the trenches, day in and day out. He walks the walk. If you're looking for the biggest lever to pull in your business, this guy is it."

– Brian Moran
Founder of SamCart

"Nic is an absolute ace, crushing the game at the top of his niche. If you're not working with him, your business isn't reaching its full potential."

– Chris Stoikos
Founder of Dollar Beard Club

"Nic's strategies have helped us reach a much bigger audience than ever before and generate a lot of sales. Pay attention to what he says, because unlike a lot of people out there…his stuff is based on a lot of experience, testing, and success. I wish we would have discovered Nic sooner!"

– Josh Turner
Founder/CEO of LinkedSelling and *Wall Street Journal* Best-Selling Author

"There's been a major shift over the years, and the marketing game has changed. What got you to where you are won't get you to where you want to go. Nicholas is this generation's Don Draper and has written the playbook on how to thrive in this new era of marketing. Attention is the new currency, and Nicholas is a master at garnering both attention and action in a very noisy marketplace."

– Jayson Gaignard
Founder of Mastermind Talks

"Nic writes from the heart. His strategies are extremely effective, but what makes him different is that he packages it in a story that can't be forgotten. Definitely in a class of his own."

– Dan Martell
Serial Entrepreneur and Investor

"It's rare to find an entrepreneur who is a great marketer, a great teacher, and an overall great human being. With Nicholas, you get all three, which is why he gets results for his clients. It's why he has a reputation for being the best in the category. It's why he consistently earns my trust and respect. Every aspiring market leader and successful business owner should pay attention to this brilliant mind!"

– Re Perez
Top Branding Leader, brandingforthepeople.com

"There are a lot of 'gurus' out there who are experts at one thing only—selling themselves. Nic is the opposite. He's the smartest, most effective person operating right now in his space. Listen to him, you make money. Ignore him, you lose money. Pretty simple."

– Tucker Max
Multiple-Time *New York Times* Best-Selling Author

"Nicholas Kusmich stands far out from the crowd when it comes to a contemporary and fresh approach to marketing. A high-integrity guy, Nic has cracked so much of the code of what it takes to be successful in the online universe. He's the kind of expert who's truly done the work, and when he talks, it can be one of the smartest business decisions you can ever make to listen."

– Emily Rosen
CEO of Institute for the Psychology of Eating

"Nicholas Kusmich is a brilliant mix of vision, tactics, and strategy. His ability to create compelling messaging that attracts the 'cream of the crop' clients is uncanny. His command of the Facebook ad space is the best I've seen. Even more powerful is how he has packaged his knowledge into bite-size steps so we can get the same results that he does. This is a guy you need to follow, understand, and emulate. Simply, there is no one better!"

– Mel H. Abraham, CPA
Author of #1 National Best Seller, *The Entrepreneur's Solution*
Founder of Thoughtpreneur Academy

"I thought I knew a lot about Facebook ads after having run them for my own company, but after talking with Nic and hearing him speak, I was blown away by how much he knew. There are 'Facebook experts' and then there is Nic."

– Gary Nealon
Founder of RTA Cabinets, an Inc. 500 Company

"Cut through the Facebook marketing clutter. Nicholas knows what he's talking about, because every time I spend a dollar using his methods, it turns into 2–20 dollars. He's a genius when it comes to marketing in general and a savant when it comes to Facebook marketing. Such a no-brainer if you want to impact more lives and scale your business."

– Dr. Isaac H. Jones
Owner of Elevays.com and Elite Coach to Leading Doctors

"I had been looking for someone who was truly the best with Facebook ads. Then in a period of three months, every single top traffic guy was saying that Nicholas was the best for Facebook. Then I heard him speak at a conference and thought the way he approached Facebook marketing was game-changing. His approach to Facebook ads is like no one else's. This guy really knows what he is doing and just dominates when it comes to Facebook. I have been working with Nicholas since then, and he's proven to be the best of the best."

– Bernardo de la Vega
Founder of Radha Beauty

"If you are looking to use Facebook to help build your business, you have come to the right place. Nicholas Kusmich is the best in the world at helping businesses leverage Facebook to grow their business. Not only have I personally seen the strategies he teaches in this book work in my business, but Nicholas also spends hundreds of thousands of dollars every day helping other businesses in all niches use Facebook ads to grow their business. This is a must-read for any business owner trying to attract more customers and drive more revenue using the power of Facebook."

– Pete Vargas
Founder of Advance Your Reach

GIVE

GIVE

THE ULTIMATE GUIDE TO USING FACEBOOK ADVERTISING TO GENERATE MORE LEADS, MORE CLIENTS, AND MASSIVE ROI

. . . . .

NICHOLAS KUSMICH

GIVE: *The Ultimate Guide to Using Facebook Advertising to Generate More Leads, More Clients, and Massive ROI*

ISBN 978-1-61961-576-2 *Paperback*
      978-1-61961-624-0 *Ebook*

INTERIOR DESIGN BY
Kevin Barrett Kane

LIONCREST
PUBLISHING

To all the people who believed in me and stood behind me even when I thought I couldn't go on, this is for you.

And to all those who said none of this would work, this is for you, too.

To all the entrepreneurs and business owners who help make the world go around, this is for you.

To my beautiful wife, Fehren, none of this would be possible without you.

And to my daughter, the apple of my eye: Daddy is doing his best to create the best world possible for you.

TABLE OF CONTENTS

HOW ARE ENTREPRENEURS LIKE SUPERHEROES?

"You create superheroes to take care of problems that can't really be solved another way."

– **Robert Rodriguez**, filmmaker, screenwriter, and musician

You may never have realized it until now, but it's true. By treading the path of the entrepreneur or business owner, you are embarking on a journey that has a lot in common with the journey of the superhero.

Both entrepreneurs and superheroes want to use their skills to serve people and make the world a better place. If you're reading this book, the chances are that you already know this about yourself. At some point in your life, you discovered that you're really good at something and realized that you could use your talents to make a difference for people.

 There's another way in which entrepreneurs are like superheroes. They all have an origin story: a reason why they are the way they are and a burning motivation that drives them to succeed. Again, you probably have experienced this. You've known times when you've struggled to balance the books and heard the voices telling you to give it up ringing loudly in your ears, only for those voices to be outweighed by your steely determination to continue.

My own origin story begins the day my dad had his first heart attack. I was four years old, and I was sitting on the couch watching TV. At the time, I didn't know what was happening. I only knew that my dad was on his knees screaming, yelling, and grunting. The next thing I understood was that paramedics arrived at the house and took him to the hospital on a stretcher.

He recovered, but that first heart attack was the beginning of an escalating series of health complications that eventually led to his demise two decades later. When I was seventeen, a stroke left him blind in one eye. He and my mom were forced to let go of the family business, which was our only source of income. I watched my mom, at the age of forty-seven, try to find a job for the first time. She applied for work folding clothes at a dry cleaner. When she returned from her interview, she looked as though she had been crying. She didn't get the job, she was told, because her English wasn't good enough.

Seeing my mom's distraught face ignited something powerful within me. That day, I made a commitment to figuring out a way to take care of her and my dad and ensure that they would never again worry about money. My dad never lived to see the fulfillment of that journey, but my mom lives with me, my wife, and my daughter. She enjoys a wonderful life, connecting with family and friends and traveling to places as rich and varied as Paris, Rome, and Sydney. My dad was never able to afford an engagement ring for her. So a few years ago, I bought her an engagement ring that she wears as a memento to him.

Why am I telling you this? Every entrepreneur, and every super-hero, has a character arc. When they set out, they face mighty challenges. Over time, if they're successful, they conquer many of those challenges, even if they sometimes face tragedy along the way. This book will help you identify where you are in your own particular character arc and give you the tools you need to take the next steps.

THE CHARACTER ARC

When I saw my mom in tears, I knew that I had to do something quickly. I started to work part time as a youth pastor. My mom also found work, and between us, we managed to make ends meet. At the same time, I supplemented my income by taking on various side hustles. Initially, I was taken in by the promises of multilevel marketing companies and got involved in schemes that promised me a huge income with very little work. For a while, I even sold Cutco knives.

For fourteen years, pastoring and some form of side hustling ran simultaneously. There were times when most of my attention was on the pastoring and others when I was directing a lot of my focus toward other ways of earning money. It was tough at times, but I learned a great deal about what it is to be a man and take care of a family.

At Christmas 2014, I stepped completely away from pastoring. For fourteen years, it had felt like a calling, but as the years ticked by, I began to realize that there were other ways of reaching the people I wanted to reach. When I first set out on that path, I believed that pastoring was the best way to connect with people and make their lives better. As I matured, however, I came to understand that there were other ways of accomplishing that goal and that it was possible to reach far more people, more effectively, through other means.

Pastoring and marketing might look like very diverse paths, but there are some remarkable similarities. I'm still making my voice heard in a way that inspires people to advance their lives. The faith journey and the business journey are closer than many people believe.

As 2016 drew to a close, I met with one of my bigger clients, a company called the Truth About Cancer. The firm was founded on the story of a man who lost his father to cancer and responded by traveling the world in search of solutions for people suffering from the disease. He created an incredible documentary about his journey, which subsequently broadened into other businesses.

Meeting with the team at the end of 2016, they told me that when they and I began working together, they had just started out. Now, millions and millions of people have heard their message, equating to an unquantifiable improvement in those people's health and tens of millions of dollars in revenue.

This is not to say that all their success is attributable to me. They have a great product and a heartfelt mission to serve people. My work has been to bring them to a far wider audience than they imagined possible. I discovered that one of my superpowers is to show people how they can bring their message to the people who most want to hear it and who are willing to pay them for their expertise.

Take a moment to think about your entrepreneurial superpowers. What do you want to bring to the world, and what motivates you to make that desire a reality? Whom do you want to serve and why?

SIGNIFICANCE AND CERTAINTY
Shortly after I left pastoring for good, in early 2015, I attended a marketing conference called the Archangel Flight School. Without pastoring to fall back on, I needed to find a way to turn my side hustles into something more substantial, and I needed to find it fast.

The event took place in the Berkeley Church in Toronto. The presenter, my now very close friend Giovanni Marsico, asked how many people in the room used Facebook ads to build their businesses, and approximately 80 percent of the attendees raised their hands. Then he asked how many people found Facebook ads profitable. I was the only person who kept my hand up.

Until that point, most of my side hustles were based on presenting myself as a marketing consultant. It was only when I sat in a room full of people who wanted to make Facebook marketing work for them, and couldn't, that I understood where my real superpowers lay.

As part of the Archangel conference, the hosts invited everyone who wished to get up on stage and share some nuggets of helpful information. The catch? Each person had only 126 seconds. I stood up and offered some insights into making Facebook advertising work.

In the eyes of the people in the room, I might as well have pulled on spandex underpants and painted a big *F* on my chest. I walked into that conference as Nicholas Kusmich, marketing consultant, and left as the Facebook guy. That was the start of a wave of opportunities that laid the groundwork for what I do today. I may have left pastoring, but sitting in a church at a conference named the Archangel Flight School, I felt as though I was being anointed.

All entrepreneurs, I believe, want to feel significant. We want to be seen as leaders in our fields. In this regard, too, we are like superheroes. Superheroes may not want the straightforward adulation that comes with pop success or sporting achievement, but they all crave, in some form or another, the knowledge that people see and talk about their deeds. If you've chosen the path of the entrepreneur, it's probable that you want to be known and respected as a leader in your field.

Finally, both superheroes and entrepreneurs need leads. What would Batman or Spiderman be without distressed members of the public to aid? As an entrepreneur, you need to know that there are people who can benefit from your abilities, and you need to know how to reach them.

Those are the promises of this book. It will show you how to position yourself in a way that frames you as a leader and an authority in your field. It will give you the tools to connect with the people you most want to serve and who are most in need of your unique talents. You'll find out how to determine your ideal market, how to respect Contextual Congruence, and how to sort your prospects into swim lanes and market to each group accordingly. Wherever you are in your journey as an entrepreneur, this book can assist in taking you at least a step further.

It's important to understand that Facebook ads are the delivery mechanism, not the purpose. I don't wake up every morning excited about Facebook ads. I wake up excited to know that

I have a chance to transform people's lives. Facebook ads are the most powerful medium I've found in which to do that. To succeed as an entrepreneur, you will need to identify your own superpowers, connect with your message, and be willing to overcome challenges.

Fortunately, by picking up this book, you are invited to become part of a community of people on similar paths, learning from and supporting one another. To subscribe to my blog, visit www.nicsblog.com/insights, and to join my free Facebook group, Facebook Marketing Mastery, visit www.nicsblog.com/group.

PART ONE

ADVERTISING IS CHANGING: FACEBOOK IS THE FUTURE

"The price of doing the same old thing is far higher than the price of change."

– Bill Clinton

1

THIRTY THOUSAND-PLUS PERCENT ROI

"Help others without any reason and give without the expectation of receiving anything in return."

> – **Roy Bennett**, *The Light in the Heart*

What do you see as the most important aspect of your business? Sales? Operations? Perhaps even research and development? I'm here to tell you that the one characteristic distinguishing highly successful businesses from those doomed to mediocrity is the ability to successfully acquire new customers or clients through advertising and the capacity to directly measure the return on investment (ROI) generated by that advertising. Why? It's because ROI measures the value you get for the time, energy, and money you invest into your business. The higher your ROI, the greater your leverage.

This book is about Facebook advertising. Specifically, it's about how to maximize the return from your Facebook advertising efforts and measure those returns. It's about the extraordinary power of understanding your market. It's about generating leads so strong that potential clients start conversations by qualifying themselves to *you*. Ultimately, it's about harnessing those tools to generate a staggering ROI and, if it's your goal, to become a celebrity and a trusted authority in your chosen industry.

It's about having the power to grow your revenue on demand. How? Let me start by telling you a story.

TAKI'S STORY

Taki Moore is a good friend of mine. He's also one of Australia's leading business coaches. Twice per quarter, once in the United States and once in Australia, Taki runs a two-day residential event he calls the Million-Dollar Coach Intensive. One of Taki's goals for the weekend is to fill the conference room with as many potential new clients as possible.

During the weekend, participants learn essential skills they can use to scale and leverage their businesses. At its conclusion, attendees who Taki feels are a good fit are invited to join his elite coaching program, Black Belt.

This is the primary method he uses to drive his coaching business. So, bringing as many *quality* attendees to his live events is an exceptionally high priority for him. When he fills his seminars, his business grows year on year. To give you an idea of the numbers we're talking about, Taki finds that the optimum number of attendees is between fifty and seventy.

Unfortunately, live events like Taki's aren't easy to fill. Bringing people to a point where they're ready to hand over money for a two-day experience takes a lot of work, and very few people are capable of successfully putting together regular events. Those who prosper in this field usually follow one of two strategies: they invest a lot of money in advertising, or they invest a lot of time in networking.

Taki was looking for a way to leverage his resources, attracting people to his events without laying out large sums of money or spending all his time networking at industry gatherings. That's when he came to me.

The previous year, Taki had engaged a vendor and experimented with Facebook advertising. The results were terrible. Vendor fees and advertising spending tore an $80,000 hole in his business, a situation from which it took months to recover. Until he spoke to me, he had sworn never to risk another Facebook advertising campaign.

Taki was understandably gun-shy. He knew that Facebook advertising *could* work for him, but he found it hard to trust that it *would*. As an added complication, by the time he was ready to start, we had only about five weeks until the first event he wanted to fill.

For a Facebook campaign, this meant moving people toward a buying decision faster than most are comfortable with. Facebook started as a network to connect students at universities. People are there primarily to communicate with friends; they don't want to feel that they are being aggressively sold to. Every good Facebook marketer understands this and recognizes how important it is not to violate the parameters of the platform.

If you use pushy sales techniques on Facebook, you will be as unwelcome as a person who turns up at a barbecue, grabs a burger off the grill, and starts loudly to try and convince anyone within earshot to buy a vacuum cleaner. Do *not* be that person.

Our challenge, then, was twofold: we wanted to encourage people to make a quick buying decision, and we needed to make sure that we did that while *building* Taki's brand, not tarnishing it. How did we do that? We followed the two golden rules of Facebook advertising.

Give Before You Ask

Most people do not log in to Facebook with the primary intention of making a purchase. This differentiates the platform significantly from overtly commercial sites such as Amazon and eBay. You cannot expect your prospects to be sitting at their laptop, or browsing on their smartphone, with credit card in hand.

This is why you must give people something they are interested in before you even contemplate asking them to make a purchasing decision. What appears to be the most direct line to a purchase is, in fact, a direct line to losing the attention and interest of the people you want to reach. When you approach Facebook with the intent to *get* something, rather than to *give* your audience something they value, you will lose.

This is the approach used by the previous vendor Taki enlisted, and the reason it failed so dramatically. We needed to avoid falling into that trap. Here's what we did instead.

We started by thinking about what Taki had that he could give away and how it would intrigue his potential clients. Next, we asked how we could present the offer in a manner that was congruent with the norms of Facebook.

To do this, Taki and I addressed the following questions:

- ▶ What problems do my ideal clients need to solve?
- ▶ What do they really need?
- ▶ What solution can I provide them with?
- ▶ How is that solution different and unique?

We soon discovered that Taki uses a very smart and unusual method of conducting a sales call. He calls it a triage call, and it offers undoubted value to his ideal clients. We packaged it up attractively and invited people to give us their e-mail addresses in exchange for a PDF "cheat sheet" taking them step by step through the process.

Offer Value at Every Step

The second golden rule of marketing on Facebook is that you must continue to offer value at every step of the process. Nothing is gained when you capture your prospect's attention by giving them something they need, only to destroy the goodwill created by this gesture through reverting to a crass appeal.

In Taki's case, we handled this by using the names and e-mail addresses we had collected to send a very soft invitation to his event. We stressed that we were letting people know it was happening and that by claiming their place swiftly, they would receive a special bonus.

We had a limited time period to work with, so we moved quickly to bring people an offer, but we didn't betray the trust they had shown us by giving us an e-mail address in exchange for information about Taki's triage call process. We continued to treat them with respect and to work within the limits of what is possible using Facebook.

Taki's Results

To promote his upcoming event, Taki spent a grand total of $1,853.68 on Facebook advertising. The campaign we coordinated together won him sixty-six new attendees to his live event. Of those sixty-six, thirty-two enrolled in his high-level coaching program. At $18,000 per year, the total worth of those thirty-two new clients to Taki's business was $576,000. Calculate the ROI of $576,000 on an advertising budget of $1,853.68, and you'll discover that it comes out at 30,973 percent.

That's not all, though. Taki reached out again to people who had requested information about his triage call strategy but hadn't registered for his live event. Of the 372 people who gave Taki their e-mail addresses, 66 had already registered, leaving 306 who had yet to do so.

Simply through e-mailing those people and inviting them to his next event, Taki ultimately saw another fifty-one enroll in his elite coaching program, generating a further $918,000 in revenue. Over the course of a year, Taki took the strategy I led him through and turned it into almost $1.5 million in additional client revenue.

He discovered that by using Facebook effectively and putting in place a strategy that attracted his potential clients rather than repelling them and following a simple step-by-step process, his ROI began to grow exponentially. You can do the same.

The Gift of Certainty

Although Taki's initial campaign gave him an astronomical ROI, the long-term effects were even more powerful. In the world of Facebook marketing, most people have no idea how to gain the attention of their ideal clients. Naturally, they feel insecure and worried about making new marketing investments. Often, like Taki, they've been burned before, and they don't want to suffer the same losses again.

Now Taki knows exactly how to place ads in a way that practically guarantees a stellar ROI. In a world where most coaches and presenters are struggling to fill events, Taki has a proven formula that boosts not only the numbers of attendees but also the quality of those who come to see him live. He has more people coming to his events, and those people are his ideal clients.

While it's obviously not possible to guarantee exactly the same results every time, the fundamental strategy is sound and can be utilized again and again.

As an additional bonus, Taki has since used this strategy to expand his business in the United States, building on his reputation in Australia and hosting events with an assurance that comes from knowing that the principles behind his client acquisition strategies are ironclad. He has taken an initial Facebook marketing budget of $1,853.68 and turned it into a continuously growing stream of new business and revenue.

FROM DECLINING MASS MARKETS TO MASTERING FACEBOOK

The way people consume media is changing. Ten years ago, advertising was usually a matter of buying up space in mass channels. Now, that approach looks dated and clumsy.

Advertising executives pay thousands, even millions, of dollars for the exposure gained through spots in newspapers, on television, and on the radio. They jettison vast advertising budgets for the privilege of a space on a billboard. Those who think of themselves as progressive throw money at Facebook and Google without understanding how the media landscape has changed and how they need to adapt their strategies.

Marketing managers spend money on advertising purely because they have a budget and they need to be seen doing something with it. They may gain some sales for their business, or they may not, but they won't be able to tell either way.

They believe that if they give their product or service enough exposure, customers and clients will naturally flock to them. Most of the time, they're wrong. At best, they have no way of determining how many sales can be directly traced to a particular ad. Even apparently successful adverts, which spark a buzz on social media, may be failures in ROI terms.

ROI on traditional advertising has been declining for a decade, and it's only going in one direction. This isn't a temporary dip. The world of marketing is changing, and those who succeed are those who understand how to ride the new wave. Most traditional advertisers don't understand the psychological stages people need to pass through before they're ready to make a purchase.

I had a conversation recently with the executives of a real estate investment firm. Their focus is on inviting people into advanced coaching and consulting programs. Every month, they spend $15,000 on advertising: $5,000 on print media, $5,000 on radio slots, and $5,000 on local television commercials. They have no idea how well the advertising works.

One of the first questions they asked me when we spoke was, "What kind of budget do we need to make this work?" This is a very common mentality, but it reveals their ignorance of the fundamentals of marketing.

The vast majority of companies still think that deciding on a budget and throwing that budget at their chosen platforms is an acceptable way to advertise. When this approach delivers subpar results, or they have no way of *measuring* their results, they lose faith in the platform as opposed to questioning their faulty strategy.

In my view, there are only two good reasons for a company to invest in paid media:

- ▶ They want to test a new sales process and generate specific metrics.
- ▶ They have a sales process that works, and they want it to catch fire.

Sometimes it makes sense to run tests to gauge the response of the market. The purpose of this approach is to assess how much money needs to be spent to generate a solid ROI. Do this when you want to understand how well your new offer plays with your customers and when you plan to use the information to fine-tune your advertising strategy.

When you already *have* that information and you know that investment in advertising will bring significant returns, the time is right to boost your advertising spend and, simultaneously, your advertising return.

When neither of these conditions is met, don't throw your money away.

> In my view, there are only two good reasons for a company to invest in paid media:
> ▷ They want to test a new sales process and generate specific metrics.
> ▷ They have a sales process that works, and they want it to catch fire.

If you're reading this book, you're one of the early adopters. You already understand that pursuing ever-declining ROI through traditional channels is not the technique you need to master to build your business, and you're keen to know what *will* make the difference. Over the course of this book, I'll walk you through everything you need to know to master the art of Facebook advertising and generate as many leads, and customers, as you can handle.

There's no point in spending $1.5 million on advertising to bring in $1 million of new business. You might as well throw

$500,000 down the toilet. If you want to measure the *growth* of your business, the metric you need to focus your attention on is ROI. Fortunately, new media channels make it incredibly easy to track ROI. You can understand exactly where each dollar is going and how much value it is generating.

When you use the tools I'm about to give you, you can dramatically increase your ROI to the point where you know that whenever you need more leads, you need only to follow the principles I'll explain in this book, and you'll wake up tomorrow with an inbox bursting with potential new clients. Even better, the people you speak to will already be enthusiastic about working with you. When I get on the phone with a new client, they often tell me that if I can find the time, they would *love* to work with me. Do your clients do the same?

I'm a terrible salesperson. I don't like to sell to people, and I'm not good at it. The reason I have so many great clients is that my *marketing* is so good that they are already sold before they even pick up the phone. I never work to convince people to do something they don't really want to do because I've already shown them that I understand their problem and that I can teach them how to fix it.

In the following chapters, we'll cover the essential differences between traditional marketing channels and the world of Facebook advertising. We'll discuss the wrong way to use Facebook and the right way. We'll explore the four parts of crafting a compelling Facebook marketing campaign.

Finally, we'll discuss how to combine these strategies for maximum impact before concluding with some questions and answers you can refer to when you need to determine whether you're on the right track.

Ready to skyrocket your ROI? Read on.

2

SHIFTING TERRAIN

"I can't change the direction of the wind, but I can adjust my sails to always reach my destination."

– **Jimmy Dean**, American actor

The way we consume content is changing. When I speak to an audience, I often take the opportunity to ask them whether they watch TV. As a general rule, about thirty hands go up. Next, I ask how many of them watch TV at network times, meaning that they watch shows when the networks broadcast them. This time, very few hands go up, perhaps 5 percent.

My third question is how many people in the room watch TV on their *own* time, meaning that they record shows, use DVR, or stream TV using Netflix, Amazon, Hulu, or similar services. Nearly 100 percent of people raise their hands.

I'm prepared to bet that even of the small percentage of people who watch TV shows on network time, the majority see the commercial breaks as an opportunity to go to the bathroom, make a cup of tea, or get a snack.

One exception to this is sports, which millions of people still watch live. Nonetheless, there's nothing to stop people chatting to friends or otherwise distracting themselves during the commercials.

By the same token, what do you do when you're in the passenger seat of a car and you pass a billboard? Are you paying attention to the message, or are you texting friends? Even when you're *driving* the car and you hit a red light, it's more likely that you're checking in to Facebook than that you're studying billboard advertisements.

Now think about what you *do* use to consume media content. How often do you check your phone? What's the first thing you do when you wake up in the morning? If you're like most of us, you keep it within reach twenty-four hours a day, checking your Facebook, Twitter, or Instagram feed multiple times per day. As quickly as social media content is created, we consume it.

Some people rail against this reality. They tell me that they are digital marketers and that they advertise on Google or YouTube instead of traditional channels. This is simply a transfer of a traditional media mindset to new media channels.

When you watch YouTube, what do you do when a video features an advertisement at the beginning? Do you watch it avidly, or do you wait impatiently until you can skip it? If you're a really seasoned YouTube watcher, you may even open multiple tabs, so you can watch one video while you're waiting for another to reach the point where you can skip the ad.

Jennifer Taylor of ScribbleLive commented in 2015 that "It's no secret that millennials and the digital natives of Generation Z have developed a built-in ad blocker. Even if you do manage to get their eyeballs on a banner or commercial, it's unlikely that the content will even register amongst all the noise in today's media landscape."

Social media is a buzz phrase, but the Internet is essentially a social technology. It was designed to connect us with one another. Traditional media platforms, such as magazines, are dying a slow death as more and more people consume the majority of their media via the Internet. Many companies already understand this and are transferring their advertising budgets to digital platforms, but very few recognize the emerging imperatives that are shaping the digital age and the power those imperatives have to shape their success.

Kodak is a tragic example of a company that played a key role in pioneering digital technology, yet fell by the wayside because the company's leaders didn't understand how the new technology was altering the way people took photographs. Once the biggest name in film, Kodak is now a mere footnote in a culture dominated by smartphones and Instagram.

Advertising in the digital age thrives on narrative. You need to tell stories that grab the attention of people who are bombarded with information on their newsfeeds and whose tolerance for things that don't interest them is vanishingly small. Unless you can do that, you will soon find that your message is lost.

You wouldn't try to sell record players in the age of the MP3, so don't be the person floundering in the surf, gasping for breath, and desperately trying to convince yourself that things will get better. The good news is that when you understand the shifts that are taking place in our media consumption, you're ideally placed to ride the wave of change, not drown in its wake.

In the digital age, the essence of marketing is understanding your ideal prospect, recognizing how they consume content, and telling them a compelling story that captivates a portion of their finite attention.

THE FALLACY OF EXPOSURE

How much would you pay to have fifty million people watch your advertisement? A prime-time spot during the Super Bowl might cost you $5 million. It's the fastest route to mass exposure on the planet. Is it worth it? What if I told you that I could get the same number of eyeballs on your ad at a cost of $10,000. Would you go for it?

You might. If you did, I'd say you were out of your mind.

What's the value of exposure? How does it help you to grow and develop your business? You don't need to show your products to as *many* people as possible. You need them to be seen by the *right* people at the right time.

One of my clients is a doctor who works with people who have type 2 diabetes. There's a strong possibility that if I put his message in front of a huge number of people, some will have type 2 diabetes and respond. Many will not. By showing his message to *only* people who have type 2 diabetes, the response rate increases dramatically. It's the difference between starting a fire with a magnifying glass and lighting a pyre covered in gasoline.

When you bring a laser focus to the question of who will see your message and tailor your advertising to precisely those people, you will start to create traction. Facebook is the perfect platform to do this. In January 2016, Facebook announced that it has 1.39 billion active users. If Facebook were a country, it would be the most populous in the world, with more people than China or India and more than four times as many as the United States.

Yet, Facebook allows smart marketers to exercise precise controls over who sees their content. You have the ability to reach

1.39 billion at your fingertips. This is what makes Facebook the most powerful platform currently available to marketers.

By aggregating the data of everyone who uses the site, Facebook probably knows more about you than you know about yourself. It knows where you check in, which restaurants you enjoy, what you like and don't like, and where you went on vacation last year. It understands your buying patterns, and it logs your activity on and off the site.

Have you ever opened your Facebook newsfeed to be reminded of an activity you had completely forgotten about? It may have slipped your mind, but Facebook has logged it somewhere in that vast algorithm, ready to present it to you whenever it becomes relevant again.

Most of us never log out of Facebook, so it knows about your other activities on the Internet. It probably knows what brand of credit card you use, what car you drive, and where you live. It understands your political and religious views, and it knows whether you are single, married, in a relationship, or whether "it's complicated."

This is what makes Facebook the premier social platform for marketers. The infrastructure and the complexity of data mining it can offer far outstrip the capacities of the competition.

No matter who your potential client is, where they live, or how they spend their time, the chances are good that they have a Facebook profile. This is why it makes sense for you to use Facebook: everyone you want to connect with is there, and you can target them based on their job title, interests, zip code, or any number of other factors.

With the capacity to reach such a colossal number of people, while targeting specific groups through the use of algorithmic data mining, Facebook has created a perfect storm for business owners.

You can put your content in front of the people you most want to reach for pennies on the dollar. This level of access was once reserved for companies with multimillion-dollar advertising budgets. Now it's at your fingertips.

Mass exposure no longer matters. Mass marketing is becoming micromarketing. You don't need to reach all the people all the time. You need to understand clearly who your ideal clients are and target your advertising at precisely the segments of the population who will benefit from it and find value in it.

FACEBOOK THE WRONG WAY AND THE RIGHT WAY

If I had a dollar for every entrepreneur or business owner who has told me that their organization is already on Facebook, I could take that money and create a 30,000 percent ROI with it.

For some reason, vast numbers of otherwise-sane people believe that simply by creating a Facebook fan page, they are doing something productive. The illusion that we are somehow marketing our products and services just by being *on* Facebook is a pervasive one.

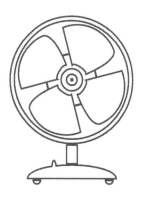

Facebook encouraged this illusion by inviting people and brands to create fan pages, then changing the rules so that subscribers see only a fraction of the posts. Individuals or companies that want to reach all of their fans must pay to boost their posts. As a result, large fan pages diminished in value. They are no longer an economical or effective method of reaching an audience. There is a huge difference between Facebook as a social platform and an advertising platform. If you think that you can post on a fan page every day and, by doing so, eliminate the need for a unique website and have followers hanging on to your every word, you will be sorely disappointed.

There is nothing *wrong* with creating a fan page and building a tribe, but it doesn't necessarily contribute to building your business. If you compound that mistake by pouring advertising dollars into boosting the reach of your posts, even when this isn't affecting your bottom line, you are falling victim to the fallacy of exposure.

Social context dictates behavior. Most people see Facebook as primarily a social platform, so boosting your social activity is unlikely to have a significant impact on the success of your business.

The opposite, even more egregious, mistake is to ignore the social component of Facebook altogether, treating it like a more traditional advertising platform. Do not assume that people will be interested in buying from you when you have no previous relationship and have invested no effort in understanding their needs or providing them with value. To most people, this is about as welcome as twerking at their grandmother's funeral.

The key to succeeding on Facebook is respecting Contextual Congruence, meaning that you must understand the social norms pertaining to the platform before you can hope to market effectively.

Received wisdom in the marketing world states that content is king. Nowadays, however, we have access to all the content we could possibly require at the touch of a button. In a world of unlimited data, *context* is king, and insight trumps information.

You cannot succeed by importing a traditional advertising mindset to Facebook and hoping for the best. Instead, you must identify your ideal prospect, build a relationship with them that extends beyond Facebook, and make offers to them in ways that *enhance* your brand, building rather than diminishing trust.

When you treat Facebook like a traditional advertising platform and seek to buy mass exposure, the best-case scenario is that you will waste money. Every time you work on the principle that exposure alone is worth paying for, you send good money after bad and damage your bottom line.

Worse, this approach will harm your relationships with prospects. Every time you approach them with a selling mindset on a social platform, you are telling them loudly and clearly that you don't understand the subtleties of the medium, increasing the chances that they will disengage the next time you have something to say to them. Like the vacuum cleaner salesperson at the family barbecue, you will make yourself unwelcome, draining your social capital and giving yourself a mountain to climb to reengage apathetic prospects.

The absolute worst-case scenario is that inept advertising can actually cause potential clients to turn on you and publicly express their dissatisfaction. The old adage that all publicity is good publicity couldn't be less accurate when applied to people talking trash about you on the Internet.

Negative posts may be perceived as reliable, giving you a huge headache and putting you into firefighting mode as you seek to limit the damage done to your reputation. I've seen this happen dozens of times, and it is an ugly sight. It takes only one employee to post an inappropriate tweet, and suddenly, you have a huge amount of the wrong type of exposure.

There's nothing wrong with creating a Facebook fan page for

your business. Ask yourself, however, whether it is really an asset to your operations or a sinkhole sucking up time and energy. Even when you receive lots of likes, comments, and shares, your page may not actually be contributing to your bottom line. Unless it plays a role in growing your business and increasing ROI, what value does it really have?

In the next chapter, we'll examine what it takes to use Facebook in the *right* way, targeting people who want to hear about your business in a style that warms them up and makes them increasingly open to future communications from you. This is the pivotal shift that allows you to move away from pointless social media activity and counterproductive efforts to create exposure and toward strapping a jet pack to your ROI.

Are you paying for conversions or merely exposure? Ask yourself this question: "Am I wasting time/money/energy on platforms that are no longer relevant?" If so, stop.

How well do you understand Facebook? Are you treating it like any other advertising platform, or are you basing your strategy on Contextual Congruence?

3

FACEBOOK THE RIGHT WAY

"Art is not what you see, but what you make others see."

– Edgar Degas

What is marketing?

Is it synonymous with advertising? Is it a way to convince people to do things they don't really do?

At its core, marketing is establishing a preeminent position through the establishment of unconscious narratives.

What does this mean?

You want people in your marketplace to consider you an authority, or even a celebrity, in your chosen field. Naturally, however, you can't do this directly. The way to do it successfully is to *act* in ways that lead people to believe that you know what you're doing and to treat you as an authority.

In essence, marketing is matching. As a marketer, I seek to connect people who have some kind of problem or frustration in their lives with the people who have the solutions they need. I'm not interested in manipulating people into believing they want what I have or changing their minds. I'm only interested in putting solutions in front of the people who want it.

Does that sound easier than trying to generate "influence" so that you can pressure people into buying from you?

I don't go into art galleries very much. Frankly, I find them boring. On the rare occasions when I do, I notice instantly that there are some paintings that stand out among the others. Why? What is it about these paintings that make them so special? Is it the brush strokes, the colors, or the techniques?

No, it's the deeper stories they convey. This quality distinguishes paintings that sell for a few hundred dollars and those that are deemed priceless masterpieces and expressions of the highest human capacities.

Lead generation and new customer acquisition is an art.

There is a science behind it, of course, and we'll discuss that more in later chapters. What makes one marketer stand out from the rest, however, is his or her ability to tell stories in a way that expresses higher values. It's the ability to position products and services in ways that make people want them. It's the ability to represent the value they bring to their marketplace in a compelling fashion.

If you've picked up this book, I'm going to make three assumptions about you:

You have something that can help people.

You know that there are people out there who would want what you have to offer, but you're not sure how best to reach them.

Therefore, you could benefit from a way of reaching those people quickly and cost-effectively in a way that is congruent with your personality and congruent with the way they consume information.

I'm biased because marketing on Facebook is what I excel at, but I believe that business revenue is driven by your ability to market your craft or product and that there's no better space to play in right now than Facebook.

Jay Abraham is one of the greatest copywriters in the world. A firm that I was working with decided to conduct a test: without telling Jay, they compared the results of his copywriting with my Facebook ads.

The company was running an exclusive event with a $10,000 entry fee. Jay wrote a two-page advertorial for *Success* magazine. Running the ad cost $175,000, and Jay's fee, which he waived, is usually $50,000. The firm received two bookings for its event on the back of Jay's advertorial. Two bookings at $10,000 each amounted to $20,000, from an initial investment of $175,000. This is without factoring in additional sales that took place at the event.

My Facebook ad, which ran only to readers of *Success*, brought in four sales. In itself, that's not really a big deal. The sample was small, and it's hard to tell how much of that return was due to the quality of the ad and how much was due to natural variation. The kicker, however, is that we spent only $1,300 to run the Facebook ads. A return of $40,000 (four sales) on a $1,300 ad spend is a massive increase on ROI over a return of $20,000 on a $175,000 investment.

Facebook can be the environment where you locate all the leads you could ever desire.

At this point, your lead generation is in one of four situations.

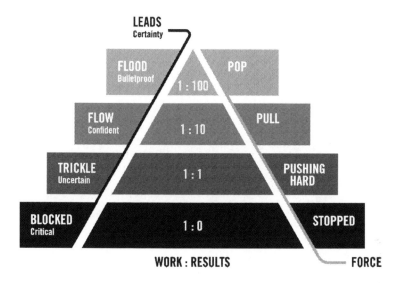

At worst, it's completely stopped. You're working hard to generate leads, but your efforts aren't paying off. Your input-to-output ratio is 1:0, and your business is in critical condition.

In a slightly better scenario, you're generating a trickle of leads but working hard for each one. Perhaps you're networking a lot and giving your card out to every potential business partner you meet, but few opportunities are coming to fruition. If this is your situation, your input-to-output ratio is 1:1, and your business is in a state of uncertainty.

Above this line, your business is healthy. When you publish a new piece of content, it generates a significant number of leads. If you need more leads, you're confident that you know how to find them. Your input-to-output ratio is 1:10, and you feel certain about your ability to create new business.

Finally, your business may be thriving. You know that each time you venture into your market, you can create a deluge of leads, as many as you can possibly handle. You have control of the lead lever, and sometimes you need to turn it off because you don't have the personnel to manage anymore. Your input-to-output ratio is 1:100, and you feel bulletproof.

Unless your ability to generate leads is already bulletproof (in which case, why are you reading this book?), I'm confident that the tools described in the following chapters can take you to the next level.

Think for a moment about how that would impact your business.

Perhaps you've had the experience of talking to a less-than-ideal client on the phone. You don't want to take them on, but you have bills to pay, and you have only a few other leads. You agree to work with them, wishing you could say no and secretly wanting to punch yourself in the face. When you have an abundance of leads, your sales conversations genuinely revolve around whether you and your prospect are a good fit. If you're not, you can decline and feel good about it because your ideal clients are waiting to connect with you.

I KNOW HOW YOU FEEL

Imagine a Pee Wee football game. With twelve seconds on the clock, little Toby's team is down by five.

The snap comes, and Toby runs a pass route, looking for space. The quarterback sees him and drops a shoulder to avoid the sack. He spins, sets himself, and throws a Hail Mary in Toby's general direction.

Toby sees the ball coming and jostles for space with the defensive back. As the ball reaches them, the defender throws up an arm and deflects it. Toby reacts quickly, spins, and collects it just before it hits the ground.

Now he's running. It's him against the clock. Four, three, two, one…he crosses the line with barely a second to spare. Touchdown! Toby breaks into a wild celebration and looks up in search of his parents.

Unfortunately, they're not there. No one is. The game was being played in front of an empty stadium. Does Toby's achievement still feel so special? Does his triumph still taste sweet, or is it hollow and empty?

I think most of us would agree that all the joy has gone out of it. Human beings are social creatures. We live to connect with others, and those connections give our lives meaning. The people you want to reach with your marketing want to connect with you.

Some years ago, I was working at my desk around 1:00 a.m., as entrepreneurs do. My then-wife knocked on the door and said: "Nic, we need to talk."

I don't believe that *any* good has ever come from those words, uttered in the context of a marriage. Instantly, I started to wonder what I'd done wrong. Had I failed to take the garbage out? Not collected the groceries? Something else? Over the next few minutes, I listened incredulously as she told me that since the very beginning of our marriage three and a half years earlier, she had been engaging in a string of extramarital affairs.

Stupidly, the next question that came out of my mouth was, "With whom?"

At the time, I was a pastor. She proceeded to list so many members of my congregation that it was a relief when she mentioned someone I *didn't* know. That night was the start of a downward spiral in my life. A few months later, I had lost my bank account and my house, and I was sleeping on a friend's couch.

Well-meaning people tried to tell me that I would be OK. I wanted to hit them. How did they know it was going to be OK? They had *no idea* what I was going through.

One person, however, did something very different. Despite my resistance, he persuaded me to join him for coffee. As we sat in Starbucks, he looked me in the eye and said, "Nic, I know how you feel."

The key distinction here is that he *did* know how I felt. He, too, was a pastor, and he had found himself in a very similar situation about four years earlier. He told me his story, and he reassured me that it was possible to get through the hell I was experiencing. When he told me it was going to be OK, I believed him. He knew how I felt.

Why am I telling you this? What on earth does it have to do with Facebook marketing?

I've come to believe that "I know how you feel" is one of the most powerful phrases in the English language. Your ability to connect with your potential clients, and to demonstrate that you understand their situation, will determine your marketing success.

As a marketer, you have one job: connect with your prospects in a way that releases as many happy hormones as possible. Good copywriting is not measured by how well your prospects understand you. It is measured by how well they feel that *you* understand *them*.

Allow me to repeat that. Good copywriting is not measured by how well your prospects understand you. It is measured by how well they feel that you understand them. When you know how to give people that experience, Facebook is the most powerful plat-  form on the planet for turning your investment into huge returns. To give you a sense of how much business I do through Facebook, my agency spends, on average, anywhere from $1 million to $3 million a month on Facebook with only a handful of clients. A recent campaign generated 92,209 leads at an average cost of $0.77 per lead in only twelve days.

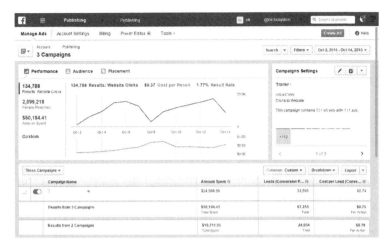

In terms of income, another recent campaign brought in approximately $306,000, using an ad spend in the region of $1,700. That's an astronomical ROI.

At a higher tier, a further campaign generated an income in excess of $1.2 million from an advertising investment of $98,000. The ROI was (relatively) much lower, but the total amount of revenue was huge for a campaign that ran for just twenty days.

Another campaign generated more than $3.2 million in only twenty-seven days.

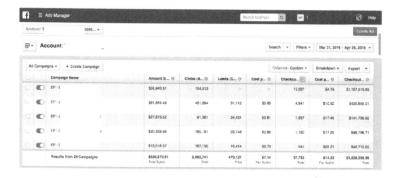

As Neil Patel puts it, nobody buys a mattress. Everyone just wants a good night's sleep. If you want to succeed on Facebook, you need to remember that no one is interested in what you're selling. They are only interested in connecting with someone who can solve their problems.

HOW TO USE THIS BOOK

I used to attend a lot of live seminars. Usually, I would absorb a huge amount of material, come home feeling inspired, and then realize that I had created four months' worth of work for myself in one weekend. Most of the time, that was the cue for me to file the material from the seminar under "I'll never look at this again."

It's impossible for a book to wholly re-create the experience of participation in a live event or the sense of excitement that comes with gathering in a room with people on a similar journey.

Nonetheless, this book is designed for you to engage with it actively. As you work your way through it, ask yourself the questions you encounter. Use the information it contains to determine your market, hone your message, and build your magnet.

There are two types of learning: just-in-case learning and just-in-time learning.

Just-in-case learning is found in mainstream education. You don't need to know the geography of the United States now, but it may come in useful someday.

Just-in-time learning occurs when material you've been seeking comes to you exactly when you need it, and you can use it to make a tangible difference in your life.

I hope that when it reaches you, this book will provide you with just-in-time learning. I want you to apply the principles and lessons you find here to transform your marketing.

Initially, don't be too concerned about getting your ads *right*. A lot of entrepreneurs are perfectionists, and they want to get everything right. Sometimes it's better simply to get things *done*.

An acceptable ad that makes it to the page is far, far better than a perfect idea that remains stuck in your head, especially the first few times you write for Facebook. Be willing to trust your instincts. Thinking too much can lead to analysis paralysis and prevent you from ever publishing your ad. Don't be afraid to collaborate with people whose opinions you trust.

Finally, as we move into the second part of this book, I invite you to ask yourself whether you're serving or selling. Some people, when I ask them this question, tell me that they serve through their sales. No. You have a choice.

> Good copywriting is not measured by how well your prospects understand you. It is measured by how well they feel that you understand them.

I'm known in my marketplace for providing the absolute maximum amount of value possible. That attitude works better for me than any sales trick or copy technique.

Whatever you do, and whatever form your business takes, genuinely seeking to serve people will win you more leads and more business than any other method.

You may be worried that if you take a service orientation, people will take advantage of your generosity. You may be worried that showing up vulnerably and transparently in your market will damage your credibility. You may be frustrated that everything you've tried so far has sunk without trace.

Take it from someone who failed consistently in the Internet marketing game for years and who can now legitimately lay claim to being the best Facebook marketer in the business. Placing yourself in service is the only way to experience true success. Bear with me, and I'll show you how to turn those anxieties and frustrations into leads. I've been there. I know how you feel.

Take the time to assess where you are on the lead-generation ladder. Is your lead generation blocked, trickling, flowing, or flooding? Understanding your current situation is the first step to creating change.

How well are you communicating with your audience? Do they feel that you understand how they feel? If not, how can you improve your communication style?

PART TWO

STRATEGY: THE FOUR M's

"Creativity without strategy is called 'art.' Creativity with strategy is called 'advertising.'"
– **Jef I. Richards**, Professor and Chair, Department of Advertising and Public Relations, Michigan State University

4

THE FIRST M: MARKET

"The consumer isn't a moron; she is your wife."

– **David Ogilvy**

Before he passed away, Gary Halbert was one of the greatest direct-response copywriters on the planet. He catalyzed millions, if not billions, of dollars' worth of transactions, and he believed that any problem could be solved with a sales letter.

In an interview, he was asked for advice on his number one sales technique. Most people anticipated that he would focus on an element of the sales letter, such as the headline or the image. Instead, he surprised his entire audience by responding, "The most important element of sales is identifying a hungry crowd." Think about that for a moment.

Who is the easiest person to sell food to? Someone who hasn't eaten in days. If you were lost in the desert and I appeared with a canister full of water, you'd give practically anything for a drink. Those bits of paper in your wallet would seem utterly worthless in comparison with the opportunity to slake your thirst.

Far too many people focus their energies on the delivery mechanism for their product or their anticipated result, forgetting that their business is driven by the desires of the market, not by their desire to bring their product or service to market.

This is a profound and humbling perspective shift.

Marketing is more like Judo than boxing. Successful marketers don't force their products into the hands of their prospects, pounding them with features and benefits until they submit. Instead, they seek to understand their market and respond intelligently, providing a solution to a problem their potential clients and customers already experience.

Your business is driven by the desires of the market, not by your desire to bring your product or service to market.

Those who start with the belief that they have a great product and try to push it into the market are treating marketing like boxing. By contrast, what is the most well-known fast-food chain in the world? What is the most successful soft drink?

You could start with a terrible product and a hungry crowd

would still buy it. I'm not suggesting you do this. You probably care about the quality of your product and the integrity of your business, as you should. The key point here is that the quality of your marketing plays a far greater role in determining the success of your business than the quality of your product.

The corollary of this principle is that it makes no sense to try and engage with everyone. That's the Baskin-Robbins mistake: by trying to be everything to everyone, you run the risk of not making a meaningful contribution to anyone.

When I started in marketing, I called myself a "marketing consultant." Who did I serve? Anyone who wanted my services. When I realized the potential of Facebook as an advertising platform, I began to style myself as a "Facebook marketing consultant." This was more precise, but it still didn't allow me to pinpoint my ideal clients.

Now I craft Facebook marketing strategies for high-growth companies. I regularly say no to clients whom I don't want to work with or those who don't match my definition of an ideal client. On average, I turn down $250,000–$400,000 of work per quarter, purely because I know that the client isn't a good fit for my skills and the way I like to work.

> The most important element of sales is identifying a hungry crowd.

This path is open to you, too. By enacting the right strategies, you could be only ninety days from becoming a microcelebrity and a trusted authority in your marketplace. Don't be the moth fluttering around desperately in search of work. Be the flame that attracts your ideal clients to your door.

This approach has several advantages. When you market well, you won't *need* to sell hard. Clients will come to you prequalified, asking you whether you have time to work with them. You will feel able to say no.

You will have the opportunity to work with your dream clients and develop the name recognition that comes from being a celebrity in your niche. They will be grateful and appreciative of your abilities and attention.

How do you reach this level? Start by picking your pond.

PICK YOUR POND

Would you rather be a big fish in a small pond or a small fish in a big pond?

When I ask this question at live events, the audience is usually split fifty-fifty. Some believe that by being a small fish in a big pond, they will never run out of potential clients.

This is a scarcity mentality, predicated on the belief that it's difficult to attract ideal clients. When you're a big fish in a small pond, that isn't a problem.

The Pareto principle, coined by the economist Vilfredo Pareto, famously states that "80 percent of the effects come from 20 percent of the causes." This could mean, for example, that 20 percent of a firm's salespeople deliver 80 percent of the organization's business, or that 80 percent of your revenue comes from 20 percent of your clients.

I suggest taking this principle a step further. Understand the 20 percent of your clients that bring you the greatest value and that you most enjoy working with, and start to look for patterns. Use these patterns to identify the top 20 percent of the 20 percent, the 4 percent of your clients whose business is most valuable to you.

YOUR PERFECT MARKET —

4%

20%

Greatest Value

All Other Clients 80%

This is the Kusmich principle, the 96/4 rule. Your perfect market lies in just 4 percent of your potential clients.

When you start to connect exclusively with this segment of your market, you will soon find that sales conversations are dramatically simplified. Instead of handling objections and attempting to convince people to buy from you, your discussions will center on whether you and your clients are a good fit.

A friend of mine, Tom, presents a perfect example.

Tom works in the search engine optimization (SEO) space in California, a huge pond. By identifying the 4 percent of his market that represents his ideal clients, he decided to specialize in offering SEO services to plastic surgeons in Southern California. He started charging those clients a $10,000 per month retainer and built a million-dollar business literally overnight.

Tom's story represents two essential elements of finding your ideal clients: they should be underserved, and they should be affluent. Underserved clients will be more willing to pay for services they value. Affluent clients have the means to do so.

This is what's known as a blue ocean, an untapped market with little or no competition. It hardly needs to be said that finding a blue ocean that matches your skills and preferences can supercharge your business.

To pick your pond, ask yourself what you stand for and against. For example, if you stand for human rights, you naturally stand against violations of human rights. If you stand for a triple bottom-line approach to business, you stand against an approach that ignores social and environmental concerns.

Think about the top 20 percent of your clients, those you most enjoy working with and that bring you the greatest value. What makes them ideal? What do they do, or not do, that makes you want to work with them?

One of my favorite qualities in clients is trust. I don't like those who try to micromanage me. I much prefer those who let me get on with my job and give them a weekly report.

Be aware of what you like about the top 20 percent of your clients, and also what you *don't* like about them. This will help you to understand which ones constitute your magic 4 percent.

Now start to look for similarities and group them together. Tom singled out high-income plastic surgeons in Southern California as his key demographic.

What's yours?

Do you like working with small companies? Large companies? Is there a particular segment of your market that excites you? The more precisely you can identify your "pond," the more effectively you can target them.

This is to everyone's benefit. Remember, you're looking to understand not only the people you most want to work with but also those you can *serve most effectively.* This isn't a sales exercise; it's a matchmaking exercise.

When you've picked your pond, the next step is to get even more granular and recognize your ideal client in much more detail.

This is where you find your fish.

Relocating to Toronto

Susan (not her real name) ran a thriving day-care business for children in her home city of Vancouver until her husband was relocated to Toronto for work, and she chose to join him. In a brand-new city, offering many childcare options, she needed a way to stand out from the crowd.

When she came to me, she was frustrated and short of ideas, unsure of what to do. She knew she could build a new business from the ground up but also that it would take years to build the level of trust and connection she had enjoyed in Toronto. She had few contacts and little name recognition, and the thought of starting again from scratch after seven years in Vancouver depressed her.

I started by asking her to reflect on her experiences at her original day-care center and to tell me about aspects of it that made it unique or unusual. She explained that without setting out to do so, the center had attracted a lot of children suffering from some kind of brain trauma, often as a result of accidents.

Parents felt very comfortable entrusting their children to Susan's care, and the center was stocked with the tools and resources brain-injured children required. In addition, the staff members were exceptionally well trained and experienced at looking after kids with brain traumas.

This information became the core of her new niche. Instead of trying to open a day-care center appealing to everyone, she decided to specialize in serving the families of brain-injured children.

The next step was to create several pieces of content that spoke to her audience and could be easily read, digested, and shared. For example, she put together a report detailing seven essential questions any parent of a child who has suffered head trauma should ask prospective day-care centers.

This report offered lots of useful information while still being quick to read and easy to understand. At the time, her day-care center was the only one in the city that could answer the seven questions effectively. This was a brilliant strategic move, positioning her both as an authority and as the only person in the city who truly understood the pains and frustrations of parents with brain-injured children and could meet them effectively.

She used her blog, other related blogs, and Facebook to engage with her community and connect with her projected audience. These people met the key criteria of any potential market: they were underserved because few day-care centers in the city had the expertise and experience to look after their children, and they were sufficiently affluent to afford Susan's services.

The strategy worked exceptionally well for her. From being virtually unknown in Toronto and struggling to establish a foothold in the city, she was soon running the leading day-care in the city for children with past or current head traumas. Her business in Vancouver took seven years to build. In Toronto, she was able to make a significant splash in her chosen pond within weeks.

This came about because she identified exactly whom she wanted to serve and produced content that connected with those people. With a little advertising to drive interest in her content, she was soon able to position herself as a specialist in day-care provision for brain-injured kids and grow her business dramatically.

This story illustrates the twofold value of finding your blue ocean. Not only does it boost your business, but it also enables you to serve the people you most want to serve and to whom you can offer the greatest value.

FIND YOUR FISH

Leo Burnett was a great advertising executive, who once said, "If you can't turn yourself into your ideal customer, you have no business doing what you're doing." To serve your clients effectively, you need to understand who they are and recognize their ideal futures.

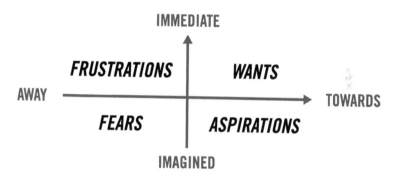

As you can see from the diagram, we are always moving toward or away from either immediate or imagined consequences.

Immediate consequences are real. A lack of leads, creating a scarcity of business, is an immediate consequence. If that's the situation for you, it's a frustration, and you want to move away from it as quickly as possible. On the other hand, you may have some leads but wish you had more. In this case, you will seek to move immediately toward more leads. This is a want.

A third possibility is that you look into the future and imagine that you won't have as many leads as you need to sustain your business. That's a fear that you will want to move away from.

Finally, you may imagine a situation where you have all the leads you need and have the freedom to turn away people who don't fit the profile of your ideal client. That's an aspiration you can move toward.

Most people tend to be more motivated by the inclination to move away from fears and frustrations than by the desire to move toward the fulfillment of wants and aspirations.

To connect effectively with your ideal clients, you need to understand their emotional drivers. What are their fears, frustrations, wants, and aspirations? This information is gold dust. It determines how you market to them and which of their "hot buttons" you need to trigger to motivate them to take action.

RIDE THE WAVE

What happens to a surfer who misses a wave and tries, too late, to catch the swell? He or she gets pounded to the bottom of the ocean.

The same (metaphorically) is true for marketers who fail to address their market as it *currently* exists, not as they wish it was. At a recent networking event, a woman gave me a postcard bearing an image of a word cloud. On the back of the card were her name and contact details. She told me that she'd love to work with me and invited me to contact her. What do you think I did with the postcard?

If you guessed that I ran eagerly to the phone after the event and dialed her number, guess again.

This isn't intended to reflect negatively on her. She may well be a lovely person. The problem, from my perspective, is that she wasn't marketing to me in the present. If there ever was a wave consisting of postcards with word clouds, that wave has passed.

Several decades ago, Kellogg's cereals concentrated exclusively on its flagship products, such as Corn Flakes. When public opinion began to turn toward high-fiber foods, the company adapted and began to promote All-Bran and Raisin Bran. This move saved its business. If it hadn't seen the wave coming and changed its focus, it would have drowned. Toyota did the same with the shift toward lowering carbon emissions and making cars more eco-friendly and now leads the market in hybrid vehicles.

> If you can't turn yourself into your ideal customer, you have no business doing what you're doing.

There is no sense in ignoring the direction in which your market is moving. Some years ago, kettlebells were the hottest fitness craze out there. Now kettlebells are over and CrossFit is hugely popular. It doesn't matter how good your product is. If you're marketing kettlebells today, you're selling yesterday's trend.

Several months ago, I realized that the biggest hazard that advertisers faced on Facebook was the likelihood of having their account shut down. I wrote a comprehensive blog post explaining how to avoid having your Facebook ads account shut down. Even today, I still receive business inquiries as a result of that post. I've had people tell me that they printed it out and kept it by their computer to refer to whenever they're writing advertising copy for Facebook.

I saw the wave, and I rode it. For maximum recognition, interest, and shares (which are basically free advertising), you need to do the same. Look for the waves in your industry and ask yourself how you can position yourself in relation to them.

Importantly, this doesn't necessarily require you to affirm a popular position. One of the most effective strategies is to call out a wave and talk about why it's nonsense. For example, if most marketers in your industry are saying that webinars are the best way to convert clients, produce a smart, well-argued piece about why webinars suck and what people should do instead. By doing this, you place yourself right at the head of an emerging wave.

However you choose to position yourself in relation to the waves in your field of expertise, you need to be aware of them, and you need to find a way to ride them.

BECOME THE BIG FISH

A very well-known figure in the financial industry called me recently. He told me that, strangely, my name kept coming up whenever he spoke to people about Facebook marketing.

He was part of a mastermind group, and other members of the group kept talking about me. He held an event in San Diego and heard my name again. Finally, a young guy he was mentoring spoke to him about me at dinner. Having heard my name from so many different sources, he became convinced that he needed to call me.

This kind of experience is flattering. It's also entirely deliberate. You can be the architect of your own image and generate massive name recognition.

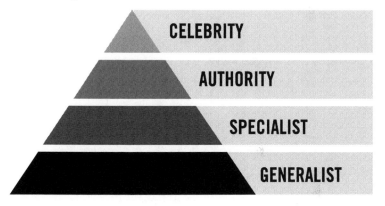

Take a look at figure 4.2. You'll see that there are four different positions you can hold in any given market.

The generalist serves anyone. In the real estate market, for example, a generalist sells houses. Above the generalist comes the specialist. The specialist carves out a niche where he or she is recognized as an expert. In the real estate business, a specialist might choose to concentrate on preconstruction lakeside condominiums.

Above the specialist, you'll find the authority. The authority has the gravitas to make pronouncements about his or her field of expertise and the reputation of knowing what he or she is talking about. Until he sold his business, Robert Kiyosaki was a good example of an authority in real estate.

Finally, we have the celebrity. The celebrity is renowned throughout his or her marketplace and commands respect and admiration. Before Donald Trump embarked on the journey toward becoming president of the United States, he was a celebrity in the real estate sphere, commanding $1 million for a sixty-minute keynote speech.

If you're currently a generalist, you need to aim toward becoming a specialist. If you're already a specialist, it's time for you to move into the role of authority. Why? There are several reasons.

The higher you move on this pyramid, the more you can charge for your services. In addition, you'll find that clients start coming to you, rather than vice versa, and that those you attract will be much easier to work with. The prestige that comes with your higher status will enable you to get more done in less time and reach a large audience of higher quality clients.

How can you boost your profile and ultimately ascend to celebrity status?

The first method is through association. The moment I first started working with Joe Polish was an enormous step up for me. Joe is one of the biggest names in marketing, and he knows *a lot* of people. Suddenly, my phone wouldn't stop ringing because Joe Polish was telling people they should call me.

Even better, these new clients weren't quizzing me about my fees or deliverability. They were *asking me whether I had availability to work with them.* That's the power of association. An excellent strategy to build up your name recognition is to start a podcast and interview significant figures in your industry. You will naturally be associated with them and benefit accordingly.

A second method of establishing celebrity is through affiliation. If you tell people that you write for *Entrepreneur* magazine, they will be impressed and assume that you know what you're talking about. Choose your affiliations carefully. Writing for the *Huffington Post*, for example, doesn't carry the same authority as writing for a publication that's widely respected in your field.

A third, perhaps counterintuitive, approach is to raise your prices. There's something appealing to the human psyche about paying more for quality services. Sometimes the easiest way we have to recognize the authority in our market is how much he or she charges.

Finally, deliver outstanding content. Content may not be king anymore, but it's still very important. By producing content that identifies a problem your ideal clients experience and that addresses it effectively, you will be perceived as an authority in your market.

CAST YOUR NET

To celebrate our most recent wedding anniversary, my wife and I visited the beautiful island of Bora-Bora. While diving with sharks, we noticed that one of the sharks had a much smaller fish attached to its belly.

Why hadn't the fish become shark food? Our dive master explained that the fish, called the remora, was performing a service for the shark. By feeding off bits of loose skin and excess food, it kept the shark clean. In exchange, the shark didn't eat it.

Whatever marketplace you're in, you'll find that there are already people who have done the heavy lifting of building an audience. In the personal development space, for example, you'll find Tony Robbins and Brendon Burchard. In the weight loss arena, Jillian Michaels is a leader.

Brendon Burchard spends at least $1,000 per day on Facebook to build his audience. If you're in the personal development space, you can literally target your message at people who are fans of Burchard. Let someone else do the heavy lifting, at least when you're starting out in Facebook marketing.

On the savanna, lions don't wander aimlessly around in search of herds of antelope. They stake out watering holes, where they are guaranteed to find plenty of game and where those animals are at their most vulnerable.

Obviously, you're not trying to eat your ideal clients! Nonetheless, the principle is very similar. By targeting the places where they are already gathered, you can reach them far more cheaply and effectively than you would by searching the whole of Facebook for them. Don't try to be the shark; be the remora.

For an epic infographic that details all the ways in which you can customize your Facebook ads to reach specific audiences, visit www.nicsblog.com/target.

MOVING TO MESSAGE

Now that you've finished this chapter, you should understand the value of getting very granular about your ideal clients and how to reach them. To succeed, you need to locate your "hungry crowd," the people who are already interested in what you have to say, and feed them.

Know whom you want to work with, and don't be afraid to say no to people who don't fit into the category of your ideal clients. Those people will be hard work and, while they may bring income into your business, will ultimately drain you of energy and enthusiasm.

When you pick your pond, find your fish, ride the wave, become the big fish, and cast your net, you will be able to recognize your ideal clients and communicate strategically in a way that makes you attractive to them.

Your next step is to decide what to say. It's time to master your message.

Assess and understand your 4 percent. Who are the 20 percent of the 20 percent of your market that you are most motivated, and most suited, to serve?

What are their fears, frustrations, wants, and aspirations? What current market trends can you capitalize on?

Measure your business against the Positioning Pyramid. Where are you (generalist, specialist, authority, or celebrity)? Who are the sharks in your industry that present opportunities for you to be a remora?

5

THE SECOND M: MESSAGE

"No matter what people tell you, words and ideas can change the world."

– Robin Williams

My wife and I were walking along the Santa Monica Pier. Amid the rich, diverse crowd of people, there was a preacher.

He was very old school, and his message was loaded with fire and brimstone. All sinners, he claimed, should repent their licentiousness or burn eternally in the pits of hell. I watched him for a while and noticed that the passersby were completely ignoring him. To the vast majority of people on that pier, he might as well not have existed.

This isn't a comment on his religion. Behind the rather intimidating front, I'm sure he had some positive things to say. It's a comment on his marketing strategies. The way he delivered his message left his prospective audience completely cold.

You're in business to change the world and work with people you love, but if no one is listening, you won't have the impact you desire. It doesn't matter how valuable your message is; unless you deliver it in a way that catches the attention of your ideal clients, it will be ignored.

Some years back, before I truly understood this, I used to hold webinars where I would deliver some great content and conclude by pitching my services to participants. When the webinars concluded, I sat back and waited for my e-mail to light up with sale notifications.

Instead of the passionate response I anticipated, however, I saw nothing. Crickets. The way I delivered my message wasn't reaching people.

To master your message, you need to know whom you want to connect with, what they need, and what you will say to them. How successfully you do this determines whether people will pay attention, engage with you, and ultimately purchase your products or services.

Failure to frame your message effectively will leave you bobbing in a sea of sameness, indistinct from the hundreds, or thousands, of people out there offering a similar service to yours. To your market, your message will seem fuzzy, just more noise in an already noisy world.

Don't be noise. Be a song.

Perhaps you're aware of the nae nae song ("Watch Me [Whip/ Nae Nae]" by Silentó). It's a catchy tune incorporating specific dance moves. There's a YouTube video of a Pee Wee football game in which the players are preparing for the next hike.[1] Suddenly, the song is played over the stadium PA system, and the players start to dance.

Even as the game continues and a touchdown is scored, the kids can barely concentrate on the game. They're more interested in showing off their moves. When your jam comes on, you gotta work it.

The same is true of marketing. When you truly master your message, it will be as appealing to your audience as a song they know and love. The right message, distributed in the right way, will capture attention and responses just as powerfully as a popular hit.

I've been in the room when Joe Polish made an offer of a Gary Halbert marketing letter to seminar attendees and told them to line up at the back of the room if they wanted it. The queue was forty-five minutes long.

How do you put yourself on the path toward this level of response? There are five essential principles.

---

1 https://www.youtube.com/watch?v=BK6eEFd5Ko8

RAGE AGAINST BEIGE

Five or six years ago, the attention of your audience was a given. Marketers released new content and felt confident that people would watch it. Not anymore.

Traditional wisdom states that marketing is a game of influence and persuasion.

Facebook marketers who are focused on influence and persuasion at the expense of capturing their viewers' attention will never have the opportunity to influence or persuade. People won't watch their videos or read their blog posts.

How many tabs do you have open when you're browsing the Internet? If you're anything like me, you probably keep upward of twenty open at any one time.

Attention is scarce, and we're highly adept at tuning out any content that doesn't offer us value.

How often do you look to the right of your Facebook newsfeed? Probably never. You know that you'll see ads.

In the 1970s, the average person saw about five hundred advertisements per day.[2] Today, that number is around five thousand. We're highly sophisticated consumers, and our radars are tuned

---

2 http://www.cbsnews.com/news/cutting-through-advertising-clutter/

to avoid unwanted advertising.

If your message blends in with the crowd, so will you. You'll be lost in the crowd. To attract attention, you need to be a breath of fresh air in a stale market, saying something that makes people sit up and take notice.

Ask yourself this: What's the last piece of commercial content you remember? Why? What made it stand out? Put yourself in the role of the consumer. What would it take, in a jaded marketplace, to make your eyes light up?

START WITH WHY

Every message has two components: the *what* and the *why*. Both are important, but the latter takes precedence.

For the purposes of this book, I'm going to assume that you already have a good product or service. The problem is that there are lots of other people who also have a good product or service. What separates yours from theirs? Why should potential clients or customers choose you over them?

Have you ever walked into a car dealership, ready to buy, and been so repelled by the salesperson that you walked out again? What happened there? You wanted the product, but something about the interaction you had didn't *feel* right. There was no *resonance*. When deciding whom we want to do business with, an experience of connection is absolutely essential.

Simon Sinek, in his famous TED Talk, breaks down company activities into the *what*, the *how*, and the *why*. Every company knows *what* it does; some know *how* they do it; few know *why* they do it. Sinek's hypothesis is that people buy your *why*.

Let's use Apple as an example. Apple creates high-quality computers, phones, tablets, and other electronic devices. It does this by enlisting the smartest talent, the best technologies, and the latest industry insights.

Why does it do this? In Steve Jobs's iconic commencement address, given to students at Stanford University in 2005, he encourages them to "stay hungry, stay foolish." He tells stories of dropping out of college to follow his curiosity and of becoming aware of his own impending mortality. It's easy to see how these experiences underpin Apple's famous motto: "Think Different."

Apple's *why* is to create pioneering tools for people who are pushing the envelope, living at the cutting edge, and changing the world. It does this by recruiting top talent and acquiring outstanding companies, and the results are the ubiquitous computers, phones, and tablets that are so much a part of contemporary life.

Do you see how starting with *why* completely changes your perception of Apple as a company?

Now let's take it a step further. Why do people line up overnight to buy a new iPhone on the day of its release when they could wait fourteen days and walk into any Apple store in the country and buy one? Is there something about the device itself? Nothing that would rationally justify the intense effort these people invest in their purchase.

They're in the grip of something much more powerful and primal. They want to be *first*. The reasoning behind their decision to pitch a tent and spend a night in the cold, staking their claim for a brand-new iPhone is not taken at the level of technology. It's taken at the level of identity.

This is where Simon Sinek's perspective breaks down. It's not simply Apple's *why* that generates such devotion. It's the *why* of its customers. What's more powerful than your *why*? The *why* of the people you want to sell to. When you understand why people want your product or service and speak directly to that desire, you will inspire them.

Science has recently demonstrated that we have three brains. The frontal lobe, or the neocortex, is the rational brain. It's the newest part of the brain, controlling complex thinking and reasoning, but it has a relatively small role in decision-making.

The emotional brain and the reptilian brain, which control emotional and instinctual expression, play a far larger role in determining the choices we make. Like it or not, purchasing decisions are driven by emotion and instinct.

You're doubtless aware of Uber, the ride-hailing platform that has taken the taxi industry by storm over the past few years. Probably, you've used Uber's services at least once. Have you considered what you're really buying?

I took the time to lift some images from the Uber website. The slogans are extremely revealing. "Moving people," Uber proclaims. "Getting more (time, value, convenience; you can have it all)." "Sharing experiences." "Owning the moment." What, you may wonder, does any of this have to do with calling a car to get from point A to point B?

Uber Technologies Inc.

The answer is that the marketers at Uber aren't really selling the idea that you need a taxi. They're selling an experience.

I recently attended a conference in Phoenix with some heavy hitters. When I arrived at the airport, what do you think I did? I requested that I be picked up in a Mercedes. The marketing got in my head. In the end, there was no one there to witness my arrival, but that didn't matter. I didn't want to simply *arrive*. I wanted to "own the moment."

People won't remember what you say. They will remember how they felt when you said it. Communicate your values and the things that move you. Make a connection.

Real Men Have Beards

The Dollar Beard Club is founded on the belief that facial hair is an essential component of masculinity. That stance was conceived in direct opposition to the more traditional Dollar Shave Club, and it permeates every aspect of the company's messaging.

The company's marketing taps into the belief that growing a beard is a primal statement and that bearded men are superior. It offers a rallying cry that speaks to hundreds of thousands of men.

It's a polarizing message. Not everyone wants to grow a beard. For those who do, however, the Dollar Beard Club offers a sense of belonging to a tribe of men who are committed to making their beards as long and luxurious as possible. Every marketing message the company produces reinforces that approach, often in a way that's very funny and irreverent.

The company's messaging encourages men to develop a strong emotional connection to their beards and to think of having a beard as a source of pride and status. A strong line is drawn between insiders (those who have beards) and outsiders (those who do not), creating an aura of exclusivity and power. Of course, most men can *choose* to grow a beard, so entry to the exclusive club is attainable to anyone willing to nurture his facial hair.

The Dollar Beard Club was willing to risk alienating some people in order to magnetize others. In commercials and promotional material, the company's CEO plays the leader of the tribe: a man who is almost Viking-like in his intensity and hirsuteness. Creating attractive characters is an essential part of forging a connection with clients, and the Dollar Beard Club does this exceptionally well.

Sometimes it's tempting to dilute your message in an effort to avoid offending people, but often, moving in the opposite direction can be more effective. If you make a strong statement, some people won't like you, but others will. If you try to please everyone, the chances are that most people will be relatively comfortable with you, but few will feel inspired to take action.

With such a strong message, it was relatively easy to boost the Dollar Beard Club's sales. Prior to working with me, it received a lot of interest and many hits on its website, but relatively few of those were converting to sales. It shifted its focus toward giving and relationship-building and developed a loyal community that has made the Dollar Beard Club into a multimillion-dollar business.

FRAME YOUR *WHAT*

Your *why* is important, but it's not enough on its own. Without your *what*, people won't know what you actually do. The problem is that unless you find a way of differentiating your *what* from everyone else's, it won't interest people.

I run a Facebook advertising agency. So what? So do many other people. What distinguishes my Facebook advertising agency from anyone else's? David Ogilvy is sometimes known as the "father of advertising." He created a model to explain the different levels marketers can play at when describing their *what*.

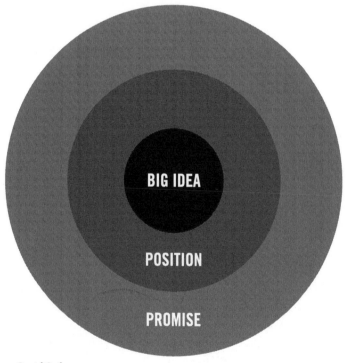

David Ogilvy

The first is the promise. Popularized by Brendon Burchard, this is what we can do for people. It's quite straightforward, and everyone has one (clue: that's the problem).

Beyond the promise comes your position in your market. If I've heard your name before, or you can demonstrate that you have authority, I'll likely pay more attention to your message than I will if you give me no reason to believe that other people trust and respect you.

The really powerful move, however, is to gain preeminence, using what Ogilvy referred to as the "big idea."

Do you remember the success of P90X? In a landscape where most programs were offering easy, painless weight loss, P90X entered the arena claiming that it would make anyone who tried it hurt, cry, and crawl but ultimately lose weight and get fit.

The product's promise was that it would cause people to lose weight. The position was directly opposed to the trend, at the time, of promoting weight loss as easy. How did P90X establish preeminence? What was the big idea?

Perhaps you remember. The company marketing P90X claimed that the huge range of different movements contained in the workout would create "muscle confusion." By asking the body to repeatedly move in unaccustomed ways, the workout supposedly prevented the metabolism from stabilizing and accelerated weight loss. Was this true? I don't know, but it turned P90X from a regular weight loss company into a billion-dollar brand.

In Canada, every bank offers unlimited checking accounts. CIBC, however, was the first bank to shout this idea from the rooftops. Even though every other bank offered the same facility, CIBC turned unlimited checking into a big idea simply by talking about it and achieved preeminence in its market.

What promise do you make to your clients?

What is your position in your market?

How will you achieve preeminence? What is your big idea?

FIND YOUR ANGLE
Mindfulness matters.

Sure it does, but anyone can say the same thing. Now that you've found your big idea, how will you make it unique? How will you turn it into intellectual property? If you want to be more productive, do the hard things first. That's a great tip, but it could have come from anyone.

That is, until Brian Tracy wrote a book entitled *Eat That Frog: 21 Great Ways to Stop Procrastinating and Get More Done in Less Time.* Suddenly, he owned the concept, and no one else could base a book on the same concept without appearing to have copied him.

For P90X, the concept of muscle confusion was distilled into a ninety-day program of extreme power. For Apple, an all-in-one smart device that could be used to check e-mail, make calls, take photos, surf the Internet, and run apps became the iPhone.

Seth Godin created the concept of purple cows. Imagine that you were out walking with your kids, and you came upon a field of cows. As you walked through the field, you noticed that one of the cows was very different from the others: it was purple.

How would you respond? Most people, in the age of smartphones, would take a few selfies of themselves and their kids by the cow and post them to social media networks. Probably, the photos would quickly spread, creating free "advertising" for the cow.

A purple cow is a *remarkable* event. If you want to attract people with your big idea, you need to package it in a way that inspires people to talk about it.

Tony Robbins freely admits that when he first started to lead weekend seminars, very little of his material was original. Most of it came from giants of the personal development industry, such as Jim Rohn and Zig Ziglar. What did he do to make his weekends remarkable? He laid burning coals in the parking lot and encouraged participants to walk across them.

It's important to recognize that he understood that his fire walks were essentially safe. They were designed to help people overcome a mental block, not transcend the laws of physics. Nonetheless, what do you think people said when colleagues asked them what they did that weekend? Do you imagine they talked in general terms about the seminar they'd been to and tried to rehash some of the material Tony covered? Of course not. They said they'd *walked on burning coals*.

What is your purple cow? What is it about your business that makes it remarkable? There are four primary ways to stand out.

The Contrarian Approach

Whatever your field of business, most marketing messages are combinations of angles that have previously proven popular. They become staid and predictable. This is the perfect environment for you to boldly proclaim the opposite.

P90X is the perfect example. In an environment where every health and fitness product was peddling the idea that weight loss was easy, P90X said it was difficult but worth it. Perhaps your peers believe that running webinars is the best client conversion mechanism, but you think that's a total myth.

Taking a position that subverts received wisdom in your market is an instant guarantee of attention, as long as you can speak with authority about the reasons your approach is better.

Make a Metaphor

I worked with a client who had created a system to attract

high-paying clients. "So what?" you may be asking. Everyone seems to have a system to attract high-paying clients.

Making the shift from generic to unique was as simple as changing the name of the program. The Velvet Rope method was born, and the client saw an immediate increase in lead volume, reduced cost per lead, and a boost in their sense of direction.

How to X without Y So You Can Z

This style of messaging can come across as a promise, but it's simple and direct and represents a good starting point or fallback strategy if you're looking for ways to think about how to frame your expertise:

- ▶ How to X (represents what your ideal prospect desires)
- ▶ Without Y (what your ideal prospect is looking to avoid)
- ▶ So you can Z (the real benefit that the prospect receives)

An example of this formula is "how to lose weight without exercise so you can fit into skinny jeans for your birthday party."

Focus on what your prospect wants to achieve, what they want to avoid, and the real benefit to them.

Create a Tool

This is a powerful strategy. Instead of telling people what to do, you simply give them a tool to accomplish their objectives. Why waste time telling them how you can help them when you can cut to the chase and simply help them? When they use the tool, they will remember that it came from you and associate their success with your teachings.

A tool needn't be complex. Checklists and resource guides are simple to create and easy to use, maximizing engagement.

POSITION THROUGH PERSONIFICATION

Personification generates resonance. Gary Vaynerchuk is a polarizing character. Some people love him; others hate him. It can't be denied, however, that the strong character he presents allows him to occupy a unique niche.

In the 2016 presidential race, both Bernie Sanders and Donald Trump presented strong characters. The Democrats declined to nominate Bernie for the presidency, while the Republicans, reluctantly at first, nominated Trump. Despite his polarizing public pronouncements, Trump ultimately won the election.

Subway completely reshaped the company's brand by introducing the character of Jared. As Jared lost weight eating Subway sandwiches, the brand morphed from being just another fast food company and started to be seen as a healthy alternative.

Flo from Progressive insurance may be annoying, but the actress who plays her is one of the most highly paid characters on television, because creating a relatable character, whether loved or loathed, drives massive engagement. Russell Brunson bases an entire training on teaching people how to establish an attractive character. If you want to develop your own character, you need four elements in place: a backstory, parables, character flaws, and polarity.

Backstory

Brendon Burchard has founded an entire business on his backstory. He was in a car in the Dominican Republic, driving late at night. He took a corner too fast, and the next thing he knew, he was standing on the roof of his car, his body bloody from a bad car accident, asking himself three questions: Did I live? Did I love? Did I matter? Every decision Brendon takes in his business is guided by those three questions.

The founders of TOMS noticed that they had an opportunity to bring shoes to people who couldn't afford them. This became the foundation of the TOMS promise that for every pair purchased, one pair will be donated to someone who needs them.

These backstories are like superhero origin stories. They define the meaning of a company's activities and form a context that informs everything they subsequently do.

Parables

A few years ago, I wanted to join an exclusive mastermind group. The guy who ran the group happened to be a client of mine. I made him a lot of money. I called him up and asked for a discount. He refused point blank, telling me that if I wanted to experience the full benefits of the group, it was essential that I invested financially in it.

What story do you think I tell potential clients when I'm on a webinar and I want them to pay full price for my products?

An advert for Dove went viral when it depicted sketches of women drawn first according to their own descriptions, then according to the descriptions of strangers meeting them for the first time. The sketches made the point that every woman is beautiful while simultaneously reinforcing the brand values of supporting natural beauty and using pure ingredients in the company's products.

How do you think this advert would have been received if Dove had simply released a statement saying that every woman is beautiful? How do you think my clients would respond if I simply told them that I wanted them to pay full price for my services?

A parable is a message wrapped into a story. The human brain loves stories.

Character Flaws

Superman is a powerful superhero, but he has a quintessential weakness: kryptonite. If he were totally invulnerable, would he be as appealing? His flaws and weaknesses make him relatable.

Don't hide your limitations; feature them. Proudly proclaim your imperfections, or explain that your product may not be for everyone. Not only will this naturally filter your audience, but it will also humanize your character. People who claim to be brilliant at everything appear untrustworthy; those who are highly skilled but not without blemishes appear authentic and trustworthy.

Buckley's cough syrup is advertised using the tag line "It tastes awful and it works." The company admits to imperfections and presents them front and center, turning them into a source of humor. Notice that the cough syrup is presented as fulfilling its primary purpose impeccably. It works. The drawback, in this context, appears minor, a small price to pay to feel better.

Polarity

Don't swim with the tide. That's a shortcut to being ignored.

You're probably familiar with the Rich Jerk. In real life, the guy behind the Rich Jerk character is nothing like him. The character plays an essential role, however. By creating polarity, the Rich Jerk generates interest, controversy, and debate.

One of Apple's most successful campaigns pitted Macs against PCs, with each brand represented by a character. The Mac character appeared young, hip, and connected, while the PC character seemed old, stagnant, and clueless.

IDENTIFY YOUR IDENTITY

It's time to get granular about your character.

There are four basic archetypes you can adopt: the leader, the adventurer/crusader, the reporter/evangelist, and the reluctant hero.

If you want to be perceived as a leader, your message to clients is that you know where they want to go and how to get there. Again, Donald Trump is an example of the leader archetype, whose message is essentially "I've got the plan. Follow me."

The adventurer/crusader is a more laidback archetype. As an adventurer, you're driven by the desire for new experiences and by your interest in causes you hold dear. Richard Branson is an outstanding example of an adventurer: he builds billion-dollar businesses but gives the impression that he's more interested in solving problems, such as how to transport people using clean energy and hanging out with his friends on his private island.

The reporter/evangelist is an ideal archetype to utilize if you don't have a solid reputation of your own to draw upon. Oprah Winfrey has built a global empire on interviewing people. Napoleon Hill, author of the most famous book about wealth ever written, was an unknown writer when he took it upon himself to ask some of the era's most successful businesspeople for the secrets of their wealth.

Finally, the reluctant hero is a good archetype to explore if you have a laidback personality. The message of the reluctant hero is that he or she has stumbled on something life changing, and now he or she feels a responsibility to share it with the world. Frodo Baggins was a reluctant hero. He found himself in possession of an all-powerful ring and pressed into a quest he hadn't asked for.

Which archetype suits your business and your personality? Take some time to think about the role you feel most drawn to, and consider how you can bring that archetype into your marketing.

Now let's think about some narratives you can place your character in.

Loss and Redemption

You had something, you lost it, and now you have it again. You were rich, you lost all your money, and then you discovered a product/service/technique that made you rich again. Alternatively, you were in great shape, you were in a car accident, and you've rediscovered your health and fitness through a method/program/piece of equipment.

Us versus Them

Apple's Mac versus PC is a perfect example of this story line.

Another common example is the juxtaposition of natural and synthetic. Place your product or service in opposition to another, or make a distinction between the qualities you uphold and those you disdain.

Before and After

Highlight the difference between a previous experience and a current experience. For example, you used to have a busy, volatile mind, but since you discovered a meditation CD, you have become calmer, more balanced, and more focused.

Amazing Discovery

The premise here is that as you were going about your business, you made an amazing discovery, and now you feel an obligation to share it. It changed your life, and now it can change the lives of your clients.

Secret Telling

The most iconic example of this story line is, of course, *The Secret*: a mysterious truth, known for centuries to the world's most successful people. Now, finally, it's available to us all. Don't tell anyone...but tell everyone.

You can adapt this story line to secrets large and small, generating a sense of excitement and intrigue around your marketing.

Third-Person Testimonials

Finally, the simplest story line you can present is the story line that comes from a client and describes how good you are at what you do.

This has the credibility of coming from an independent party, so it can be more direct and still be powerful. Sometimes the best story you can tell is to show a prospective client a case study from someone you've already worked with.

From Message to Magnet

This chapter covers a lot of ground. We've discussed the necessity of crafting a message that will be heard amid the noise of the marketplace and explored how to do that in a way that generates compelling narratives that will draw your clients in and open them up to what you want to share with them.

It's important to understand that your message, and your character, must feel authentic to your company's marketing. People can pick up on a message that has been faked. That doesn't mean your message must represent exactly who you are as a person. Rich Jerk isn't actually a jerk.

What's important is that your message draws out *aspects* of your brand, and your character showcases *elements* of your brand's personality, even if those elements are exaggerated for dramatic or comic effect.

In the next chapter, we'll explore the form your message takes: the magnet.

► KEY TAKEAWAYS FROM CHAPTER FIVE

You need to know whether you are a noise or a song in your industry. Be honest.

To become a song, make sure that you understand your prospect's *why*. Evaluate your promise, your position, and your big idea.

Construct your "IP": How are you personifying your business? Are you a leader, an adventurer/crusader, a reporter/evangelist, or a reluctant hero?

Know your story line. Which of the narratives above fits your personality and your experience most closely? Loss and redemption, us versus them, before and after, amazing discovery, secret telling, or third-person testimonial?

6

THE THIRD M: MAGNET

"Remember that the happiest people are not those getting more, but those giving more."

– H. Jackson Brown Jr.

What is a magnet?

In short, it's a piece of valuable content containing a small amount of your message that you present to your marketplace with the intention of creating a connection.

It's the first date, the cup of coffee. You're not trying to secure a heavy commitment at this point. Your prospects don't know much about you. They're willing to give you a shot, but at this stage, they're only dipping a toe into the water. Don't scare them off by getting too heavy too fast.

Traditional business wisdom, exemplified by Alec Baldwin's Blake in the 1992 film *Glengarry Glen Ross*, states that a salesman should "always be closing." If this was ever true, it's no longer the case. People are jaded and used to being pitched to. The harder you pitch, the worse you look.

How do you feel when someone pitches to you? Probably, you don't enjoy it. We love to buy, but we hate being sold to. A far more productive method of marketing is to start with the intention of providing something of value to members of your community. When you focus on giving and put the necessary structures in place to direct people to your programs and other offerings, monetization will take care of itself.

This chapter will teach you how to create a highly attractive magnet that will convey your message to people in a way they can hear, manufacture celebrity, and bring a flood of leads into your business. You know your market, and you've honed your message. Now is the time to create a tool that will attract the right people into your business.

Remember, this is the first point of contact between your ideas and the market. The quality of your magnet will determine whether you are greeted with a flood of leads or merely a trickle. At its best, inserting your magnet into the marketplace is like opening a dam. Every time I post my blog explaining how to avoid having your Facebook ad account shut down, I start receiving new leads *every single day*.

It acts as an autopilot mechanism, directing people toward my business so that I don't need to constantly get on sales calls, send out e-mails, or advertise. Additionally, it frames the conversations I'm having with prospects so that they are already primed to become clients.

Before we move on, take a moment to visualize what difference quality magnets could make to your business. What would they make easier? What stresses would they reduce or even eliminate? How would you feel knowing that you had a powerful magnet in your back pocket, ready to be brought out whenever you needed new leads?

THE PURPOSE OF A MAGNET

What will a magnet do for you?

First, it will give you a channel where you can be heard. If you had a choice between making a thousand phone calls and distributing a magnet to a thousand people via Facebook, which would you choose?

Unless you *really* love to get on the phone, this is a no-brainer. A magnet gives a huge pool of people a chance to get to know a little about you and what you offer and to have a positive experience of what you can do for them.

Second, it will generate a platform for you. In a digital world, you need some form of platform to operate successfully. This could take the form of blog subscribers or subscribers to your YouTube channel. It could be the people who are fans of your page on Facebook.

For most business owners and entrepreneurs, however, by far the easiest and most profitable way to generate a platform is to build an e-mail list. An e-mail list is an asset to your business. Treat the people who subscribe well, and you'll never need to invest in paid marketing again. They have taken the step of saying that they believe you will provide them with value and that they want to hear from you, and you must respect their trust.

What percentage of people do you think will buy from you on their first encounter with your work?

If you're extremely good, you may convert perhaps 3 percent of leads to a sale in one interaction. More typically, you will be doing well to hit 1 percent. People who are always selling alienate 99 percent of their potential client base, purely because those people are not ready to buy at the first time of asking.

Flip that around and start offering people something they are interested in, and then tell them that if they give you their e-mail addresses, you'll send them more good stuff.

On average, one person on your e-mail list is worth anywhere from $1 to $10 to you per month. A list with a thousand active names, therefore, has a value of between $1,000 and $10,000 per month to your business, in perpetuity. People buy from those whom they know, like, and trust. Creating a platform gives you the opportunity to form a relationship based on knowledge, liking, and trust with your clients and potential clients.

That's why you need a magnet that will draw people to your conversion mechanism and encourage them to join your e-mail list.

THE PERFECT MAGNET

The perfect magnet has four components: it is short, actionable, goal-oriented, and easy. Remember these elements using the acronym SAGE.

We live in an age driven by micro-content, not macrocontent. If your first attempt to engage with your marketplace is a ninety-minute video, how many people will work their way through it? Whatever form your magnet takes, be it blog post, video, PDF, or something else, it must be consumable within four to seven minutes. Remember, you're competing for attention in a saturated market.

S *Short*

A *Actionable*

G *Goal-Oriented*

E *Easy*

Your audience may be willing to give you a shot, but they won't be ready to give you a commitment straight away. Keep it short.

Who was the twenty-second president of the United States? If you don't know from memory, you can find out in seconds by asking Siri, Google, or any number of other search engines. Twenty-first-century consumers don't need more information. They have all the information they could ever need, at their fingertips, twenty-four hours a day. What they *do* need is *insight*.

They need someone who can tell them how to turn all that information into results. That's what your actionable magnet will do for them. For the same reason, people don't need more information that they will read, nod their heads at, and file away indefinitely. They need information that takes them toward their goals.

It's important to realize that in four to seven minutes, you cannot possibly solve major personal or business challenges. Nor should you try. Your intention is to provide them with the first step.

If you're in the weight loss space, don't try to tell them how to lose twenty pounds. Talk to them about one food that burns fat and reduces appetite. I worked with clients in the relationship and pickup industry. They didn't use their magnet to try and teach men how to approach unfamiliar women and get phone numbers. They used it to teach easy methods for building self-confidence.

Attempting to take people from A to Z using a single magnet will overwhelm users and require you to make hyperbolic claims that you can't live up to. Focus on step one.

This alone is a very powerful move. When people allow you to lead them one step toward their goals, they start to believe that you can take them further. They also start to trust *themselves* and believe that with your guidance, they can reach what may have appeared an impossible objective.

An example: Imagine that you're offering an online program to teach people how to play guitar. A good magnet would be a video or a resource sheet explaining how to play a single chord. Show your prospects that you can help them take one step toward their goals, and they will start to believe that you can assist them in achieving their larger goals—and they will also associate their success with you.

Finally, don't fall into the trap of thinking that you need to make your magnet complicated in a futile effort to prove how clever you are. It may once have been the case that complexity was a virtue but no longer. People want magnets that are easy enough for them to make use of, not baffling examinations they don't understand.

Short, actionable, goal-oriented, and easy—these are the qualities that will make your magnet appealing. Tailor your magnet depending on the precise outcome you want to achieve.

- ▶ A short, actionable magnet will build momentum.
- ▶ An actionable, easy magnet will engender a sense of progress.
- ▶ An easy, goal-oriented magnet will generate confidence.
- ▶ A short, goal-oriented magnet will create excitement.

Educate, Engage, Inspire

Let's get more granular. What exactly do you want your magnet to *do*?

Every magnet should educate, engage, or inspire—preferably all three.

Teachers have always been respected. Those who have wisdom and choose to share it with others exhibit some of the noblest human qualities.

When you educate people, you place yourself in a position of authority. In their eyes, you have the power to provide them with the resources they need to progress. For your business, this is a very good thing. By engaging with people, you build trust. When you publish a magnet, of course, you can't engage with people on an individual basis. What you *can* do is give them a sense that you are engaging with their concerns.

Imagine that I want to craft a new magnet for people struggling to make headway using Facebook ads. I may open by saying that I've polled my audience and discovered their three biggest Facebook ad problems.

Now, even though I haven't asked the end user of my magnet for *their* feedback, they feel involved in the process. They may well be struggling with some of the same problems. Instantly, they feel a connection and become more willing to consume the content I'm sharing with them.

Inspiration is *not* motivation. Your job is not to be a cheerleader for the people who see your magnet, telling them that they can do whatever they set their minds to do. Your job is to give them a tool that takes them a step closer to their goals. When you do this, you will naturally inspire them. They will feel a sense of achievement and a desire to go further. Associating their success with you will nurture an experience of loyalty.

What Form Should My Magnet Take?

There's a simple matrix you can use to determine the value of different styles of magnet.

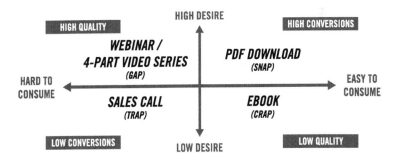

As you can see, the key factors are the ease with which a magnet can be consumed and the desire your prospects feel to engage with it. A magnet that is hard to consume and that your prospects don't feel much desire for is obviously a terrible idea. Examples include sales calls and strategy sessions, which most people will instantly identify as glorified pitches. Don't fall into this trap.

When your audience's desire is low, and you're offering them something that is easy to consume, they will probably show a brief interest before lapsing into apathy. When was the last time you read an e-book? Now, when was the last time you downloaded an e-book, *thinking* that you would read it sometime?

I rest my case.

If you have sparked a high level of desire in your potential clients, but you're offering them something that is hard to consume, they must already trust you enough to dedicate considerable time to your material.

People want webinars and video series. They provide an opportunity to dive deeply into material that can't be covered in a few minutes. On the other hand, they require a level of commitment that takes time to develop. You can't offer access to a ninety-minute webinar to a cold prospect and expect him or her to respond enthusiastically.

For the purposes of making initial contact with your market, focus on short, snappy resources that will pique people's interest and give them something they value immediately. Think PDFs, resource guides, checklists, and similar approaches.

What are the benefits? These magnets generate high-volume, low-cost leads, with high potential for conversions. Importantly, they are easy for *you* to create. There is no need for you to sit down and write an e-book when you can put together a PDF in a fraction of the time.

Some people ask me whether they should use video for their magnets. The answer is yes, *if* you're good with video. Video is relatively hard to create. When I produce a three-minute video, it takes an hour and a half to shoot. Additionally, cold prospects will be looking for any reason to reject your magnet. If they don't like what you're wearing or one of your facial expressions, or the audio crackles, that can be enough for them to stop watching. Only use video if you know that you can make it work for you.

Building a Magnet

The first time they open your magnet, your prospects probably don't
know who you are. This is why it's
essential to introduce yourself.

Tell them who you are and what you do for people. This might seem like a "promise," but it's essential to orient those who have no idea of your credentials or position in the market. The next step is to tell them what the *magnet* will do for them. It should take only a few seconds for them to understand who you are and what value your magnet offers to them. If it's something interesting to them, they'll keep reading (or watching).

In the main body of the magnet, break the content down into several segments. You want your prospects to feel a sense of progress as they work their way through the magnet. Give them a few steps to work through, without succumbing to the temptation to make the magnet excessively long or complex.

One of my magnets is an eight-part guide to writing outstanding Facebook ads. It breaks the content down into small, manageable chunks that make it easy to consume, understand, and act on.

Finally, offer people a next step. Tell them what you want them to do after they've used your magnet. Do you want them to sign up for a webinar series? Make that offer, and tell them where to click. Do you want them to call you? Let them know that you have some slots open for phone consultations, and show them where to book.

Invite them into your conversion mechanism, and make it feel like a natural continuation of the conversation. Not everyone will be ready to move so fast, and that's OK. You will reach out to those who aren't another time. You need to direct people somewhere, however, and it may as well be into your conversion mechanism.

If you want your magnet to look visually appealing, hire some-one from fiverr.com to design it for you. It's a quick and high-ly cost-effective service. Whatever you do, though, keep your magnet short and snappy. Communicating ideas clearly and simply is a mark of how well you understand them. Writing a clumsy, confused twenty-page diatribe on the state of your industry is not.

Naming Your Magnet

Choose the name of your magnet with care.

I've known a simple name change to double the quantity and halve the cost of high-quality leads, and I have a simple, yet effective, template you can use to determine the name of your magnet.

Start by asking yourself what it is. One highly successful mag-net I worked on promised gym owners and personal trainers five strategies they could use to retain clients for longer. Now consider the benefits of your magnet. Whom is it for? How will those people be better off from using it?

In this case, continuing to work with an existing client is far less energy intensive than onboarding a new client. Happy, satisfied customers generate referrals, and the security of regular long-term clients is good for the business overall. If you are a gym owner, would you want this information? It's a no-brainer.

When you understand what your magnet is, and whom it's for, ask yourself what it's *like*? Is there a metaphor that describes it? Now list the top three descriptive words you've come up with, and add three technical words that explain the purpose of your magnet. Technical words lend your name authority and gravitas.

At this point, you need to engage in a process of trial and error. Play with different combinations of words until you find the one that feels right.

For this example, I asked myself which words communicated the value of the magnet most effectively. Who uses a gym? A community? A group? A tribe?

What does the magnet help gym owners to do? Keep clients? Lengthen contracts? Retain customers?

Finally, what *is* the magnet? A checklist? A guide? A system?

The Tribal Retention System, by Chris Brown of Superfit Business, was born.

How to Assess a Personal Injury Firm

I worked with a personal injury law firm that was using traditional forms of media to bring in new customers and clients. The company was spending large sums of money on radio and TV advertising, with no means of tracking the results.

They came to me wanting to use Facebook to attract their ideal customers and convince those people to pick up the phone and give them a call. They knew whom they wanted to reach: people who had been in an accident and required a personal injury attorney. What they lacked, at that time, was a compelling magnet.

I asked them to tell me what most people don't know when they have just gotten into a car accident, and what they *need* to know before they can make an informed decision about how to proceed. It took some prodding, but they eventually revealed that going to a lawyer unprepared is a risky business. There are several questions anyone who has been in an accident should ask to ensure that they are receiving solid representation, and most people don't ask those questions.

We had a magnet. Together, we created a quick guide to the five questions people should ask when they first consult a personal injury attorney. Naturally, the document was framed in a way that was 100 percent honest and ethical, while making it clear that my clients could answer the questions most effectively. At the bottom of the document was a call to action, inviting readers to phone if they needed to talk through the questions.

At the time of writing, they continue to use this magnet to attract their ideal clients. When we first began to work together, they weren't receiving any phone calls at all that could be traced to their advertising efforts.

After they started utilizing a strong magnet, they began to attract three to five phone calls per week. Approximately 30 percent of those people visit the law firm for an in-person meeting, and 90 percent of *those* become clients, paying a retainer for the services of my clients.

That may not seem like a huge number, but it's worth remembering that an inbound phone call is a strong lead and that the lifetime value of a single client to a personal injury firm is several thousand dollars. They don't need a massive number of leads. They only need to open a channel that brings in the right high-quality clients.

This method is quite simple. Think about information your potential customers need to know, and deliver real value to them in a concise, actionable way. Facebook allows you to aim your magnet precisely at the people who will benefit from it at a relatively minimal cost.

FROM MAGNET TO MECHANISM

Your magnet is your first impression. Just as you wouldn't show up to a first date wearing a ratty T-shirt with spinach in your teeth, you won't benefit from creating a magnet that is poorly thought out and difficult to read.

On the other hand, it's surprisingly simple to make a good first impression with your magnet. You don't need the most mind-blowing content or incredible design. You need to provide people with insights that they can use, presented in a way that is simple to consume and brings them a step closer to a larger goal. Take the time to think about what you do and how you can help people, and you will certainly find the material you need to put together a magnet that will generate a flood of leads at a low cost per lead.

Now you need to understand what to do with those leads. You need a mechanism.

> **▶ KEY TAKEAWAYS FROM CHAPTER SIX**
>
> You're creating a magnet. Great. Is it SAGE (short, action-able, goal-oriented, easy)?
>
> Will it educate, engage, and inspire? How do you know?
>
> What format will it take and why? For most magnets, a PDF download is the simplest and most effective format.

7

THE FOURTH M: MECHANISM

"All you need is the plan, the road map, and the courage to press on to your destination."

– **Earl Nightingale**, American radio personality, writer, and speaker

Some years ago, I received a last-minute invitation to speak at an event in Washington, DC. The client gave me only about twenty-four hours' notice and persuaded me by saying that he would organize my plane ticket and send a driver to collect me at the airport. When I landed, the driver was waiting as promised. I got in the car, and the driver asked me where I was going.

Of course I had no idea. I agreed to take the gig on the basis that someone else was taking care of the logistics. I thought the driver would know where he was taking me. The car was full of gasoline, and the driver was ready to drive. We had the tools we needed to reach our destination, but neither of us knew where we were going.

Unless you know your destination, your efforts are doomed to futility. This is why you need a mechanism that supports you in building relationships with potential clients and brings them closer to buying from you.

Taki Moore's objective was to fill his live coaching events. What's yours? Do you want to fill a coaching program? Sell a product? Bring prospects into your sales process? When you understand where you want to take people, you can reverse engineer your mechanism to move them toward that goal, step by step.

Your next step is to plan a route. When you want to get somewhere, you have numerous options. You can walk, bicycle, take a car, ride a train, or travel in a plane or helicopter. You may want to stop on the way or move directly from point A to point B. Depending on the destination and the distance you need to travel, some options will make much more sense than others.

The same is true for marketing.

There are, however, some essential basics. College freshmen

know that the 101 courses are the foundations of their degree. Once those foundations are solid, more advanced courses build on top of the knowledge they have already acquired. It doesn't make a lot of sense to start pulling fancy marketing moves until you've mapped out the core competencies and started to practice them successfully.

FIRST, THE AD

Your mechanism starts with an ad. That ad directs people to a landing page. The landing page leads to a thank-you page. When you have a potential client's e-mail address, you can start to correspond with them, usually via e-mail. Begin by getting your ad right. Your goal here is not to sell a product. Too many people make that mistake and lose the interest of their prospects before they've given that interest time to develop. You are focused only on getting a click-through to the next phase of your process.

What makes a perfect ad? There are three elements.

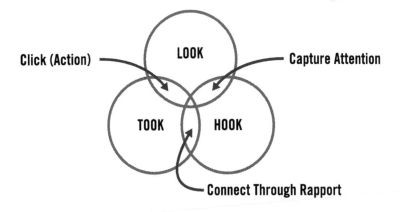

Look

The single most important aspect of creating a captivating ad is a great image. The reason it's a cliché that a picture is worth a thousand words is because it's true. The human brain responds strongly to images, especially those that awaken emotion in us.

As you scroll down a monotonous Facebook newsfeed, what captures your attention and compels you to investigate a story? Probably, the first thing to capture your attention will be an image.

How do you use this principle to your advantage? The image should "pop," by which I mean it should stand out from its surroundings. This is incredibly simple to do. Take a standard image and boost the contrast slightly. You'll notice that the picture seems more defined and catches the eye more effectively.

Alternatively, use a black-and-white image. In an environment full of color pictures, it will make an impression. Please, however, don't be tempted to make desperate grabs for attention by giving your image a garish red border or covering it in bright pink text. People are wise to marketing tricks nowadays, and you will only make yourself look bad by doing the Facebook equivalent of yelling, "Look at me!"

Also, make sure that you keep the image relevant to your product. What's an example of a popular graphic, guaranteed to garner attention? An attractive woman in a bikini. Now, what happens if you use that image, and your product or service has no relevance to the impression you've created? You'll get clicks but no conversions. Don't mislead your market. It does them a disservice and tarnishes your brand.

Hook

Always open your ad with a question that invites an implied yes.

If I ask my wife whether she'd like to go on vacation, her instant response will be an enthusiastic yes. If you're a gym owner, and I ask you whether you'd like a system that will help you to retain clients, will you be interested? Almost certainly.

The mind loves to engage with questions, and people who have answered yes to a question feel more positive about themselves and more positive about the person who asked. It's the beginning of rapport.

By the same token, inviting them to answer a question places you in a position of authority. Who has more power in a conversation: the person asking a question or the person answering? Bosses ask more questions than subordinates. Lawyers ask more questions than witnesses. When you invite a potential client to answer a question, you encourage them to see you as a source of authority.

Ultimately, marketing is nothing more than a series of small yesses that lead toward a big yes. You want your prospects to believe that you have something they value and to be willing to

Nicholas Kusmich
Written by Nicholas Kusmich [?] · Just now · 🌐

Want the exact 10 step formula I use for every FB Ad I write that has generated hundreds of millions of clicks, millions of leads and tens of millions of dollars in new revenue? → http://bit.ly/2f2n02c

Let's be frank, unless you're a seasoned copywriter; writing ads are confusing. You look at a blank white screen and don't know what to write to get your desired result. Heck, if you're not careful, you could end up losing a small fortune.

Well not anymore! I'm the guy behind the highest ROI FB campaigns around. I have countless hours and untold amounts of money in the trenches making FB ads work... and today I want to give you my FREE Perfect FB Ad Template so you too can bypass all the learning and go straight to a proven formula that works!

Click here to download your free template → http://bit.ly/2f2n02c

The Perfect FB Ad Template. How to create winning ads without wasting time or money [FREE DOWNLOAD]

Discover my proprietary 10-phase Ad Formula that has generated tens of millions of dollars, so you never have to worry about how to create a highly converting,...

CLICK HERE TO DOWNLOAD THE TEMPLATE

follow you on a journey that leads to their betterment.

An excellent way of accomplishing this aim is to use a copy template I refer to as "feel, felt, found." I know how you feel because I've felt that way myself until I found this method/product/idea.

> Sometimes life feels like it's out of control as a parent, maybe even chaotic. I knew for me, trying to balance all of the housework, kids and other responsibilities often left me feeling a little on the downside because I felt like I was failing at all of it. That is, until I discovered one simple but often overlooked "thing". Once I knew and applied it, our house and my life did a complete turnaround. Way more peace, and way more fun in our home.

When you follow these principles, you will find it much easier to connect with your audience on an emotional level. As we've discussed earlier in the book, it's emotion, not rationality, that will win you a following.

It's *essential*, however, that you come from a place of authenticity when you use this strategy. People can sniff out fakes very easily, and if they feel that you are trying to manipulate their emotions, they will completely lose interest in what you have to offer.

Took

Some time ago, I wrote an ad inviting people to claim a free PDF. One person, in the comments below the ad, wrote, "Yes, I want it. How do I get it?"

Click the link, my friend. You click the link.

While this episode frustrated and amazed me, it also made it very clear that I should never assume that people will understand what I want them to do, unless I explicitly tell them. Now, whenever I write an ad, I have the person who isn't familiar with the custom of clicking a link in mind. When I want people to click, I write, "Click here."

Don't leave anything to chance. Make it extremely obvious what action you want your prospects to take, and let them know what they can expect to happen when they give you that click.

One final point here: scramble your URL, so that people don't simply copy and paste it into a new tab. Why? You want to track the number of visitors who come through your ad, and anyone who copies and pastes the URL will scramble those statistics. Even though you're paying for the click, it's worth the small outlay to be able to analyze the behavior of site visitors.

The whole point of your initial ad is simply to get the click. You're not looking to sell anything. You're taking the first step in a mutually beneficial relationship, which starts when they reach your landing page.

For an ad template that takes you through each of the ten elements you need to include in your Facebook ads, visit www.nicsblog.com/template.

THE LANDING PAGE

The landing page is the beginning of your real relationship with your audience.

You know that they're interested in what you have to say to them because they've clicked through from Facebook. Do a good job on the landing page, and they will give you their e-mail address in exchange for your magnet.

Once again, it cannot be emphasized enough that the vast majority of people won't buy so early in the process. By pushing for a sale, you'll drive them away. Companies that spend a lot of money sending cold potential consumers directly to an offer are wasting money (mostly). They're like men who meet a woman they like and try to take her home the very same night. They may sometimes succeed, but they'll upset and alienate a lot of people on the way, and their overall reputation won't be enhanced.

You want to create an opening to communicate with your

IN THIS FREE TEMPLATE, I'LL SHOW YOU:

THE ESSENTIAL ELEMENTS

The 10 essential elements needed in every FB Ad that causes the highest CTR's and Conversions while pre-framing your prospect to want even before they see it.

A SECRET KEY

The most underutilized piece of Ad real estate that MOST marketers are ignoring which is actually harming and reducing your CTR's.

IMAGE HACKS

The right types of images to use in order to grab the most attention (without being douchey) and increase engagement.

STELLAR STRATEGY

The specific order of each element so you can for the most effective result. Miss any one of these and the result won't be the same.

and more...

92,209 Leads in 12 Days

$3,228,259.39 in 27 Days

Hi, I'm Nicholas Kusmich the world's highest ROI-ing Facebook Ads Strategist, and I help high growth businesses scale using Facebook Advertising.

The Perfect Ad Template's proprietary 8-phase Contextual Congruence Strategy has been responsible for generating hundreds of millions of clicks, millions of leads and tens of millions of dollars in revenue.

Without it, you will waste your time staring at a blank white screen guessing how to create your next ad and then wondering if that ad will convert.

With it, you'll remove all the guesswork and will never again waste time or money set up an ad and get even better results from your ad campaigns. Use and enjoy!

Nicholas Kusmich

WHAT ACTUAL CLIENTS HAVE TO SAY ABOUT NICHOLAS...

Creating high converting ads is only a click away...

DOWNLOAD NOW >>

prospects on a continuous basis, eventually warming them up to a sale. Your landing page is like a handshake. Make it warm and inviting, and back that up with something prospects will value. This way, they're much more likely to give you their number.

To facilitate the progression from Facebook to landing page, make the lander look and feel similar to the original ad. A lot of people create an appealing visual aesthetic and copy style when they're writing an ad, only to abandon what's worked for them on their landing page. You want people to feel comfortable when they click through and for the experience to be consistent.

Aggressive copy, or a totally different color scheme, will make the landing page feel disconnected from the original ad, and the trust your prospects were beginning to feel will quickly disappear. They will wonder whether they've stepped into a trap and become wary of giving you their e-mail address. In advertising parlance, this is known as the scent, or the trail. When the colors, tone, and image remain congruent, the trail is easy to follow. When they don't, it goes cold.

Another aspect of this congruence is a willingness to display information about who you really are on your landing page. There was a time when marketers believed that the fastest way to conversions was to remove any extraneous information from their landers in the belief that anything that distracted people from taking the next step was counterproductive. This is no longer the case.

Most websites include a footer with contact details, terms of service, privacy policies, and other similar information. There's no reason for your landing page to be an exception. Demonstrate that you are a real person/company who can be reached if necessary and that your aim is to help your prospects, not to trick them into doing something they'll later regret.

Robert Cialdini wrote a book entitled *Influence*. In it, he discussed the concept of microcommitment. As soon as people have made a small commitment in a given direction, they are much more likely to feel a sense of investment and take the next step.

Traditional marketing wisdom states that it's a good idea to place a form on the landing page, asking for people's name and e-mail address. When you ask people to click through to a second page to claim their PDF/report/resource guide, however, you are inviting them to take a microcommitment. Ask them for their name and e-mail address on the second page, and you will be rewarded with a higher sign-up rate.

Remember that when they come to your landing page, people are encountering you for the first time. They are trying to get a sense of who you are, just as they would if you are meeting for the first time in person.

An image of your face will reinforce the impression that you are genuine in your desire to connect with them and serve them. A ticker that tracks the number of people who have already downloaded your magnet will reassure them that others are taking the action they're considering.

Testimonials from satisfied customers and logos of companies you're affiliated with or places where you've spoken publicly will only strengthen the impression that you are genuine and trustworthy. Succeed in this objective, and you'll win both the interest of your potential clients and their e-mail addresses. It's time to say thank you and to divide them up into swim lanes.

For an entire perfect landing page template showing you visually what you need to include on your page, visit www.nicsblog.com /landingpagetemplate.

The journey from ad, to landing page, to e-mail capture, to thank-you page has been a journey of increasing momentum.

At this point, your new prospect is beginning to warm to you. He or she has taken some positive action, and he or she feels good about himself or herself. The cardinal mistake a lot of marketers make at this point is to close the door. They present visitors with a thank-you page and allow the relationship to cool before they continue the conversation.

Here's what I suggest you do instead.

Everyone understands the concept of swim lanes. There are the fast swimmers who appear to have been born in the water and can pound out fifty lengths of the pool before breakfast. They swim in lane 3. There are the moderate swimmers, who take a more leisurely approach. They may not be fast, but you know they will get there in the end. They swim in lane 2. Finally, there are the slow swimmers. Sometimes it seems as though they're never going to finish a length of the pool, but when they do, it means a lot to them. They swim in lane 1.

Your potential clients fit roughly into these three categories.

The fast swimmers are excited and passionate. They're the people who look at your magnet, totally get where you're coming from, and are ready to buy. They make decisions and take action quickly.

Moderate swimmers may like what you're doing, but they need more connection before they're ready to make a purchase. It has been estimated that, on average, people need seven points of contact before they're ready to buy. Moderate swimmers fall into that category.

Slow swimmers, as the name suggests, are very cautious and take longer to make a decision. They need to be very sure they're doing the right thing and often consult with many people before they make a commitment. They may read everything you send them for eighteen months, or even longer, before suddenly flipping into buying mode and deciding that they're ready to make a purchase.

Once you have captured a lead, you need to provide swim lanes for people, so they can self-select.

Give the fast swimmers an offer on your thank-you page. Let them know that if they're ready, they can buy right away. The moderate swimmers will say no to that offer, but they've already said yes to your magnet. Continue to provide them with valuable content, and they will say yes sooner than later.

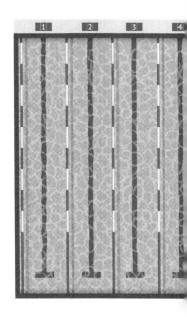

Slow swimmers will continue to consume your content for months, perhaps for years. It's tempting to assume that they'll *never* buy from you, but if you remain patient and continue to deepen your relationship with them, they will eventually be ready to make a purchase.

I've been a slow swimmer. When I first took an interest in Internet marketing, I subscribed to the list of a leader in the industry. At the time, his price points were way beyond what I could afford. Nonetheless, I read every book and e-mail he wrote and watched every video. I followed him for three years before I was in a position to buy.

It pays to make a conscious effort to accommodate every type of client.

Reducing Cost per Acquisition by More Than Two Thirds

For contractual reasons, I'm not allowed to name the massive supplement company that I worked with on honing its Facebook game. Suffice to say that you've heard of them, and their annual revenue is in eight figures. They produce high-quality supplements without synthetic ingredients, aimed at people who care about their health and the health of the planet.

When they came to me, they were already very successful, but they felt they could improve their results. Their marketing was based primarily on affiliate marketing, otherwise known as joint ventures. Most of their joint venture partners are heavily influential in the health space and command large followers on Facebook. These are food bloggers, trainers, fitness models, and the like.

Before we started working with them, they wrote ads and targeted those ads at the audiences of key influencers. By connecting with audiences who were already interested in food, health, and fitness, they achieved good results. What we did, however, was to go directly to partners and offer them a new framework for relationship.

We wrote ads in the voices of the influencers and connected with their followers directly. Meanwhile, we gave those influencers commissions on every sale. This had the effect of making the ads appear as endorsements. Audiences began to receive good information from people they already followed and trusted, influencers received a commission, and sales grew dramatically.

The company was used to paying, on average, $10 to acquire a new customer. This subtle strategy brought that cost down to $3. Running ads in the voices of influencers and presenting them to an audience of people who were already excited by those influencers dropped the average cost per acquisition by more than two thirds.

THE WHOLE PACKAGE

Throughout this part of the book, we've investigated the keys to determining your market, discovering your message, and creating your magnet. Now we've discussed the best ways to build your mechanism.

If you do all of these effectively, you will be able to identify the people you most want to reach, decide what you want to share with them, produce a piece of content that will intrigue them, and take them from Facebook to your landing page and your e-mail list, from where you can continue to provide them with valuable content until they're ready to make a purchase from you.

PART THREE

USING THIS BOOK:
TAKE YOUR MESSAGE TO THE WORLD

"Reach for the stars."

– **Christa McAuliffe**, teacher and astronaut

FOUR PAGES IN

"Action is the foundational key to all success."

– Pablo Picasso

I remember the moment my dad got the call. His oldest friend, Louis, had passed away.

Denise, Louis's daughter, made the call. She asked for Nicholas Kusmich Sr. When I passed the phone to my dad, I saw his face change within seconds. He was heartbroken. Louis had died the previous night, and the funeral would take place a couple of days hence. When he hung up the phone, tears were rolling down his face.

Louis and my dad grew up together. They were inseparable. As adults, they lived several hours apart, but they still kept in touch. Every time Louis came to town, he called my dad up, and they

143

went out to the Polish deli, where they spent hours trading stories and laughing.

They didn't see each other all that much, but it didn't matter. My dad didn't have a lot of friends. Louis was his best.

The days leading up to the funeral were very hard. My dad didn't talk much. I guess he didn't know what to say. I went with him to say good-bye. It was a dreadfully cold, Toronto winter's day, and both he and I were bundled up in an effort to keep ourselves from freezing. We both hated the cold.

The funeral was small, perhaps only fifteen people: Louis's family, my dad, and me. We gathered around the casket for a short service, shivering in the bitter conditions. The wind whistled around us while we bid Louis a final farewell, my dad and Louis's family crying as he was lowered into the freezing ground.

Something happened to Dad that day. I think he felt his own encroaching mortality and realized that his time might be short. When we got home, he pulled out some lined paper, a three-ring binder, and a Bic ballpoint, and he started to write.

He wanted to write a memoir for me or for whomever else might one day wish to read about his life. He wrote about Louis—the day they met, the conversations they had, even the funeral that day.

Sadly, he was right. He didn't have much time. It wasn't long before I was driving like a maniac, following the ambulance carrying my dad to the hospital. One of the nurses took me aside and asked whether, if he survived but lost his brain function, I wanted him kept alive as a vegetable—a question no son should have to answer.

I never had an opportunity to make the decision. Dad made it for me. He departed this world with his family by his bedside.

He wrote only four pages of that memoir. I still have them; sometimes I even read them. I keep them as a reminder that I, too, have a story to tell. We all do. Don't wait until it's too late to share that story. Don't leave having gotten only four pages deep.

Most people who are in business do what they do for a reason. I assume you're no different. You have a message you want to share and a desire to make the world a better place. The tools in this book will help you to frame your stories and your messages in ways that allow you to make a difference.

Take what you've learned and use it. Make a commitment to bring your message, your product, your service to a world that needs it so that you can look back at the end of your life and know that you've truly given of yourself.

I think you're in business because you want to make a difference for people and make the world a better place. To do that, you need to gain mastery of your lead generation.

As I mentioned in chapter 3, I'm making three assumptions about you based on the fact that you have picked up this book. The first is that you have something to say, something that can help people. The second is that you would like more people to see and hear your message. The third is that you could benefit from tools that can help you to bridge that gap.

The landscape of advertising has changed. If you are going to keep your business afloat in the modern world, you need to approach marketing in a new way because the traditional approach is slowly dying.

If you want to bring your message to the people who are most likely to be interested in it, there is no better platform than Facebook. No other platform allows you access to more than a billion people for pennies on the dollar and enables you to fine-tune your targeting to ensure that you put your message in front of those who want to read or see it.

That privilege, however, comes with new rules. Facebook demands that you *give* before you ask because it is based on social connection. You *must* honor that connection before you seek to create a buying relationship, otherwise you will alienate potential clients.

I know firsthand how powerful Facebook can be. I've shown dozens of clients how to use it to present their products and services effectively and to transform their business outcomes, all while staying true to the messages they want to deliver and the changes they want to see in the world.

Brendon Burchard says that if you're not spending $1,000 per day on Facebook, you haven't entered the world of digital advertising. I agree with him. In fact, if you have a winning offer, you should be spending $5,000 to $10,000 or more a day on advertising. In this day and age, Facebook is, hands down, the greatest direct response advertising platform on the planet. If you have a business you want to grow, and you're not at least exploring what Facebook can do for you, you're missing a huge trick.

Take the tools in this book and use them to create change. If you have further questions, and you want to be part of a supportive community, join my Facebook group, where I regularly provide members with advice and guidance.

Reach the people who need what you have to offer. You're here to be of service, and you have a story to tell. Tell that story. Don't stop four pages in. Marketing matters not simply because it will help you to sell more (although when you utilize the exercises, formulas, and procedures in this book, it will).

Marketing matters because you will change more lives with your marketing than with your product.

► **KEY TAKEAWAYS FROM THE CONCLUSION**

There's only one takeaway from this chapter. Take everything you've learned from this book and use it to reach people who need to hear your message. Do it.

FREQUENTLY ASKED QUESTIONS

Is Facebook the right platform for my advertising right now?
As you can probably tell from the content of this book, I love Facebook. Perhaps you think I'm biased. You may be right, but I have good reasons to prefer Facebook to any other marketing platform. There really is no other medium in the world that allows you to target specific subsets of people so precisely for such a small financial outlay.

Of course, the caveat to this statement is that if you don't know what you're doing, advertising on Facebook can feel like throwing good money after bad, but that's true of any platform.

What kind of Facebook ad budget do I need to get results?
Clients ask me this question every day, and I know straight away that they're still stuck in the mindset of traditional media. Facebook advertising is not about how *much* you spend. It's about how effectively you target your campaign.

Done well, advertising on Facebook is an investment. What is the lifetime value of a customer for you? What percentage of that amount are you willing to spend to acquire a customer? When you know the answers to these questions, you will have more of an idea on how to approach your Facebook campaigns.

What if I told you that I could generate three dollars for each dollar you spend? If that were the case, you'd want to spend as much as possible, knowing that the more you spend, the more you'll get back. Calculating how much you should spend on advertising is not gambling. It's mathematics.

What are the metrics I should be paying attention to?

There are three primary types of metric on Facebook: vanity metrics, important metrics, and vital metrics.

Vanity metrics include signs of engagement that don't move people toward taking action, such as "likes," comments, and shares. It's satisfying to see people taking an interest in your content, but nothing useful can be deduced from these numbers.

Important metrics are factors such as click-through rate and cost per click. Of every hundred people who see your ad, how many people click on it? How much do you spend, on average, for each person who clicks on your ad? While these metrics can be useful indicators, there are more accurate ways of measuring what really matters.

Vital metrics are those that get to the heart of the issue. The most common are cost per lead and return on ad spending (ROI). When you know how much you are paying for each lead, you can make adjustments to bring that cost down and test their effectiveness.

ROI is the single most important metric in determining the success of your advertising, and it's a metric many people ignore completely. Your ROI tells you how much income you are generating in comparison with your spending. It's essential that you understand this, otherwise how can you determine whether your advertising is succeeding?

How can I find an audience?

Many businesses see Facebook as a place to find new audiences. They want to make offers to people who they think will be interested in engaging with them. What most people don't realize is that there are different types of audience, and some will be more receptive than others. Here's a rundown, from coldest to warmest:

1. **Interests and behaviors.** This is the coldest type of audience you will find, but it's the one most businesses focus on. Fitness companies, for example, target people who are interested in fitness and assume those people will be ready to buy from them.

2. **Connections.** These are people who "like" or follow a fan page. They have indicated an interest in what you have

to offer, although they haven't demonstrated clear intent to make a purchase. The larger this audience, the more likely it is to yield results.

3. **Lookalike.** This is an audience created to mimic your current customers. Imagine that you have a thousand customers on your database. You can upload the customer data to Facebook and ask the platform to find you an audience of similar people on the basis that they, too, will be interested in what you have to say. Facebook will cross-reference all the data you supply, find people who are closely matched, and show them your content.

4. **Retargeted.** A retargeted audience is significantly warmer than the previous types but still not ideal. Perhaps you have experience of being retargeted. You visit a retail website and almost, but not quite, make a decision to buy a pair of shoes. Suddenly, you see the same shoes advertised everywhere you go on the Internet. They show up on Facebook, for example, or the sidebar of your Google mail page. When done badly, retargeting can be annoying and creepy. When used ethically, however, it can be powerful. It's based on the principle that most people won't make a purchase on their first exposure to an item they're interested in, so it pays to give them reminders.

5. **Custom.** This is the warmest audience available on Facebook. It consists of people who are already familiar

with your business. They know, like, and trust you. If you've built an e-mail list or customer database, you can upload it to Facebook. Facebook will locate these people for you, giving you the capacity to create a Facebook ad that goes only to people on your e-mail list. Now, if you need to communicate a message that you would usually send via e-mail, you can use Facebook to send exactly the same message to your custom audience. This gives them two opportunities to connect with your message, multiplying your impact. It usually provides the best results and the highest ROI.

Am I using the right types of advertisement?

When you scroll through Facebook, you're doubtless aware of the small blocks of ads that pop up on the right-hand side of your screen. Probably, you ignore them nine times out of ten. You know that they are placed there in an attempt to sell you something, and you will only click if you're interested in buying.

Newsfeed ads, however, are much more unobtrusive. It's likely that you scroll through your newsfeed regularly, looking for content that interests you. When you see content that looks natural and catchy, you may well click on it. The same is true of your prospects.

As always, make sure you advertise in a way that is congruent with Facebook as a platform and that you provide value to your audience.

Should I use retargeting?

Yes, absolutely. Most people will say no when they are first presented with an offer. It takes time for them to develop trust in you and become ready to make a purchasing decision. Unless you have a strong, proven retargeting strategy, you're not playing the Facebook advertising game effectively.

How can I keep abreast of the latest developments in Facebook marketing?

This book is the culmination of close to a decade of marketing practice and tens of thousands of hours in the trenches, executing campaigns that work. Nonetheless, Facebook is an evolving platform, and marketing is an ever-changing discipline. For a full list of my latest resources, trainings, and updates, visit *www.nicsblog .com/resources*.

ABOUT THE AUTHOR

Nicholas Kusmich is an international speaker, founder of the H2H Media Group, a director of The Council of Marketers, and the creator of the Art of Lead Generation. Nic is best known as the world's leading Facebook advertising strategist and for delivering the highest returns on investment in the industry (at his peak, upward of 30,000 percent).

In his working life, Nic serves A-List clients including potent thought leaders, *New York Times* best-selling authors, and top Inc. 500 companies, creating advertising campaigns that truly convert. He specializes in implementing his proprietary Contextual Congruence methodology, which generates mass conversions on social platforms through understanding and respecting the mindset of users and forging genuine connections.

When he's not working, Nic can usually be found relaxing with his beautiful wife, Fehren, and their baby daughter, Eden, in their home in Toronto. He loves flashy shoes, which he matches with colorful socks from his collection of more than fifty pairs. He's a firm believer that every man should own at least one good pocket square.

For more information about Nic's work and to subscribe to his *Insights*, visit www.nicholaskusmich.com.

Made in the USA
Middletown, DE
07 July 2017